DUKE ELLINGTON

JAZZ COMPOSER

DUKE ELLINGTON

JAZZ COMPOSER

KEN RATTENBURY

YALE UNIVERSITY PRESS   LONDON & NEW HAVEN

Grateful acknowledgment is made for permission to reproduce excerpts from the following music:

Trilby Rag, by Carey Morgan. © 1915 Joseph Stern, assigned to E. B. Marks Music Co., U.S.A. Used by permission of Carlin Music Corp. and International Music Publications. *Charleston Rag*, by Eubie Blake. © 1944 Warner Bros., Inc. (Renewed). All Rights Reserved. Used by Permission. *Jumpin' at the Woodside*, by Count Basie. © 1938 Bregman, Vocco & Conn, Inc., U.S.A. Reproduced by permission of Chappell Music Ltd. and International Music Publications. *Boogie Woogie*, by Count Basie and Milton Ebbings. © 1946 Bregman, Vocco & Conn, Inc., U.S.A. Reproduced by permission of Chappell Music Ltd. and International Music Publications. *Rhapsody in Blue*, by George Gershwin. © 1927 Harms Inc., U.S.A. Copyright renewed. Reproduced by permission of Warner Chappell Music Ltd. and International Music Publications. © 1952 WB Music Corp. (Renewed). All Rights Reserved. Used by Permission. *In a Mist*, by Bix Beiderbecke. © 1928 by Robbins Music Corp. *Kitten on the Keys*, by Zez Confrey. © 1921 Jack Mills, Inc., U.S.A. Subpublished Francis Day & Hunter Ltd., London WC2H 0EA. Reproduced by permission of EMI Music Publishing Ltd. and International Music Publications. © 1921 (Renewed 1949) Mills Music, Inc. c/o Filmtax Copyright Holdings, Inc. International Copyright Secured. Made in U.S.A. All Rights Reserved.

Designed by Richard Hendel
Set in Electra + Gill types
by Tseng Information Systems, Durham, NC
Printed in the United States of America by Edwards Brothers, Ann Arbor, Michigan

Library of Congress
Cataloging-in-Publication Data
Rattenbury, Ken, 1920–
 Duke Ellington, jazz composer /
Ken Rattenbury.
  p. cm.
 Bibliography: p.
 ISBN 0-300-04428-3 (cloth)
 0-300-05507-2 (pbk.)
 1. Ellington, Duke, 1899–1974—Criticism and interpretation.   I. Title.
ML410.E44R3   1990   89-16544
781.65′092—dc20   CIP
                       MN

A catalogue record for this book is available from the British Library.

The paper in this book meets the guidelines for permanence and durability of the Committee on Production Guidelines for Book Longevity of the Council on Library Resources.

10 9 8 7 6 5

To my wife, Elsie,

who loves all this jazz music

just as much as I do,

for her wonderful support and

encouragement over the years

CONTENTS

PREFACE

To begin on a personal note, I have been involved with jazz music as a musician all my working life (as a pianist from 1933 until 1940, when I changed to trumpet). This means that I began only a few years after the music of Duke Ellington had first appeared on record. In the 1920s the New Orleans music of King Oliver, Jelly Roll Morton, and Louis Armstrong initially attracted me, I suspect, through its abrasive, assertive, boyish brio; but the smoother sounds of contemporary Ellington intrigued me then, through the strange-sounding ensembles and nonstandard quality of some of the solo instrumental performances. The tones of Ellington's brass and reeds did not, sometimes, conform to expectations or convention. Overall, and unquestioningly, I simply enjoyed the music, and began collecting jazz records with the acquisitiveness of a magpie, sustained by an enthusiasm which has never waned. I still cannot get enough of this jazz music.

Duke Ellington's life and music have received generous coverage biographically, historically, and discographically. His career as a jazz composer and performer, which began in the early 1920s and continued until his death in the early 1970s, has been well reported, if at times somewhat overdramatized. The sound of his music is available at the touch of a switch, and discographical data have been exhaustively assembled, cross-checked, and published. Examples from each of his five working decades are still in circulation, owing to frequent reissues and the compilation of lavishly presented anthologies. If we are seeking simply to be entertained, the mixture of music and minutiae may be potent enough for us. To be taken for granted in this way would never have upset Ellington, who said on numerous occasions when cornered, "Too much talk stinks up the place." He was not to be drawn out on matters of mechanics, being so protective of his modus operandi and so astonishingly cavalier about the fate of his original manuscripts that a full score by Ellington is a rare object indeed these days. So far, and possibly as the result of this basic shortage, musical analysis of Ellington's compositions has been largely restricted to discussions of isolated fragments of notation in short score, with the aim of laboring a novel shift of harmony or unraveling an intriguing skein of voicing. This sort of random sampling has by no means been sufficient to evaluate any work as a structured composition. It has merely scratched the surface, and worn disfiguring holes in the fabric of jazz criticism and evaluation. Some repair and reinforcement are in order.

I have had four aims in writing this book:

1. to assess the extent to which Duke Ellington drew upon black music traditions of blues, ragtime, and jazz to achieve the mature synthesis of the years 1939 to 1941;

2. to examine the processes through which Ellington attained his status as the foremost genuine composer in the jazz field, when earlier influential figures had been performers who based their work by and large on extemporization;

3. to recognize and acknowledge the flair and infinite care with which Ellington selected his musicians—players able, by their musicianship and creativity, to contribute in a unique way to the "Ellington sound";

4. to support my conclusions by discussing scores, transcribed in full and analyzed in depth, from the years 1939 to 1941—the period that saw the full flowering of the Ellington style.

Before anyone else in jazz, Duke Ellington accomplished a genuine, methodical integration of black folk-music practices with white urban ones. Through his own dedicated, personal effort and acute powers of aural observation—through the acts of writing and presenting his own works—he chronicled the development of jazz at a crucial stage. To follow the progress of this remarkable musician's career is to document musically the evolution of jazz through several stages, the last of which corresponds to the stable, recognizable form that the music assumes today.

ACKNOWLEDGMENTS

During the writing of this book I have received generous help, encouragement, and cooperation from many people both inside and outside the jazz fraternity. Their painstaking and prompt responses to my enquiries, which in many cases were repeated, unearthed a large amount of valuable material on Ellington and his works that had not surfaced in the standard literature on jazz. Some of the standard literature is useful nonetheless: I have found particularly helpful and reliable the collection of sixty-six specialized books published by the Jazz Book Club, London, during the 1950s and 1960s.

But it is above all through the vast experience of the following jazz people and institutions that I have gained so much real and specialized knowledge of Ellington and his music: Birgit and Benny Aasland, Duke Ellington Music Society, Järfälla, Sweden; Tony Agostinelli, jazz archivist, Roger Williams College, Rhode Island; Belwin-Mills Music, London; J. Richard Berlanger, librarian, University of Missouri; Edward A. Berlin, musicologist, author of *Ragtime: A Musical and Cultural History*; Jan Breuer, musicologist, Sweden; Campbell, Connelly & Co., music publishers, London; Chappell Music, music publishers, London; George Chisholm, OBE, eminent jazz trombonist; Ron Clough, archivist and collector of memorabilia relating to Ellington, specializing in early recordings; Alan Cohen, jazz saxophonist, composer, arranger, transcriber of Ellington's works; Russell Davies, television presenter, arts critic, reviewer, jazz musician; Peter Dickinson, composer, former head of the music department, University of Keele; Geraint Ellis, jazz cornetist, teacher, authority on trumpet styles in jazz; John Fisher, light entertainment producer for BBC television; Janice Fournier, Ellington Oral History Project, Yale University; Dave Gelly, jazz critic for the *Sunday Observer*, tenor saxophonist; Marion Gillies, jazz writer; Kenny Graham, jazz composer; Vic Guder, former vice-president of the professional division of United Artists Music, Los Angeles; André Hodeir, composer, critic, author of books on jazz evolution and form; the late Derek Jewell, biographer of Ellington, former jazz critic for the *Sunday Times*; Art Lange, associate editor, *Down*

Beat; the late G. E. "Eddie" Lambert, author of the first full-scale biography of Ellington published in Britain (1959); Leeds Music Co., music publishers, London; MCA Music, music publishers, London; Dan Morgenstern, director, Institute of Jazz Studies, Rutgers University, New Jersey; Steve Race, pianist, composer, author, broadcaster; Johannes Reidel, professor of music, University of Minnesota; Stephen L. Roberts, librarian, American Embassy, London; Alan Rushton, conductor, choirmaster, pianist; Charles H. Russell, president, New York chapter of the Duke Ellington Society; Philip Speight, producer of jazz programs and documentaries for BBC television; Clark Terry, trumpeter and flugelhorn player, former sideman with Ellington; D. Thistlethwaite, expert on the mechanisms and restoration of player pianos, Rugeley, England; Eric Townley, jazz reviewer, commentator, archivist; United Artists Music, music publishers, London; Steve Voce, jazz journalist, commentator, reviewer, broadcaster, collector; Martin Williams, acquisitions editor, Smithsonian Institution Press, Washington; and Dick Zimmerman, Maple Leaf Club, Los Angeles.

AN INTRODUCTION

TO ELLINGTONIA

Duke Ellington was possessed by music. He acknowledged his lifelong obsession in these words:

> Roaming through the jungle of "oohs" and "ahs," searching for a more agreeable noise, I live a life of primitivity, with the mind of a child and an unquenchable thirst for sharps and flats. The more consonant, the more appetizing and delectable they are. Cacophony is hard to swallow. Living in a cave, I am almost a hermit, but there is a difference, for I have a mistress. Lovers have come and gone, but only my mistress stays. She is beautiful and gentle. She waits on me hand and foot. She is a swinger. She has grace. To hear her speak, you can't believe your ears. She is ten thousand years old. She is as modern as tomorrow, a brand-new woman every day, and as endless as time mathematics. Living with her is a labyrinth of ramifications. I look forward to her every gesture. Music is my mistress, and she plays second fiddle to no-one.[1]

Born into a relatively well-to-do family in Washington on 29 April 1899, Ellington had a gift for melodic invention and exceptional powers of observation, imagination, and concentration. By taking full advantage of these abilities, he applied himself to the task of integrating the improvisatory elements of a music almost wholly dependent on emphatic ostinato rhythms (originating in the drum culture of a far-off black society) into the strict harmonic and instrumental conventions of music from the Old World. Ellington died of cancer in Presbyterian Hospital, New York, after fifty-three crowded and triumphal years in the business of making jazz music.

The number of Ellington's compositions has been variously estimated in the jazz and lay press to be anywhere between 1,000 and 5,000. A reliable figure is 1,012, based on the lists of copyrighted compositions published in Ellington's autobiography *Music Is My Mistress*[2] and in Mercer Ellington's memoir *Duke Ellington in Person*.[3] Of this number around 750 works are by Ellington alone, 200 are collaborations with his own musicians (half of these with Billy Strayhorn), and 50 are collaborations with others.[4]

Owing to the astonishing lack of care and respect afforded to Ellington's original manuscripts during and after his life, a definitive census of his works may never be accurately accomplished. It is not difficult to calculate that by normal standards Ellington the composer was outstandingly prolific. Over fifty years he and his collaborators produced twenty compositions each year, or one about every eighteen days; as for the compositions that Ellington wrote himself, these average out to one every twenty-four days. The sheer volume and variety of Ellington's work pose a problem to the student of his working methods. What criteria should be used to select compositions worthy of detailed study? Which works best represent his style, and which are the most rewarding and revealing to look at?

To answer these questions I have decided to consider first the principles that guided Ellington's ear and hand throughout his career: his personal approach to the mechanics of composition and orchestration, and the qualities and standards of musicianship which he adjudged to be minimum requirements for the successful realization of his music. I will then take a survey of his work from the formative, questing years between 1923, when he organized his first regular band, to 1938, by which time the benefit of stable, experienced personnel and the incentive of a growing recognition of his talents allowed him to reach a peak of creativity and facility. During this period early forms of black music making exerted a strong influence: blues and ragtime had been the common musical currency in the South during the half-century preceding Ellington's emergence as a working jazz musician and composer at the beginning of the 1920s. I will also explore the white music of Tin Pan Alley, and the question of whether its influence on Ellington was in any way reciprocated. I hope to have shown by this time that Ellington's contribution to the jazz repertoire consisted of his having assimilated and combined elements of black (African) and white (Euro-American) music with a high degree of expertise.

I decided to present a selection of Ellington's mature works in full score, to look into his methods of composition and orchestration, and at the same time to trace his allegiance to previous and contemporary influences. I chose further to concentrate on works recorded between 1939 and 1941. The decision to examine this period was initially inspired by the evidence of my own ears, when I detected an ageless style, a steadfastness of concept, and a striking instrumental virtuosity in the interpretation of Ellington's music. But the choice of period still needs to be justified. Certainly, no man-made article ever attains a polished and finished roundness by accident. Work has to be done on it; industry powered by perseverance, dedication, method, observation, and self-criticism—in short, professionalism. The late Marshall McLuhan's view of professionalism is apposite to the circumstances of Ellington, who was continually and inextricably involved, in a truly creative sense, with his musician colleagues: "Professionalism is environmental. Amateurism is anti-environmental. Professionalism merges the individual into patterns of total environment. Amateurism seeks the development of the total awareness of the ground-rules of society. The amateur can afford to lose. *The professional tends to classify and to specialize, to accept uncritically the ground-rules of the environment. The ground-rules provided by the mass response of his colleagues serve as a pervasive environment of which he is contentedly unaware*" (italics added).[5]

The period 1939 to 1941 witnessed the peaking of Ellington's qualification as a jazz composer. It exemplified his mature style, which was formed out of his influences and associations and the criteria he used in writing, performing, and recruiting suitable, sympathetic sidemen.

At the end of this book I include some statistical and discographical data, and brief biographical appreciations of some of the more than one hundred musicians who were influential in producing and performing Ellington's music. They are listed on a selective roll in appendix B. The entries there include notes on the musicians' styles, and relevant excerpts from Ellington's autobiography *Music Is My Mistress*.

African blacks were first brought to the United States as slaves in 1619. Although there is no way of finding out exactly what their music sounded like, something is known of its form:

Antiphonal song-patterning, whereby a leader sings phrases which alternate with phrases sung by a chorus, is known all over the world. Nowhere else is this form so important as in Africa, where almost all songs are constructed in this manner. A peculiarity of the African call-and-response pattern, found but infrequently elsewhere, is that the chorus phrase regularly commences while the soloist is still singing; the leader, on his part, begins his phrase before the chorus has finished. This phenomenon is quite simply explained in the terms of the African tradition of the primary use of rhythm. The entrance of the solo or the chorus part on the proper beat of the measure is the important thing, not the effects attained through antiphony or polyphony. Examples of call-and-response music in which the solo part, for one reason or another, drops out for a time, indicate clearly that the chorus part, rhythmical and repetitive, is the mainstay of the songs, and the one really inexorable component of their rhythmic structure. *The leader, receiving solid rhythmic support from the metrically accurate, rolling repetition of phrases by the chorus, is free to embroider as he will.* (italics added)[6]

When Ellington's scores are scrutinized, the device of antiphony is seen to have been employed in every one.

Black African styles were not straightforwardly accepted by the white musical establishment: "In most areas of the South, specific legislation outlawed drumming, but the Blacks substituted hand-clapping and foot-stomping in their own private gatherings. Thus, the African rhythms could be practiced and perpetuated without offending their White masters. One important exception to this situation was the Place Congo, a square in New Orleans, where, until the Civil War, slaves were allowed to gather to dance, sing and play . . . several types of drums, pebble-filled gourds, jews-harps, jawbones, thumb pianos (African sansa) and the 4-string banjo."[7] It is clear that the African style was heavily biased toward pure rhythm,[8] and that in the main the instruments employed were far shorter in expressive tonal range and mechanically less sophisticated than the instruments used in white bands. It would therefore seem that the music itself would have erected some barriers against acceptance: to ears attuned to the lenitive niceties of white musicians with conservatory training who performed conservatively, the bizarre percussion sounds of African bands must have seemed like abrasive clatter that overpowered the element of melody. But by the mid-nineteenth century opportunities widened for the Afro-American musicians to learn and practice the techniques of the white schools, and the abolition of slavery accelerated this trend. For example, around the turn of the century John Robichaux, a Creole bandleader and drummer active in downtown New Orleans, had prefigured some of the sophisticated devices later used by Ellington and his contemporaries.[9]

Wilfrid Mellers sums up on the black and white musical alliance with these observations:

The improvisatory "reality" of folk art and the conventionalised "artistry" of commercial music had to meet . . . if jazz was to become the representative music of our industrialised world; for just as man in the big city cannot turn his back on the world of commerce, so a dispossessed minority, if it is to create an art relevant to urban society as a whole, must to some degree absorb the values of that society. Duke Ellington has shown that this marriage, which seems unholy, can be consummated without sacrilege, dishonesty or evasion; this is his historical importance, which complements that of Gershwin. Ellington, starting from jazz, came to terms with Tin Pan Alley; Gershwin, starting from Tin Pan Alley, attained the integrity of jazz.[10]

To me, the main attraction of jazz lies in its unpredictable performance, or in the precise, highly rhythmic interpretation of scores written expressly for jazz musicians. In either circumstance, conventional brass, reed, and stringed instruments are coaxed into producing microtones, glissandi, and portamenti well beyond the standard twelve-tone notational system—thus harking back to the vocal tones and inflections of rural blues, work chants, and traditional laments. Ellington was the first genuine jazz composer to incorporate these effects comprehensively, although the sounds of the rural field shouts, work hollers, and blues had already made some inroads into instrumental interpretation.

Contemporary Activity during Ellington's Formative Years

The sixteen years or so between the time Ellington organized his first dance bands in Washington in the early 1920s and the time when his orchestra gave its most polished, sophisticated performances were a period of critical, rapid development in jazz (see fig. 1). Ellington's most influential colleagues during this period were Joe "King" Oliver (1885–1938), Ferdinand Joseph La Menthe "Jelly Roll" Morton (1885–1941), Benny Moten (1894–1935), William "Count" Basie (1906–85), and the first great improvising jazz soloist, Louis Armstrong (1900–1971).

Oliver, a trumpeter, leader, and composer, played in a New Orleans style oriented toward blues and ragtime. The improvisations of his ensemble and his head arrangements left generous room for solos. His best-known compositions include *Dipper Mouth Blues*, *Canal Street Blues*, *West End Blues*, and *Doctor Jazz*. Morton, a pianist, leader, and composer, made recordings in the late 1920s with the Red Hot Peppers which display an effective transfer of blues and ragtime piano styles to the instrumentation of the jazz band; his composed passages have a loose, improvisatory feel and bear a resemblance to the work of Oliver. He is best known for his compositions *King Porter Stomp*, *Milenburg Joys*, *Wolverine Blues*, and *The Pearls*. Moten, a leader and pianist, was a forerunner of the swing bandleaders of the mid-1930s to 1940s. His arrangements, highly rhythmic and dominated by riffs, were largely written out. He made much use of the interplay of trumpet, trombone, and reed sections and was important in the development of the Kansas City style. Basie, also a leader and pianist, played in a style that was bluesy, rhythmic, technically simple, and direct. His orchestrations depended largely on riffs and

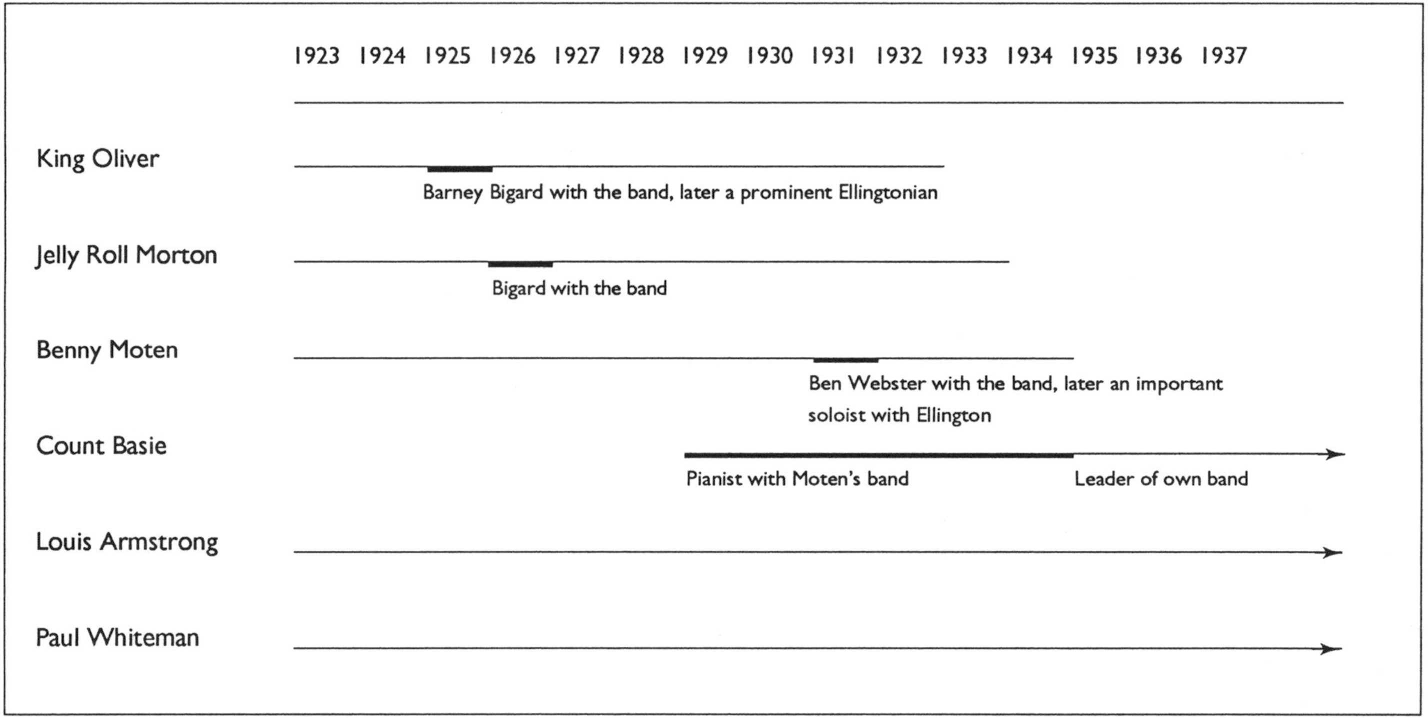

Figure 1. Contemporaries of Ellington and their periods of activity

included many head arrangements evolved from repeated performance. Like Ellington, Basie recognized the value of a stable team of soloists: among those who played with him regularly were Lester Young, Buck Clayton, and Paul Gonsalves (who later joined Ellington's band). Armstrong moved from New Orleans to Chicago to begin his professional career in 1922 with Joe "King" Oliver, with whom he remained for two years. He was in the mainstream of big band jazz from 1930 to 1946, working as a featured soloist with his own groups and others, many of which fell far short of his own standards. His significance lay in his technically brilliant, creative trumpet playing, his guttural style of singing, strongly influenced by the blues, and his consummate showmanship, which stimulated worldwide interest in a music which before had attracted mainly a localized black following.

Another contemporary of Ellington was the bandleader Paul Whiteman (1890–1967), of whom Wilder Hobson observed: "Whiteman drew very little from the jazz language except some of its simpler rhythmic patterns . . . there was little more than a trace of the personal expression, improvisation, 'counterpoint' or rhythmic subtlety of natural jazz . . . His band included some fine jazz players, but their improvising talent was subordinated in the 'symphonic' orchestrations. The Whiteman orchestra [was] a large, expert dance orchestra [or small concert group]." [11] Whiteman may be regarded as the first pop bandleader. He contributed nothing to the development of orchestral jazz, and his grotesque, overstated arrangements were mere caricature. But Whiteman did employ some of the most remarkable, genuine jazz improvisers of the day: Jack Teagarden (a trombonist from Texas with a real feeling for the blues), Bix Beiderbecke (a cornetist with a lyrical, highly melodic style), and Frank Trumbauer (a C-melody saxophonist who like Beiderbecke was given to tuneful, spacious improvising). I believe that the efforts of his sidemen alone assure Whiteman a place in jazz history.

Ellington was therefore not the only pebble on the beach, but after fifty years he has turned out to have been the most rounded and the least eroded by time and changing fashion. In an article published under his name in *Rhythm* in 1931, Ellington discoursed on his views on jazz and rhythm. [12] Some of the article may have been ghostwritten by Irving Mills's public relations organization. But the technical and musical insights contained in the article display such fine critical faculties, and so clearly result from an insider's awareness of the aesthetics and mechanics of successful jazz performance, that they could only have come ultimately from the composer himself. A few pertinent excerpts from the article follow.

"Our very lives are dependent on rhythm, for everything we do is governed by ordered rhythmic sequences; that modern dance music of the best type is completely rhythmic is only in accordance with the natural law." Here Ellington has touched on a fundamental fact of life: that the insistent rhythms of jazz (or for that matter of any music supported by a surging, repetitive, percussive pulse) have a visceral effect on the receptive listener. Other writers later explored this same topic.[13] In jazz this phenomenon is known as swing.

"Everyone who really understands the dance band of today knows that it is the rhythm section which is by far the most important; without a solid basis of impeccable rhythm, no matter how brilliant the melody section, the band can never be successful." In other words, a dance band or jazz band is only as good as its rhythm section. "Long association between players should result in their being able almost to anticipate each other's thoughts, so that the first desideratum, viz., that they should play as one man, is not hard to attain." This statement is particularly relevant to Ellington's own groups, where the individual, often nonstandard timbres and quirky improvisational skills of the carefully selected musicians were welded together into the unmistakable and virtually inimitable Ellington style. "We do not use any printed orchestrations. These are much too stereotyped. For a band to keep in the top flight today it must be original. I therefore make all my own arrangements." Ellington felt strongly that orchestrations and compositions must be suited to the talents of his sidemen. Further emphasis on this theme: "What little fame I have achieved is the result of my special orchestrations, and especially of the co-operation of the boys in the band, I cannot speak too highly of their loyalty and initiative . . . We have made the band our work and our hobby." Thus Ellington appreciatively acknowledged the individuality, talent, and enthusiasm of his musicians.

"I am always being asked how I write the trick phrases and rhythms that my band plays . . . Always I try to be original in my harmonies and rhythms . . . I put my best musical thoughts forward into my tunes and not hackneyed harmonies and rhythms which are almost too banal to publish." Ellington's ambition to break away from the banalities of contemporary ballroom music is clearly stated here; he had a high regard for harmonic subtlety. Although the melodic conventions of the blues and the rhythms of early ragtime remained integral to Ellington's work throughout his career, he had already decided in 1931 that these were but a beginning. In looking ahead, Ellington recalled the tyrannies of the Deep South: "It is my firm belief that what is still known as 'jazz' is going to play a considerable part in the serious music of the future . . . The music of my race is something more than the American idiom. It is a result of our transplantation to American soil and was our reaction in the plantation days to the tyranny we endured. What we could not say openly we expressed in music and what we know as 'jazz' is something more than just dance music."

In the article Ellington mentions the names of several prominent soloists:

Harry Carney (baritone saxophone), Johnny Hodges (alto saxophone), Charlie "Cootie" Williams (trumpet), and Joe "Tricky Sam" Nanton and Juan Tizol (trombones) were still with Ellington in 1939. With the exception of Williams, who left in November 1940 to join Benny Goodman's orchestra, they were still there throughout 1941. Fred Guy (banjo, later guitar), Sonny Greer (drums), and of course Ellington himself maintained the stable rhythm team so highly recommended in the article. The rhythm section varied only in 1935, when Wellman Braud (double bass) was replaced by two double bass players (which was unusual in jazz at the time), Hayes Alvis and Billy Taylor; in 1939 Taylor was replaced in turn by the brilliant musician Jimmy Blanton.

I will conclude this introduction to Ellingtonia by quoting from Wilfrid Mellers. "Throughout the 'thirties and 'forties, Duke Ellington was pre-eminent, if not unique, in preserving the authenticity of jazz while achieving, too, tenderness and sensitivity—the essential human values within the context of a hard, brutalised, industrialised world. His stature cannot be separated from the fact that he discovered how to make creative—not escapist—use of elements derived from pop music, in association with the heritage he received from jazz."[14] My aim is to find out just how Ellington came to achieve all this.

ELLINGTON'S APPROACH

TO COMPOSITION

THE "ELLINGTON

EFFECT"

The term "Ellington effect" was coined by Billy Strayhorn, who collaborated with Ellington as a composer, arranger, lyricist, second pianist, and deputy leader from 1939 until his own death in 1967. It denotes Ellington's unique sound, which had three sources: his attitudes toward music and rhythm (some of which are discussed in the preceding chapter), the contribution of his sidemen, and his facility at the keyboard, which was responsible to some extent for his pianistic approach to jazz orchestration.

General Observations by Ellington Himself

During an interview on Radio Stockholm on 29 April 1939 (his fortieth birthday),[1] Ellington responded as follows to a request for definitions of "true" jazz and "swing": "We always say that 'jazz' is representative of American music. . . . My definition of 'swing' is . . . that part of rhythm that causes a bouncy, buoyant terpsichorean urge . . . makes you want to dance and bounce about! 'Swing' today is a commercial label on the music itself, but we always thought it was an emotional element; we've always accepted it as that. It's something you feel when the music is played. 'Swing' in a foxtrot is the same as the lilt of a waltz." The interviewer asked: "Will 'swing' and modern (popular) music, do you think, influence the 'serious' music of the future?" Ellington replied: "There's a lot of 'serious' music already that has injected in it a few jazz figures, or a little jazz flavor. On the other hand, of course, . . . our jazz composers . . . there are many of *them* who are guided by the 'serious' or 'conservatory' influence—theory!" Later in the year Ellington commented further on the elusive, effervescent, euphoric quality that distinguishes the best jazz performances: "No *notes* represent swing. You can't *write* swing because swing is the emotional element in the audience and there is no swing until you hear the notes. Swing is liquid, and though the same group of musicians may play the same tune fourteen times, they may not *swing* until the fifteenth time."[2]

In autumn 1958 Ellington toured England with his orchestra, and contributed an article, "The Future of Jazz," to the souvenir program. In it he was unequivocal on the subject of improvisation:

> There are still a few die-hards who believe . . . there is such a thing as unadulterated improvisation without any preparation or anticipation. It is my firm belief that there has never been anybody who has blown even two bars worth listening to who didn't have some idea about what he was going to play, before he started. If you just ramble through the scales or play around the chords, that's nothing more than musical exercise. Improvisation really consists of picking out a device here, and connecting it with a device there; changing the rhythm here, and pausing there; there has to be some thought preceding each phrase, otherwise it is meaningless.

In an appreciation of the cornetist Rex Stewart (1907–67)[3] that appears in his autobiography *Music Is My Mistress*, Ellington recalls the manner of his own early training: "Although he was born in Philadelphia, Rex Stewart came out of the same Washington school system as I did, and his intellectual ambitions were typical of the Washingtonian of that time, when people believed that if you were going to be something you ought to learn something. Some people learn from going to college, others from just reading. Some learn from conversation. *All my musical education, for example, was received orally. When they asked you questions, they knew if you knew what they had taught, but if you brought them papers . . . well, somebody else might have written them for you!*" (italics added).[4]

Over the years the inner workings of the Ellington phenomenon have continued to fascinate students of his music. For instance, the jazz writer, critic, and historian Leonard Feather has noted that Ellington was fully aware of the desirability of form and presentation and always deeply involved with his gifted soloists, and that it was "his personal triumph that the overall band 'effect' was even greater than the considerable sum of its parts."[5] Sidney Finkelstein has pointed out Ellington's overt respect for jazz tradition: "Ellington's music is fundamentally his own, shaped by his taste and musical thinking . . . the performance [of his music] is a kind of collective creation, restoring, within the narrow confines of a single band, the social character of New Orleans music."[6]

He has noted further: "The old stomp, rag, and slow blues often return, so changed that they are apparent only as the skeleton of the music."[7] According to Mellers, "Ellington is a new type of composer in that he has written, not merely for specific forces or a specific function, but for a particular group of human beings, each with his own distinctive characteristics. . . . The more respect the band shows for the identities of the individuals who comprise it, the better it will be, so long as the cohesive power of the composer-arranger operates effectively. This is why there must always be a two-way relationship between the composer and the players."[8]

Joachim-Ernst Berendt on styles:

Ellington created his "jungle" style . . . expressive "growl" sounds of trumpet and trombone . . . voices in a jungle night.

The "jungle" style is one of the four styles identified with Duke Ellington.

The "mood" style, moody and sad . . . partakes of the real blues-feeling, even in pieces which are not real blues.

The "concerto" style . . . small "concerti" for different soloists in the orchestra.

The "standard" style, which did not contribute too much that was new . . . [but] was clothed in typically Ellingtonian colours and sounds.[9]

Before Ellington appeared with his orchestra at the University of Michigan on 11 November 1972, a writer for the *Michigan Adviser* observed: "[Ellington] describes writing music as a 'crap game'; 'Throw away the dice and sometimes it comes out right.' . . . Igor Stravinsky said Ellington is the greatest American composer, an observation with which Dave Brubeck, jazz pianist and composer himself, has concurred in these words: 'He expresses our culture more than any other American musician.' "[10] Mercer Ellington, Duke's son, recalled his father's musical idiosyncrasies as follows:

He objected to the word "jazz" because in the early days it was used by the lowest elements of society—the people in brothels—to identify music linked with orgies. This was really a kind of defense mechanism that was not concerned with his disapproval of this form of life but with the broad use of its jargon in connection with the music.

His dislike of formal training was another example of this kind of anomaly. When the formal institutions bestowed honorary degrees on him, he kept them, displayed them, and cherished them. He didn't just toss them into the trash can. But formal training, to him, implied adhering to the rules and a lack of creativity. He didn't like the rules in anything. To discard a rule was a source of inspiration to him because he immediately saw the way to make it work in reverse.

Ellington never wanted to be involved in anything that anybody had already set down in a pattern. Although he himself indulged in intricate patterns that verged on the atonal, he thought of music as a means of communication that projected a mood. However "free" the act of composition in music . . . once a piece was composed, he believed it should hold its own dimensions, be heard in an individual form from day to day, so that it would evoke the same feeling whenever it was performed. Whether today's audience would hear it in the same way as yesterday's was beyond his control, as was the variable quotient in jazz solos.[11]

Ed Anderson, a lyricist and friend of Ellington's family, recalled: "I had the nerve to say to [Ellington]: 'Don't you think that you should go to a conservatory like Juilliard and study; don't you think it would be helpful to you?' I said this in good faith. I didn't say this as any kind of criticism. And he said: 'If I were to go and study I think I'd lose everything I had.'"[12] And the concert pianist Don Shirley once commented: "[Ellington was] experimenting constantly with sound, and really enjoying the idea of contradicting the rules and regulations. Primarily because he didn't know any of 'em! And it worked. That's important—making it work."[13]

Ellington seemed to possess an ear and an instinct that enabled him to recognize in a musician some personal, often nonstandard timbre and style that accorded with his own conception of how orchestral jazz and solo jazz should sound. In 1924 he recruited the trumpeter Bubber Miley, who remained with Ellington until 1929 (he left the band owing to ill health and died in 1932). This association brought Ellington closer to the blues and turned him some degrees away from the dance band tradition which had dictated the style of his earliest groups, organized for the most part to provide unchallenging music for social functions in Washington. Gunther Schuller has assessed the importance of Miley's contributions to Ellington's sound and repertoire:

> The interesting question is how were Ellington and his men . . . able to create a unique kind of big band jazz, in the late 1920s and early 1930s? Bubber Miley was largely responsible for the initial steps through his introduction of a rougher sound into the band. Ellington himself is quite clear about Bubber's influence: "Bubber used to growl all night long, playing gutbucket on his horn. That was when we decided to forget all about the sweet music."[14] He . . . helped teach the same techniques to the band's trombonists—Charlie Irvis and his replacement in late 1926, Joe "Tricky Sam" Nanton. It was Miley and Nanton who developed the band's famous "jungle" effects through their use of the growl and plunger [mute].

Actually, Miley's influence extended far beyond these effects. He was

Example 2.1   *Creole Love Call* (Ellington)

not only the band's most significant soloist but actually wrote, alone or with Ellington, many of the compositions in the band's book between 1927 and 1929. Although the extent of Miley's contribution has not yet been accurately assessed, there seems little doubt that those compositions that bear Bubber's name along with Ellington's were primarily created by Miley. These include the three most important works of the period— recorded in late 1926 and early 1927—*East St. Louis Toodle-Oo, Black and Tan Fantasy*, and *Creole Love Call*.[15]

Miley is not given credit for having collaborated with Ellington in the composition of *Creole Love Call*, either on the sheet music, first published in 1926,[16] or in the list of works in *Music Is My Mistress*[17]—only Ellington's name appears.

The harmonic sequence in *Creole Love Call* departs from the classic twelve-bar blues (four bars of I, two bars of IV, two of I, two of V, two of I; see chapter 3). Here bar 7 retains the IV, and the tonic major chord does not reappear until bar 8. The recording of the piece is notable for Ellington's innovative use of the voice. In ex. 2.1 Adelaide Hall's wordless obbligato has been added to the extract from the original sheet music.

Bubber Miley possessed a gift for uncluttered melodic invention, nowhere more apparent than in the main theme of *East St. Louis Toodle-oo*, a tune of simple, arpeggio construction with a pronounced folksiness. Ellington's scoring, for three low-register saxophones and tuba, provides a rolling, somber, almost funereal accompaniment to Miley's simple yet subtle invention (ex. 2.2).

Example 2.2 well illustrates what Billy Strayhorn described as the Ellington effect.[18] In the early days Miley was clearly responsible to a large degree for much of the musical ambience that has usually been credited almost entirely to Ellington. On the evidence of recordings from the late 1920s, it appears that Ellington was guided toward a personal compositional style by the powerfully individualistic sounds of such key men as Bubber Miley and the trombonist Joe "Tricky Sam" Nanton. Clearly, Ellington was deeply dependent upon his musicians during these crucial and formative years.

The main strain of the second collaboration of Ellington and Miley mentioned by Schuller, *Black and Tan Fantasy* (ex. 2.3),[19] is a twelve-bar blues theme in the minor that appears to be stylistically close, in its traditional harmony and simple, triadic construction, to the principal strain of *East St. Louis Toodle-oo*.

The British writer on jazz Francis Newton has described the highly selective processes that led to the creation of Ellington's distinctive sound: "[Ellington's] most lasting gift to orchestral jazz is the discovery that bands can have a distinctive 'sound', i.e., orchestral color, the pallette being mixed by the

Example 2.2   *East St. Louis Toodle-oo* (Ellington and Miley)

composer from the colors of the original musicians, carefully chosen for the purpose . . . The Ellington sound is quite unmistakeable. It contains a mixture of New Orleans colors—especially the liquid 'Creole clarinet' . . . the 'blue' sound of muted brass . . . and a well-mixed reed sound."[20]

Example 2.3 'Black and Tan Fantasy (Ellington and Miley)

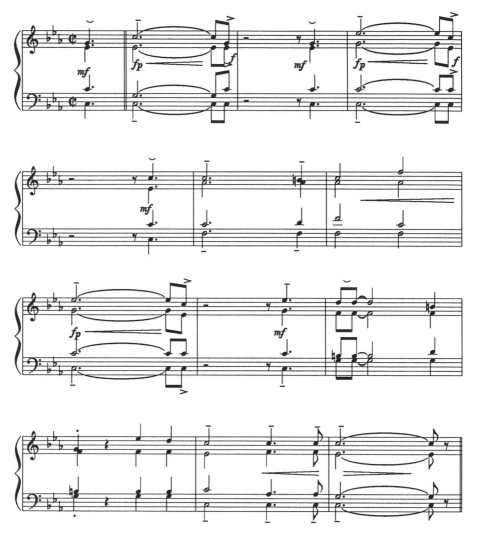

Strayhorn coined the term "Ellington effect" in an article in *Down Beat* in July 1952, when he had already worked closely with Ellington for thirteen years. His impressions were republished in *Hear Me Talkin' to Ya: The Story of Jazz by the Men Who Made It*, which contains 150 interviews with jazz musicians. Strayhorn's observations deserve to be quoted in full:

In 1934, in Pittsburg, I heard and saw the Ellington band perform for my first time. Nothing before or since has affected my life so much. In 1939, I became his protégé, enabling me to be closer and see more.

His first, last and only formal instruction for me was embodied in one word: Observe. I did just that and came to know one of the most fascinating and original minds in American music.

Ellington plays the piano, but his real instrument is his band. Each member of his band is to him a distinctive tone color and set of emotions, which he mixes with others equally distinctive to produce a third thing, which I like to call "The Ellington Effect."

Sometimes this mixing happens on paper and frequently right on the bandstand. I have often seen him exchange parts in the middle of a piece because the man and the part weren't the same character.

Ellington's concern is with the individual musician, and what happens when they put their musical characters together. Watching him on the bandstand, the listener might think that his movements are stock ones used by everyone in front of a band. However, the extremely observant may well detect the flick of the finger that may draw the sound he wants from a musician.

By letting his men play naturally and relaxed, Ellington is able to probe the intimate recesses of their minds and find things that not even the musicians thought were there.

Lately (this was in 1952), personnel changes have prompted the comment that what I call "The Ellington Effect" has been replaced by something different. This, I believe, comes about from listening with the eyes instead of the ears. The same thing has happened every time there has been a change during my stay, and, even before my time, the advent into the band of the very people who have left brought forth the same remarks.

The same comment accompanied *my* arrival, but has long since simmered down into a "whodunit" game indulged in by the band (which always puzzles me, because I think my playing and writing style is totally different from Ellington's).

"The Ellington Effect" has touched many people, both listeners and performers . . . and will, as long as there is, and after there is—Ellington. (italics added)[21]

The following extract, from an article written in the year of Ellington's death by the American jazz critic Gene Lees, summarizes Ellington's unique, unorthodox methods:

A lot of men organized the sections [of a jazz orchestra] in the way that is common to most big bands—rhythm section, trumpets, trombones and saxes—and voiced them, by and large, together . . . Duke didn't do it that way. He put his colors together up *through* the sections, matching and mixing colors in all sorts of odd ways. He was the first man—in jazz, that is—to use a wordless female voice as an instrumental color. (italics added)[22]

His band was, in a sense, like a brilliantly strange assemblage of *objets trouvés*. In Ellington's world of color, the answer was a firm "Why not?" And these strange distinctive musicians, interestingly, always sounded better in the Ellington band than out of it.

Duke Ellington took the world as he found it, both in life and in music, tolerating impossible discrepancies in men and circumstance. That is how he was able to make a functioning unit of men with utterly distinctive musical sounds. Therein lies the essential difference between "classical" and jazz composition. Classical composition assumes, with a certain narrow variability, a "correct" trumpet sound, or a "correct" trombone or violin sound. Jazz tolerates all sorts of oddity and individuality, and Duke went beyond toleration . . . He turned idiosyncrasies to his advantage.[23]

And here are some observations by Ellington himself on the conditions under which he habitually worked as a composer. In 1958 Ellington was questioned on the wisdom of persisting at his age with his rigorous, unbroken schedule of international tours and one-night stands in the Americas. He responded thus: "I'm much too impatient to [give up the work and touring] . . . I have a fear of writing something and not being able to hear it right away. In fact, if the band hadn't always been there for me to try my pieces on, I doubt if I'd have gotten nearly as much writing done as I have. The business of just being a composer, in my case, isn't easy. Look at the hundreds of good composers who come out of the conservatories each year, write hundreds of symphonies and never hear them played. No, I prefer being sure my music will be played and will be heard, and the best insurance is having one's own band all the time to play it."[24] Ellington acknowledged the relentlessness of his program of commitments in an interview granted before a concert at the Crown Centre Hotel, Kansas City, on 12 May 1973: "I'm working somewhere almost every day of the year, and I compose more songs now than ever before . . . Each month has something that has to be ready for someone . . . [I am always] running behind."[25]

The bulk of Ellington's work exists only in the form of recordings. Owing to the scarcity of full orchestral scores of his works, it seems important to reconstruct the atmosphere of the recording studio and the practices followed during a typical session: these shaped the final form that Ellington's music took. Two recollections of his recording sessions covering roughly the same period provide insights into Ellington's method and confirm his all-round consistency of approach: the first is that of the cornetist Rex Stewart (in Ellington's band from 1934 to 1945), and the second is that of Fred Stone, a session trumpeter and composer based in Toronto, who belonged to Ellington's brass section for six months beginning in March 1970, during which he toured fifteen European countries.

Stewart remembered this sequence of events at a typical recording session: Ellington would usually arrive late, then warm up at the piano for a quarter-hour or so. If he played fast, the band knew it was to record a stomping, roaring piece; if he played slowly, they were to record a lament. Ellington would then invariably suggest to the musicians that they make sure the piano was in tune; this in fact meant that they themselves should be. He would then produce some frayed scrap of manuscript paper with, say, a few notes scribbled down for the reeds, then produce something similarly cryptic for the trumpet and trombone sections. The session finally proceeded, with much trial-and-error repetition and numerous suggestions and criticisms by Ellington for performance, until at last all were ready to record. Stewart's own words hint at the state of controlled chaos which attended such sessions: "And that's the way things went—*sometimes!*"[26]

Stone recalled Ellington's recording sessions as follows: "The Ellington Orchestra is the only musical outfit I know where the members are hired solely on the basis of their strength and individuality. It is the only orchestra I know where you are not required to become an exact percentage of the section you're playing with; where you are not required to match the sound of the previous member. You must function as an individual—and you are judged solely on your personal musicianship. The Duke uses his band as his personal workshop, his laboratory; the recording sessions are the results of his experiments, and the orchestra an extension of his character."[27] Stone's account was essentially a straightforward journalistic report of the orchestra's day-by-day activities while it was on tour, especially in between the concerts, but in an addendum he also described his own experiences and offered firsthand observations on the general atmosphere and pace of work in a recording studio. In essence his recollections run on lines parallel to Stewart's, but a few of his remarks shed additional light on the covertly frantic circumstances attending one of the sessions:

> Ellington will end an evening by saying, "Okay, recording session at 10 in the morning" . . . Next day, about 10:30, people start to wander in.
>
> At 12, Duke shows up. With no music . . . Sits down at a piano, plays a chord or two, a cluster of notes, then he'll write it down.

Twenty minutes later he's finished—and he hands [the manuscript] to the copyist he carries with the band.

He uses a code system, whereby it doesn't mean anything except to Tom Whaley, the copyist . . . Tom scores it, he knows exactly what Duke wants. They pass it out and Duke picks up the mike . . . and says, "Okay, put this one down."

The engineers are right out of it. "We can't! We haven't got the microphones ready" . . . Ellington looks at them and says, "Look, either you get it down now or we're getting the hell out of here. This is the way we do things . . . first time round."

And the fact is that 90 per cent of the time he's right—it *is* best first time round. But it's not easy on the recording people, that's for sure. (italics added)[28]

In general Stone's account suggests that Ellington had seen little reason to modify in any way the methods he had already evolved and accepted by Stewart's day.

The recollections by Stewart and Stone of Ellington's seemingly casual approach are firmly substantiated by the reported experiences of two men who were prominent and influential in the publishing and recording industries in the 1940s. Jack Robbins, head of Robbins Music Corporation (who published much of Ellington's music), recalled his numerous cables and calls to Ellington on tour, asking for lead sheets of new compositions already recorded by the orchestra. In most instances Ellington did not respond at all; but when pressed he would sometimes call on an arranger to transcribe the tunes off the records. On one occasion Ellington's own notes had been scribbled on an empty paper bag. Herb Hendler, then artists and recording manager for RCA Records, remembered an occasion when he had heard quite by chance that Harry James had recorded one of Ellington's tunes, the title of which included the word "light." At first Ellington said he did not recollect any such tune, but then remembered vaguely that the lyricist Don George had provided words that did contain a reference to light. The song turned out to be *I'm Beginning to See the Light*, one of Ellington's most successful songs. In his description of Ellington's routine in the recording studio, Stone made some comment on how Ellington used the piano to determine orchestral voicings. His observation is pertinent to the discussion which follows.

Ellington's keyboard facility predisposed him toward a pianistic approach to orchestral scoring. This is clear from a comparison of his scoring for full orchestra and small groups with, for example, a duet for piano and double bass (see chapter 7). This suggests that his approach to part writing was guided by an almost total, straight transfer of his piano chording style to the orchestral score. When the individual ensemble parts are scanned laterally, and in

Example 2.4

Parallelism

(a) Ko-Ko

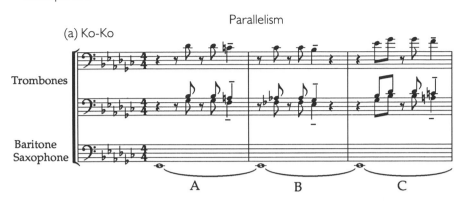

Trombones

Baritone
Saxophone

A   B   C

Parallelism*

(b) Concerto for Cootie

Reeds

71   72

* and some contrary motion in the lower treble part

Parallelism

(c) Subtle Slough

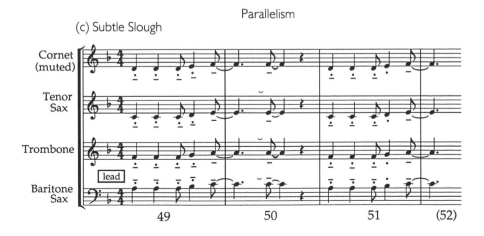

Cornet
(muted)

Tenor
Sax

Trombone

Baritone
Sax

lead

49   50   51   (52)

Example 2.4 (continued)

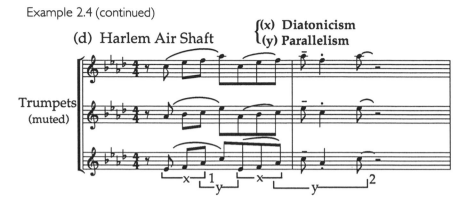

(d) Harlem Air Shaft

{(x) Diatonicism
{(y) Parallelism

Trumpets
(muted)

relation to one another, they display a cheerful unconcern with the presence of academically undesirable consecutive intervals or false relations. Parallelism and diatonicism abound in Ellington's voicings—natural consequences, it seems, of picking out the notes of a chord at the keyboard, one by one, and transferring them to the score either literally or approximately. As a result of this essentially vertical approach (in jazz usually referred to as block scoring), consecutive seconds, fourths, fifths, sevenths, octaves, and ninths are the rule rather than the exception in his writing for ensemble. Several instances of these nonacademic practices, typical of Ellington's part writing, are illustrated in ex. 2.4.

The part writing in ex. 2.4 strikes me as being wholly pianistic in style. In orchestral tuttis Ellington frequently thickened and extended a chord to allot a different note to each available wind player.[29] Gunther Schuller has offered similar observations on the subject of Bubber Miley's contribution to the Ellington effect.[30] As examples he has chosen extracts from works which had also been the result of early collaborations between Ellington and his musicians: "[In] *Misty Mornin'*, based on somewhat altered blues changes, in the 15th and 16th measures of [Arthur] Whetsol's trumpet solo, the unique inner voicings that helped to make *Mood Indigo* so special are tried out briefly."[31] Schuller has included short extracts from the two compositions. I have marked in ex. 2.5 the reminiscent voicings noted by Schuller, and identified them in the following key:

A = first-inversion triads
B = second-inversion triads
C = dominant ninths
There are two false relations occurring between the triads marked (X) and (Y) in bar 3 of *Mood Indigo*: (1) C-natural, middle part (X), to C-sharp, top (melody) part (Y); and (2) A-flat, lowest part (X), to A-natural, middle part (Y).

Example 2.5   *Misty Morning*
              (Duke Ellington and Arthur Whetsol, 1928)

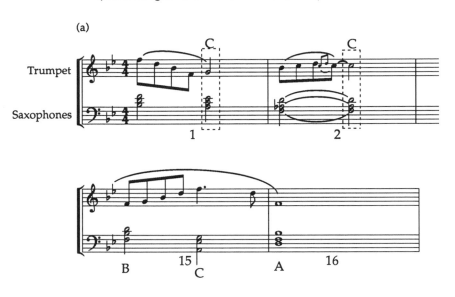

(a)

Trumpet

Saxophones

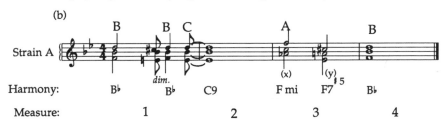

Mood Indigo (Ellington, Barney Bigard, and Irving Mills, 1930)

(b)

Strain A

Harmony:

Measure:

Schuller continues, expanding on both the intuitive and the pianistic approaches:

> Such voicings were unorthodox and wrong, according to the textbooks. Ellington did not care about the textbooks. His own piano-playing gave him the most accessible answer to voice-leading problems. [The above] examples have the kind of parallel motion a pianist would use, and Ellington applied to the orchestra the voice-leadings he used on piano. It must be remembered that Ellington was an almost completely self-taught musician. As such, contrapuntal thinking has always been foreign to him, but the parallel blocks of sounds he favors so predominantly

are handled with such variety and ingenuity that we, as listeners, never notice the lack of occasional contrapuntal relief. To Duke's ears, reacting intuitively, and unfettered by preconceived rules, the effect of this kind of "piano" voicing, though novel, was good.[32]

On the evidence provided by the extracts examined above, taken from either end of the years leading to his maturity as a jazz composer, it appears clear that Ellington's realizations owed little to the tenets of classical counterpoint. It is also apparent that he saw no reason to change the methods he had adopted in the first instance as being suitable for his purposes.

Several questions arise from these observations, some of which may be answered only by posing other questions. Did Ellington's technical limitations as a pianist, particularly noticeable at the beginning of his career, in the mid- to late 1920s, restrict his compositions? Or did they enhance them, by preserving a link with the basic black musical forms—blues and ragtime—and their immediate, although Europeanized, derivatives? Ellington's touch and technique on the piano have never seemed to me any more classical than his methods of scoring for the ensemble; the two are inextricable. Might Ellington, who came from a comfortable, comparatively affluent home, have repudiated his "poolroom education" in music had he been encouraged to seek acceptance from the white, European musical establishment, or sought such acceptance on his own? And had he done so, would he thereby have strained his allegiance to the folk origins of jazz, and destroyed much of the substance of his emerging individualism as a composer? I hope to answer these questions in later chapters.

In my analysis of three transcriptions of Ellington's own piano performances, the influence of the blues, ragtime, and European impressionism may be identified.[33] From a purely physical standpoint, one does not find on reading through the transcriptions that Ellington needed a cast-iron, legitimate, trained piano technique to execute his performances accurately. If his technique had been honed to a Lisztian perfection, perhaps his music would have lost the earthiness that accounts for much of the charm and individuality of black jazz.

Some Preliminary Conclusions and Comparisons

In 1934 the English composer and conductor Constant Lambert published *Music Ho! A Study of Music in Decline*, with which he became one of the first formally trained, white, European musicians to recognize, analyze, and publicly approve of the superior qualities in Ellington's music. Bearing in mind that these conclusions were arrived at in 1933 (very early in the period of discovery, experimentation, and development leading to the years of Ellington's mature style), it is not surprising that Lambert, for all his tutored insight, should have referred to Ellington's orchestra as a dance band. The qualities which in Lambert's view raised Ellington and his band above the norm are stylistic integrity, structural discipline, compositional ingenuity, harmonic adventurousness, sophistication, and professionalism (my own view, now based on more evidence, coincides with Lambert's). Constant Lambert's conclusions suggest to me that the principles Ellington enunciated in 1931 had been implemented to a marked degree.

Lambert's book is in essence a critical survey of the whole of the world's music since the First World War (which was, coincidentally, the vital, formative period leading to Ellington's mature style and the Ellington effect). He made his observations in the early 1930s, when Ellington's music had already crystallized into a recognizable style, but Lambert's assessments contained not enough awareness of antecedent forces. This may be due largely to its timing: in the twenties and early thirties, black music had not attained the momentum of expansion it enjoyed in the later thirties and beyond. Some of Lambert's comments on the future and significance of jazz are revealing:

> The development of jazz is clearly in the hands of the sophisticated composer . . . The scoring and execution of jazz reach a far higher level than that of any previous form of dance music, and in Duke Ellington's compositions jazz has produced the most distinguished popular music since Johann Strauss.
>
> The difficulty of making a satisfactory synthesis of jazz is due to the fact that it is not, properly speaking, raw material but half-finished material in which European sophistication has been imposed over coloured crudity. There is always the danger that the highbrow composer may . . . leave only the sophisticated trappings behind. This includes what has happened in that singularly inept albeit popular piece, Gershwin's *Rhapsody In Blue*. The composer, trying to write a Lisztian concerto in jazz style has used only the non-barbaric element in dance music, the result being neither good jazz nor good Liszt, and in no sense of the word a good concerto. Although other American composers, and even Gershwin himself, have produced works of greater calibre in this style, the shadow of *Rhapsody In Blue* hangs over most of them and they remain the hybrid child of a hybrid. A rather knowing and unpleasant child too, ashamed of its parents and boasting of its French lessons.[34]

The general harmonic background supplied by the popular music of Tin Pan Alley and Broadway in the 1920s and 1930s, against which Ellington experimented during this period, is important; the parallelism so frequently appearing in his own work was by then commonplace. Gershwin's harmony appears truly representative of the fashion of those days. For example, in the opening bars of *Rhapsody in Blue* (ex. 2.6), parallel chording occurs in bars 1, 3, 4, 5, 6, and 7. The distance between the basic source inspirations followed by the two composers seems quite wide, however: whereas Ellington's harmony is personal and based on blues chromaticism (see chapter 3), Gershwin seems to have been obsessed with parallelism, and his method displays a calculated formulation of standard functional progressions over which he could assemble his jazzy strains. In this respect, my own reservations concerning Gershwin's assumption of the blues connection in *Rhapsody In Blue* have to do with his overt and cavalier annexation, and his attempted concretion in the score, of the "blue note" phenomenon (again, see chapter 3). He has achieved this by returning obsessively in his themes to the minor third, sixth, seventh, and ninth degrees of the scale, as well as to the augmented ninth, in a calculated attempt to convey an impression of genuine blues. These pseudo "blue notes" are marked "X" in ex. 2.6.[35]

This deliberate selection of blue-sounding notes is maintained with little respite throughout the work, and is its principal melodic inspiration. The sustained clarinet glissando which opens the piece, although containing the whole range of microtonal adjustment possible, is theatrical in the extreme, and I feel it is a most obvious and contrived scene-setter.

In genuinely improvised blues, notes in these positions are usually variable in pitch, subject to microtonal adjustment up or down in performance, whereas in Gershwin's oeuvre they are deliberate, tempered, and somewhat self-conscious. These are blue notes that impersonate the real thing, a little too good to be true (or perhaps more accurately a little too true to be good). They have been slotted into the twelve-note system with supporting harmonies tailored to fit—after the event of their selection.

In extempore blues performance this sustained contrivance normally is not possible (for it is not the natural way of playing), nor does it appear with such artificiality in Ellington's music, which in deference to the ethnic roots of the genre invariably settles for a balance between gentle discipline and guided extemporization. Ellington's approach, ever faithful to the overriding folk element inherent in the blues, remains close to the practices of the original blues singers, who performed to their own accompaniment or without any, and of blues instrumentalists, who perform with basic strummed accompaniment.

A distinction must be drawn between the improvising jazz soloist and the genuine jazz composer. Jazz, the shape of which was at first cast firmly in a totally improvisatory mold, was not long in breaking it. The emergence of such jazz composers as Ellington and Jelly Roll Morton in the 1920s saw to that. Extemporization alone would appear to offer much musical liberation,

Example 2.6   Introduction to *Rhapsody in Blue*
                (George Gershwin, 1924)

but this theory has flaws and limitations in application. To avoid complete anarchy, players need to adhere to a preconceived, mutually recognized pattern
of chord changes upon which to build, this procedural route to be traversed
many times. And if one listens to, say, a dozen recorded improvisations by one
performer, one may soon perceive a font of basic ideas, comfortably rehearsed,
that recur repeatedly (with modulatory adjustment). But although this is not
technically improvisation, neither is it composition in the strictest sense. It

does, however, focus on the gulf opening between an improvised music and a composed one.

In 1933 Lambert discussed Ellington's work in this connection:

> The best records of Duke Ellington, on the other hand, can be listened to again and again because they are not just decorations of a familiar shape but a new arrangement of shapes. Ellington, in fact, is a real composer, the first jazz composer of distinction, and the first black composer of distinction. His works—apart from a few minor details—are not left to the caprice of the instrumentalist; they are scored and written out, and though, in the course of time, variants may creep in . . . the first American records of his music may be taken definitively, like a full score, and are the only jazz records worth studying for their form as well as their texture . . . And, although his instrumentalists are of the finest quality, their solos are rarely demonstrations of virtuosity for its own sake.[36]

And on Ellington's unique talents and significance as a jazz composer he wrote:

> The real interest of Ellington's records lies not so much in their colour, brilliant though it may be, as in the amazingly skilful proportions in which the colour is used. I do not only mean skilful as compared with other jazz composers, but as compared with so-called highbrow composers . . . Ellington's best works are written in what may be called "ten-inch record form" (the 78 rpm. disc), and he is perhaps the only composer to raise this insignificant disc to the dignity of a definite *genre*. Ellington [in 1933] has shown no sign of expanding his formal conceptions, and perhaps it is as well, for his works might then lose their peculiar concentrated flavor . . .
>
> [Ellington] has crystallised the popular music of our time and set up a standard by which we may judge . . . other jazz composers, whether American or European.[37]

THE INFLUENCE OF

THE BLUES

*Jazz is commonly thought to have begun around the turn of the
century, but the musics jazz derived from are much older. Blues is
the parent of all legitimate jazz and it is impossible to say exactly
how old blues is—certainly not older than the presence of Negroes
in the United States. It is a native American music, the product
of the black man in this country, or, to put it more exactly the way
I have come to think about it, blues could not exist if the African
captives had not become American captives.*

Although the observations above, from *Blues People: A Study of
Negro Music in White America*, by LeRoi Jones (Imamu Amiri Baraka), are
somewhat overgeneralized, at their core is a point central to my argument and
analysis: that the genre of the blues is "certainly not older than the presence
of Negroes in the United States," and that it is "a native American music."
Owing to the lack of reliable and unprejudiced transcription, this assumption is nearly impossible to support from the standpoint of twentieth-century
musicology. Wiley Hitchcock has observed: "Though extensive scholarship
documents the existence of the blues in the 20th century, there is almost no
mention of the form previous to 1900. Since statements by blues performers
such as W. C. Handy and Big Bill Broonzy indicate that the blues were sung
before 1900, we can only speculate about their origins. It seems probable,
however, that the blues tradition developed after the Civil War, when blacks
were no longer forced to work on the property of their white masters."[1]
In the introduction to his book *Blues Fell This Morning*, Paul Oliver comments in similar fashion, and specifies some of the forms of black music that

predated the blues in the Southern states during the nineteenth century (and, one might speculate, before it): "With some speculation on the origins of the blues, it has been possible to trace its process of evolution and change in a sequence which becomes progressively more clear after the turn of the century. Buried deep in the fertile ground of the Revivalist hymns, the spirituals, the minstrel songs, the banjo and guitar rags, the folk ballads, the work songs and the field hollers lie the roots of the blues which began to take form at some indeterminate time in the late 19th century."[2] On the subject of metrical form: "From such beginnings evolved the folk blues, which originally had 8- and 16-bar forms related to the spirituals and ballads, but ever more frequently took shape in a pattern of 12-bar stanzas."[3] Blues before the advent of the phonograph record—the instrument of almost total recall—remains basically an unknown quantity. But the innumerable recordings made during the last sixty-odd years chronicle the extempore delivery of the blues and the use of microtones incapable of being accurately written down using only the twelve semitones of the European chromatic scale. The unpredictable nature of blues performances, full of surprises, would have offered little chance for accurate notation by the would-be transcribers of the nineteenth century.

As Hitchcock says, scholarly research has "documented the existence of the blues," but the data are almost exclusively historical, sociological, and anecdotal: the musicological significance of nonstandard pitching is usually confined to a sentence or so. Dena J. Epstein's painstakingly researched and splendidly documented study of black folk music before the American Civil War, *Sinful Tunes and Spirituals,* contains some evidence that in addition to percussion of indeterminate pitch, idiosyncrasies of nontempered pitching similar to those which characterize twentieth-century blues melodies and extemporization were present embryonically in the music which had been imported into America. The two following extracts from Epstein's book are the recollections of persons said to have been in occupations requiring sensibility, sensitivity, and scholarship. Both observe some noticeable departures from white European style and usage. In 1861, after staying in Charlotte County, Virginia, a schoolteacher from New England, Mrs. Roger A. Pryor, described the funeral of one of her host's old "servants": We [walked] behind hundreds of negroes following the rude coffin in slave procession, singing antiphonally as they went, one of those *strange weird hymns not to be caught by any Anglo-Saxon voice . . . a strange weird tune no white person's voice could ever follow"* (italics added).[4] And from 1863, a report by a minister from New England who attended a church service in Carrolltown, Louisiana: "[A] low, mournful chant [began] . . . a strange song . . . what is termed in music, a minor . . . *the weird chorus rose a little above, and then fell a little below the keynote"* (italics added).[5] As for the problems which bedeviled the nineteenth-century transcribers, which seemingly were aggravated by some prejudice, "By no means were all the transcribers concerned with these unconventional sounds. Some were so confirmed in their tolerance to European musical norms that they either did not hear the departures or did not feel they were worth preserving. Still others saw it as their duty to 'correct' what they regarded as crudities and uncouth vulgarities."[6]

Given these preconceptions and prejudices, it is not surprising that the white musical establishment should have taken so long to analyze the African style according to its own conventions and academic disciplines, and eventually to accept it. This process is now briefly observed and acknowledged. In 1914, three years before jazz was awarded the accolade of a phonograph recording (and then performed by white players, in the Original Dixieland Jazz Band), H. E. Krehbiel commented on the African origins of the style: "Although based on the same principles as European music, [African music] suffers from the African's lack of European technical skill in the fashioning of his crude instruments. Thus, the strangeness and out-of-tune quality of a great many of the played notes."[7] These imperfections would undoubtedly have been present in some circumstances; for example, poor intonation in performance could have been accounted for by basic errors of dimension—in the placing of frets (home-made banjos and guitars), or in the gradation of the wooden keys of the *balafo* (the African xylophone, structural ancestor of the modern xylophone and vibraphone). But Krehbiel does note some recurring patterning in the style of pitching of black musicians and singers: "There is a significance, which I cannot fathom, in the circumstance that the tones which seem rebellious to the Negro's sense of intervallic propriety are the fourth and seventh of the diatonic major series and the fourth, sixth and seventh of the minor."[8] Ernest Borneman, writing on "The Roots of Jazz" in 1959, is still wrestling to explain and analyze the African phenomenon of nonstandard pitching in terms of the musical conventions observed by the Europeans: "It seems likely that the common source of European and West African music was a simple hemitonic pentatone system. Although indigenous variants of the diatonic scale have been developed and preserved in Africa, modern West Africans who are not familiar with European music will tend to become uncertain when asked to sing in a tempered scale. This becomes particularly obvious when the third and seventh degrees of a diatonic scale are approached. The singer almost invariably tries to skid around these steps with slides, slurs, or vibrato effects so broad as to approach scalar value."[9]

These observations point a way toward serious consideration of a method by which the microtonal elements in black music may be absorbed into the music systems followed by the Europeans. The result would be a fusion of the elements of freedom (characteristic of black music) with those of discipline (characteristic of white music), to produce a music recognizable as a cooperation between black and white. In the introduction to his book *Blues Fell This Morning*, Paul Oliver sums up thus:

> Complex though the beginnings of jazz were, in the assimilation of the marching parade music, of ragtime, the spasm bands and the popular music of the turn of the century, its final emergence as a coherent art form, the blues played a major formative part. Because of the dependence of jazz on blues—the acceptance of the fact that the blues has proved to be a basic element in every aspect of the music as no other single feature has proved to be, the blues has been studied in some detail. Through the blues have been traced links of jazz music with earlier Negro traditions of the spirituals, the worksongs and the hollers. The influence of the blues was a musical one, eventually to be developed into a purely musical nonvocal form of expression.[10]

Paul Oliver's final observation provides the brief for the remainder of my discussion, which deals with one essential question: that is, how did Ellington accomplish in his works an integration of the African way with music into the academic European systems of composition, construction, and performance?

Ellington and the Blues

Duke Ellington was born only thirty-four years after the emancipation of the slaves in 1865. His father, James Edward Ellington, was first a butler at the White House and later a blueprint maker for the U.S. Navy.[11] The young Ellington always had a piano of his own to play, and was taken to hear all the popular musicians whenever they were booked into Washington. Duke was fascinated by piano players, both those with local reputations and those with national ones. These experiences were the beginning of what he later described as his "poolroom education in music":

> There was one great poolroom on T Street—Frank Holliday's poolroom, next to the Howard Theatre. It was not a normal, neighborhood-type poolroom. It was the highspot of billiard parlors, where all the kids from all neighborhoods came.
> Of course, all the piano-players used to hang out there too . . . Claude Hopkins was there. Shrimp Bonner was another. Phil Wood, who used to play piano at the Howard Theatre, was a good songwriter too. Roscoe Lee, who became a dentist, would be there. He, and Claude Hopkins were reader piano-players, like Doc Perry, Louis Brown, who came by from time-to-time. Les Dishman was the great left hand. Then there were

Clarence Bonner, Sticky Mac, and Blind Johnny. *These* cats couldn't read, but there was a wonderful thing of exchange which went on between them and the guys who did. (italics in original)[12]

Ellington also remembered other local players: Ralph Green, Louis Thomas, Caroline Thornton, and Gertie Wells, all unschooled, "natural" musicians. Regrettably, the paucity of precise information and absence of re-cordings make somewhat speculative the question of exactly which sources in-fluenced Ellington the most, particularly with regard to the "blue" inflections that flavored his own music so strongly. An exception to this generalization concerns Claude Hopkins, who recorded with, among others, the tenor saxo-phonists Bud Freeman and Coleman Hawkins and the trumpeter Joe Thomas, and who clearly forged a link between the blues and Ellington.[13] There is also some confirmation from Ellington himself that he had listened intently to the "natural" playing of other piano players in Washington and learned from them, as he recalled in his autobiography: "The whole thing suddenly became very clear to me, just like that, and *I got all the Negro music that way. You can't learn that in any school. And there were things that I wanted to do that were not in books*" (italics added).[14] He recalled in particular an encounter with the renowned ragtime and stride pianist and composer James P. Johnson in Washington:

> Percy Johnson was a drummer and a buddy of mine . . . One day, he invited me over to his house . . . He had a player-piano and he put on a roll by James P. Johnson . . . Percy slowed the mechanism down so that I could see which keys on the piano were going down and I digested John-son's wonderful sounds. I played with it until I had his *Carolina Shout* off pat . . . I really had it perfect, so that when James P. Johnson himself came to Washington to play at Convention Hall, my cheering section and pals waited until he played *Carolina Shout*, and then insisted that I got up on the stand and cut him! I was scared stiff, but James P. was not only a master, he was a great one for encouraging youngsters. He went along with the whole scene, and when I finished *Carolina Shout* he applauded too. I didn't play any more that night, but just leaned over the piano and listened to the one and only. What I absorbed on that occasion might, I think, have constituted a whole semester in a conservatory. Afterwards he elected me his guide for a tour of all the Washington joints, and I stayed up until 10 a.m.[15]

Notwithstanding the influence of the blues on his music, Ellington did not experience any of the discomforts of living out the blues personally. The songs of the visiting bluesmen related privations, the knowledge of which he absorbed at second hand. Toward the end of his life, Ellington recalled in characteristically oblique fashion his comfortable start: "I don't believe a man plays the blues because he *has* the blues. It's like any art—sculpture, for instance; a sculptor can carve the figure of a crying woman without *being* a crying woman" (italics in original).[16] That Ellington's admitted approach to his profession was largely intuitive—his facility developed during patient and protracted trial and error—appears to me to add to his achievements. His significance as a jazz composer may have been founded on his ability to capture on score the singular nuances and surprises, both melodic and harmonic, of the vocal blues and their accompaniments: "According to the textbooks, Ellington's part-writing is incorrect; according to his ear (and ours) it is correct, for the rules of European harmony were not devised to produce the effects that Ellington had in mind. His genius is to be equated with his ear, which is the servant of his experience. Any music-maker of whom this is not true is not a composer."[17]

The Blues Scale

Nonstandard pitching is a phenomenon of vital significance in Ellington's music. The tempered chromatic scale, a staircase of twelve notationally equal semitones, can only partially accommodate the microtonal gradations of pitch encountered in the slurs, glissandi, and wide vibrati of an extempore blues performance. It seems reasonable to suspect that another scale may be present—a blues scale (ex. 3.1).[18] In any performance of the blues, there will be instances where a note sung, blown, plucked, or bowed may not quite conform in pitch to the conventional twelve-note system. The note may be a microtone above or below one of these twelve, say between the major third of the scale and the minor third, or between the flattened fifth and the perfect fourth. It is difficult to notate such variances other than by explanatory annotation. In transcriptions from recorded blues one sees, for example, "¾-tone flat," "bend," and "slow gliss." In recorded blues the liberties in pitching are taken most frequently in the neighborhood of the third, seventh, and fifth degrees of the diatonic scale; these are the blue notes. Whenever this nontempered pitching occurs while the accompaniment persists with the basic major triad, there is a momentary contradiction, saved from bizarre "wrongness" by controlled correction (resolution) on the part of the improviser.

In ex. 3.1, the positioning of the three blued areas within the diatonic scale is displayed. One blued region is enclosed within each tetrachord, and the alliance between tetrachords is negotiated by the third blued area frequently encountered between the dominant and subdominant degrees of the scale.

Example 3.1   The Blues Scale

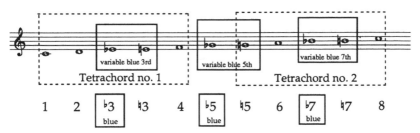

This may well be the "African scale" mentioned earlier, or at least the common ground for black and white music which Ernest Borneman had broached in his writings in 1959.[19] The firmest directives to cadential resolution are issued by the blue notes on the seventh and fifth degrees, where the flattening of these notes toward the sixth and fourth degrees of the scale forces modulation through a perfect cadence into the second inversion triad on the subdominant. The errant blue note, the flattened mediant, frequently refuses to obey the white man's rules, which would insist on a rise by half-step to the subdominant. Within these patterns lies the clue to the formulation of the classic twelve-bar and eight-bar sequences of cadences evolving from the moment the black musicians adopted instrumentation and some discipline from their white masters (see ex. 3.2 for the most widely used progressions). In practice

Example 3.2   The 12-Bar Blues

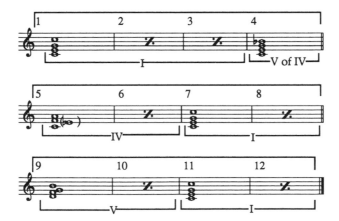

Example 3.2 (continued)   The 8-Bar Blues

(b)

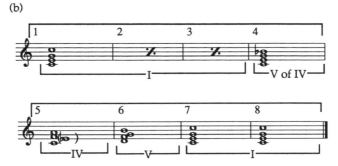

these may have varied in the number of bars employed, duration being dictated by the variable parsing within the frequently spontaneous lyrics of the bluesmen's songs.

The Relation of Blue Notes to Basic Harmony

When notated to the nearest semitone in the twelve-note system, the variable blue notes illustrated in ex. 3.1 solidify into conventional chords when these are extended beyond the octave, as in ex. 3.3. The ambivalent major-minor probability in blues construction is also shown in ex. 3.3, then illustrated in greater detail by the harmonic analysis in ex. 3.4. The chords formed by the passing blue notes against the accompaniment are marked there as blue harmonies.

Example 3.4 is a twelve-bar blues line on five staves. It is given to establish a link, in the purely harmonic sense, between the music of the blues artists and the white orchestral conventions of voicing and resolution. The following is an outline of its characteristics; each paragraph corresponds to one of the staves.

1. *Basic harmonies*. These are presented first, as basic guidance for extemporization. Here the original and truly archaic pattern has been enhanced by arranging a plagal cadence between bars 2 and 3, and an interrupted cadence through bars 9, 10, and 11.
2. *Blues melody*. This has been assembled consciously to include instances of typical activity around the third, fifth, and seventh degrees of the diatonic scale. Such predictable stylistic tendencies can be recognized in recorded blues performances from all periods in jazz.
3. *Blue note discords*. These have been indicated when a disagreement

Example 3.3

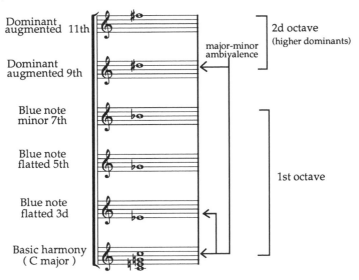

Example 3.4   A Blues (blue notes marked*)

Example 3.4 (continued)

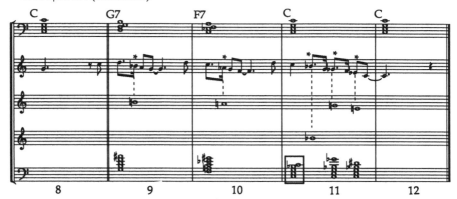

occurs between melody and accompaniment. In performance the extempore blue note rarely settles squarely on the precise semitone that
would be demanded in a conventional context, but often the lowering
or raising of pitch may be only barely noticeable.

4. *Blue note concords.* Where a minor seventh has been played and the
   basic accompaniment to the performance includes this blued note (or
   indeed, even where it does not), no perceptible disagreement will be
   apparent from the written transcription; only in performance will the
   variable pitching of the played note be perceived to be fractionally off-
   center (as in the discords described in paragraph 3, above).

5. *Blue harmonies.* These make the firmest point so far regarding Ellington's approach to harmonization, based on his recognition of the passing clashes which habitually occurred between blues extemporizations
   and their accompaniments. These fluid circumstances may be readily
   frozen into solid, vertical harmony, as noted in ex. 3.4.

The blues scale would appear to offer a direct route connecting the two
bases of inventiveness involved here—the one pure, the other applied—and
to enable one to trace the source of the dissonances which became characteristic of Ellington. The first four bars of Ellington's composition *Main Stem*
(1942) illustrate his use of a blue note, sharply accented on the strong first
beat of each bar. This motif is repeated with some variation throughout the
work. Ellington's inborn predilection for blue notes and his flair in weaving
the dissonances of the blues into his orchestral writing (hinted at in ex. 3.5)
move the spheres of black and white music into nearly identical orbits. As
Wilfrid Mellers has observed in a similar vein, "Ellington explored impressionistic harmony, not so much because it was 'modern' (by the twenties it was
no longer), but because he realized intuitively that it was the only harmony
that might be relevant to blues-derived jazz, since it was at once sensuous and

non-developing . . . Ellington's harmony is another feature that links him with the world of pop music; and it is probable that he first inherited Debussian and Ravelian harmony from Tin Pan Alley, rather than from direct sources."[20] Or, in Ellington's own words, "Today, you need the conservatory, with an ear to what's happening in the street."[21]

Example 3.5   Main Stem

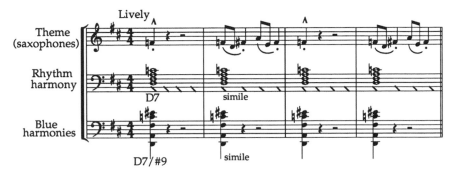

"Blues Is the Essence of Jazz"

Some time ago, two jazz critics (one, coincidentally a recording director), and a musician came together to discuss "if the blues is essential to the jazz idiom." Pianist Billy Taylor—the participating musician—said, "I don't know of one giant who didn't have a tremendous respect and feeling for the blues, whether he played the blues or not. The spirit of it was either in his playing or he wasn't really a giant as far as jazz was concerned . . ." Neshui Ertegun, director of Atlantic Records and a respected critic, followed up, "Let me ask you one question. Do you think a man like Lester Young would play a tune like *Body and Soul* in the same way, if he had never played the blues?" Billy Taylor's answer was, "No." And Leonard Feather summarized, "I think what it boils down to is that *blues is the essence of jazz*, and merely having a feeling for the blues means having a feeling for jazz. In other words, the chords, or notes of the chords which are essential for blues are essential for jazz —the flat third, seventh, etc." To which Billy Taylor countered, "Well, I hesitate to oversimplify in that particular case, because I tend to go back to the spirit. It's not the fact that a man on certain occasions would flat a certain note, bend a note, or do something which is strictly a blues-type device. It's just that whatever this nebulous feeling is—the vitality

they seem to get into the blues—whatever it is, makes the difference between Coleman Hawkins' *Body and Soul* and a society tenor [saxophone]
player's *Body and Soul.*" [22]

The premise expounded by these professional jazz people is that blues is
a manner of playing, in a personal, convincing, inventive way, any phrase
which may come to mind, either extemporized or remembered, and that
extempore blues constructions on basic tonic, subdominant, and dominant
harmonies, with all their flexibility immediately beneath the third, seventh,
and fifth degrees of the scale, are equally at home when incorporated into the
paraphrasing of any established melody, or into an extemporization based on
the chords beneath the melody. Feather and Taylor agreed to divide musicians
working in popular music into two distinct categories: the artists, represented
by Coleman Hawkins, who are well equipped to enhance a theme from the
imagination of someone else without straying from its preset harmonies, but
who have an innate feeling for the blues; and the artisans, epitomized by the
"society" tenor saxophonist, capable only of reproducing the theme as they
read it from the score.

In truth, the improvisation by Hawkins on *Body and Soul* referred to above
does not overtly display a preponderant blues influence; it merely follows the
interesting changes of a good pop song, and blue notes appearing in relation
to the underlying harmonies are purely ornamental and not structural. The
pervasive, enduring, ever-present blues inflections in jazz are better illustrated
by ex. 3.6, where two extemporizations are compared (transcribed, then transposed for ease of analysis to a common key). On the face of it the styles are
disparate—the recordings were made twenty-one years apart by different soloists—but clearly both men were strongly influenced in their melodic thinking
by the blue note phenomenon; also, their rhythmic structuring displays the
sense of rubato so typical of free blues. So however incongruous it may seem
to mention Louis Armstrong and Charlie Parker in the same breath, their
responses to the blues directive are identical.

Few could recognize more quickly than Ellington the difference between
the likes of an Armstrong or Parker and the "squares" of this world: Ellington
was a fine judge of talent from very early in his career as a composer and
bandleader. In 1924, for example, he recruited the trumpeter James "Bubber"
Miley (1903–32). "It has been suggested that in Ellington's early compositions
he contributed the 'art,' while the 'folk' element of blue improvisation came
from his collaboration with his first trumpet, Bubber Miley. The collaboration
would not have worked if the 'blue' passion had not been latent in Ellington." [23] Born in South Carolina, Miley moved to New York at an early age and
grew up there. After working in jazz in New York he toured in the early 1920s

Example 3.6

Louis Armstrong:
Gully Low Blues (1927)

Charlie Parker:
Parker's Mood (1948)

Chord Sequence

* = dissonant blue notes
† = consonant blue notes

with the folk and blues singer Mamie Smith, then known as the "first lady of the blues." (Sidney Bechet also played with her from time to time; she was the first black singer to make a recording.) Miley was recruited by Ellington in autumn 1924 and remained with him until February 1929; he later was associated briefly with Jelly Roll Morton. (Morton had little time for Ellington —and the feeling was mutual—but he was not averse to benefiting from the talents of one of Ellington's former sidemen, even though these talents had by then been eroded by ill health.)

With the recruitment of Miley, Ellington moved decidedly toward the blues as an inspiration for his writing and the overall tone of his band; earlier the prime influence had seemed to be ragtime (see chapter 4). Miley possessed a singular talent, unique in 1924; he had evolved a technique of producing a growling, vocalized sound by humming in his throat while producing the trumpet's own sound, at the same time manipulating a plumber's rubber plunger cup in front of the bell of his horn, at varying distances from it, to manufacture nearly human, wordlike articulations. To camouflage the basic trumpet timbre almost completely, a small metal mute was also inserted into the bell. The presence of blue notes in his solos (see ex. 3.7), combined with the vocalizations, is evidence of a lineage connecting the field hollers of the slaves with the box of tricks of the blues instrumentalists. After Miley left the band the effect of his ideas on his leader's music proved lasting and profound. His folksy trumpet style was perpetuated by his successors, Cootie Williams (from 1929 to 1940 and from 1962 to 1973), Rex Stewart (1934 to 1945), and Ray Nance (from 1940 to 1965 with some brief absences, and for a short time in 1973). Early in 1928 Miley recorded *Take It Easy* with Ellington and his orchestra (ex. 3.7).

+	= plunger held close to bell, almost completely closed
o	= plunger waved away from bell (about two inches)
♩	= note on which the throat growl is employed
⌄	= slight flattening of the center note (say by a quarter-tone), either by slackening the lip pressure without recourse to valve movement, or by depressing the valve halfway
⌣	= a bend, which has the same results as for the triplet above, but which is achieved only with the lip
(a)	= blue note, where the soloist has either flattened the mediant against the root major triad persisting in the accompaniment, or played the augmented ninth against the sustained dominant seventh. See bars 6 and 7.
(b)	= instance where the soloist is at variance with the accompanying harmony, though not on the primary blue notes on the flattened mediant and minor seventh. The soloist either has augmented the fifth of the chord (as in bars 2, 12, and 14—in performance the augmentation is to the extent of a quarter-tone), or has seemingly mispitched (see the B-flats in bars 12 and 13 and the E-natural in bar 13.

Example 3.7 *Take It Easy*

As usual, the small, pear-shaped metal mute was inserted into the bell of Miley's trumpet, to remain in place throughout. The cup-shaped rubber plunger provided the vocalized wah-wah effects.

By selecting Miley as his first trumpet soloist, Ellington gained access to the quirks of pitch, style, and sound of the fathers of country blues. Miley's impersonation of the human voice was a major ingredient of the band's extemporizations. Ellington's orchestra was conventional only in that its instrumentation was common to bands specializing in popular music, such as those of Gus Arnheim and Paul Whiteman, both prominent in the 1920s and early 1930s.

"The man in the street gained his knowledge of jazz from the symphonic perversions of Paul Whiteman which, in attempting to make jazz 'respectable,' deprived it of all validity. The soaring strings, souped-up textures, chromatic sequences inflated the feeling; the bulging brass elephantised the sonority, until the result was an exact musical equivalent for the 'substitute living' of the worst aspects of Hollywood."[24] The orchestras led by Ellington, Arnheim, and Whiteman each contained trumpet, trombone, saxophone, and rhythm sections, but Ellington's group was decidedly apart from the others. Its players and the ear of its leader were unique, and consequently so was its sound. Arnheim and particularly Whiteman sought to be all things to all listeners; Ellington did not. His men were not simply so many trumpeters, trombonists, and reed and rhythm players.

Joe "Tricky Sam" Nanton (1904–46) played trombone in Ellington's orchestra from 1926 to 1946. He had begun his professional career with the pianist Cliff Jackson in Washington, then worked from 1923 to 1924 with Frazier's Harmony Five and in 1925 with the banjoist Elmer Snowden. Nanton possessed a technique of vocalized delivery similar to that of Miley and using similar accessories, but producing an even more gruff and human-sounding timbre. A typical solo by Nanton is shown in ex. 3.8.

Nanton's solos are simpler in construction than Miley's (the trombonist did rather have his hands full, having to wrestle simultaneously with slide and plunger). They were delivered with great authority and a shouting directness,

Example 3.8   Four bars from Nanton's solo in *Ko Ko*

"ya-ya" = [+o]-[+o]

Example 3.9   Tricky Sam Nanton's solo in *Sweet Chariot*

and it is interesting to examine them in full, for they fairly leap out from the background of Ellington's orchestrations. More often than not they were executed in the top register of the instrument (see ex. 3.9), possibly because of a desire to minimize the shift of slide.

Nanton's solo from 1930 is typical (ex. 3.9). The extemporization follows almost exclusively the notes of the underlying triads. Only on four occasions does Nanton step out of this line: in bar 1, where he plays the blue C-flat at (a); in bar 4, where the dominant thirteenth (B-flat) appears at (b); in bar 6, at (c), where he interpolates the flattened fifth of the root chord (to express this as a positive note rather than as a nontempered step, as in the blues, was an innovation in jazz at the time)—a peak of surprise in this context; and in bar 8, where he plays the major seventh (C-natural) as the modulatory pivot into the dominant seventh in bar 9, where the ninth is used as a passing note.

The solo is executed entirely in the upper register of the trombone. Apart from offering relief from acute elbow bending, the force which must be applied to produce such high tones adds emphasis and passion to the whole statement. Throughout Nanton's solo a range of feeling is expressed by means of adroit manipulation of the plunger: freely and with near human articulation during the first two bars, bottled up, strangulated to a degree, during bars 3 to 7, and reverting to outspoken directness in bars 8, 9, and 10. Ellington used Nanton repeatedly to inject the sounds of pain, passion, and, occasionally, ironic laughter into his works. Nanton's gruff cries, suspended within his spartan constructions of I–IV–I, linked Ellington definitively with the seminal sounds of archaic vocal blues. In this respect Nanton's uncannily accurate impersonations were invaluable, and he defined the style throughout his career.

By their manner of playing, Miley and Nanton allowed Ellington to manipulate the blues style, and to inject its shape and sound into the orchestral body of his music. The two men were born only a year apart, and to a considerable extent both absorbed the mannerisms of the vocal blues into their instrumental techniques. But unfortunately no bluesmen born a generation before Miley and Nanton were recorded (no "jazz" and little else of black music was recorded before the First World War), and there is therefore no proof of the styles current around 1900. Modern recordings of elderly bluesmen and younger musicians who embraced the style can at best only hint at the sounds and constructions from the period preceding Miley and Nanton.[25]

Johnny Hodges: An Extraordinary Blues Player

Johnny Hodges, alto saxophonist, was born in Cambridge, Massachusetts, where he studied music privately, then played with the bands of Bobby Sawyer (1925), Lloyd Scott (1926), and the drummer Chick Webb (1927). He developed into an instrumentalist of startling accomplishment; his tone could be described (inadequately) as silky; he was a master of controlled, uninterrupted glissandi, poised portamenti, and anguished, almost explosive accenting. This repertoire of techniques gave him full access to the nontempered intervals characteristic of the blues. His approach differed from that favored by Miley and Nanton in that he rarely used the growl in his playing (even though it is quite possible to use it on reed instruments), relying in-

Example 3.10   Johnny Hodges's final chorus in
              Things Ain't What They Used To Be

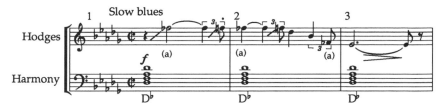

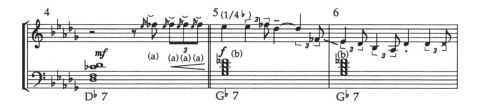

stead on the attractions of ravishing tone and perfectly controlled nontempered pitching to achieve his dramatic projections. He played with Ellington from 1928 to 1951 and again from 1955 until 1970, when he died unexpectedly. Hodges's strength lay in the simplicity of his extempore construction; he rarely strayed from the basic inversions of the chords, but added cunning touches of blueness in the form of suspensions and impeccably executed glissandi. He virtually dictated the rules of the game for the alto saxophone in Ellington's music, and was never satisfactorily replaced. During and after the 1930s, no doubt inspired by the succession of leisurely, lush tunes which Ellington produced during this period, Hodges recorded a series of lyrical paraphrases of these melodies, contributing hugely to their great success in Tin Pan Alley.

Hodges was featured in formal blues sequences throughout his career in the Ellington Orchestra. In 1940 Ellington's only son, Mercer, provided a riff tune, *Things Ain't What They Used to Be*, which effectively became Hodges's property for the next thirty years. Example 3.10 is a transcription of Hodges's final extemporized chorus from the original small-group recording of the piece made in Hollywood in 1941.[26] His fondness for the blued third is apparent throughout the extract.

(¼-flat) = one quarter-tone flat only
(a)   = blue note
(b)   = dissonance created by a major sixth in the solo against a minor seventh in the accompaniment
(c)   = eleventh of the dominant chord against the major third (mediant) in the accompaniment
(d)   = augmented fifth of the dominant, creating a momentary, bluesy clash

The three extempore solos in this chapter, by representatives of Ellington's trumpet, trombone, and reed sections, reveal the extent to which the freedoms inherent in the blues scale tinted the styles of the three musicians. Nanton and Hodges were still with Ellington during his prolific period of 1939 to 1941; Miley had died in 1932. One of those who later played trumpet with Ellington, Cootie Williams (1929 to 1940), used several unorthodox playing techniques, including half-valving. Although these were not pure blues inflections in realization, they nevertheless added some color to Ellington's performances, which retained their blues inflections and flavor until the end of his career.

For Ellington composing was not an abstraction: it was an activity invariably directed toward performance. But where does the improvisatory quality of the blues come in? The elements of the blues were present in the solo styles and timbres of Ellington's carefully chosen musicians. He wrote strong themes for them. He orchestrated settings for their improvisations, devised carefully modulated sequences, and gave his soloists an orchestral background that was either calm and unobtrusive or agitated and involved, depending on the mood and tempo of the piece, thus enabling his improvisers to relax.

Ellington integrated pure improvisation with written music in several ways:

1. By means of harmonic progressions which he organized as the bases for extemporization. Frequently these were conventional blues structures

of eight or twelve bars, with an almost obligatory, muscular plagal cadence somewhere close to the core of the sequence. (It bears repeating,
however, that the blues is a way of playing and not simply a certain
sequence of cadences.)

2. Through the choice of musicians with whom he worked. Ellington
   made sure to avail himself of the idiosyncratic, nontempered gradations
   of pitch encountered in the blues, by using the improvisatory talents of
   such atypical musicians as Miley and Nanton. The special techniques
   evolved by these men and their successors, imitative of early vocal
   blues, were integrated into the fabric of Ellington's writings.

3. By means of chordal voicing in his orchestration (see ex. 3.5). Ellington
   was aware of the enlivening blues dissonances created when the blues
   scale is superimposed over a basic triadic accompaniment (for example,
   augmented or minor ninths, and augmented elevenths or flattened
   fifths, on the dominant seventh chords).

The augmentation or diminution of primary triadic intervals, building into
the impressionistic chordal structures shown in ex. 3.4, was the closest that
conventional harmony could come to incorporating the effect of the nontempered intervals formed by blues improvisation against a basic blues accompaniment. Ellington's sensitive ear was quick to recognize the common ground
between black and white conventions. His significance as a jazz composer
and orchestra leader lies in his ability to imbue his writing with the color and
character of the classic blues within the constraints of conventional notation
and the need for discipline within the ensemble.

THE INFLUENCE

OF RAGTIME

Ragtime developed during the last half of the nineteenth century. It combines the irregular pulses and displaced accents of black music—syncopation—with the structural formalism of conventional melody and harmony. Ellington, born in 1899, heard ragtime both at its peak as a form of popular music and as the transitional element which introduced the new jazz style. Many other changes were taking place at the same time:

There had to be a growth within the techniques of instrumental jazz itself. This begins to happen in the Mid-west logging and turpentine camps where the workers played instrumental blues for guitar, or, more commonly for two guitars, one playing the rhythm-harmony, the other the tune and embroidery thereon. Since these pieces stressed the rhythmic excitement rather than the vocal melancholy of the blues, they were sometimes known as "Fast Western." Though a harsh, rough sonority could be extracted from two guitars, the plangency of the instruments was not naturally suited to this rawly masculine music; so the Fast Western blues players seized avidly on the broken-down upright pianos that came their way in the shanty-town bars and brothels. . . . At the same time as the urban folk art of barrelhouse piano was evolving in the bars and brothels, the Negro tried consciously to create a notated form of piano music that would be his contribution to "art." This was piano rag: which is as distinct from barrelhouse piano in that it has no reference to either the blues or to improvisation . . . Rag derived, like banjo music, not from the blues, but from those more sophisticated White sources that had found a home, along with slavery, in the Southern States—French quadrilles, military two-steps, that were closely related to, then merged, to create rags in 16-bar strains—never in the [elastic] 12-bar strains of the blues.[1]

Some traces of the blues do however appear in classic ragtime, suggesting that the partition between blues and rag was not quite as soundproof as the above observations imply. One example is Carey Morgan's *Trilby Rag*,[2] which dates from 1915, toward the close of the ragtime era. Even a sampling of the masses of notated ragtime which survive from the period make clear that the popular forms of black music had moved away from the blues and toward the musical conventions of the Old World in matters of composition, presentation, and form. Ellington was particularly adept at integrating improvisatory black music into conventional structures, but he was by no means the only black musician to do so. Others, notably Jelly Roll Morton, James P. Johnson, Willie "the Lion" Smith, and Thomas "Fats" Waller, favored a more casual approach to both writing and playing than Ellington did. They were all pianist-composers and proficient improvisers, and all were born between 1885 and 1904, when ragtime developed and was recognized.

The musical climate in which Ellington and his contemporaries lived was formed as early as 1847, when Louis Moreau Gottschalk (1829–69) published his piano piece *La Bamboula, danse des nègres*, said to be based on African themes heard in Congo Square, New Orleans. But Gottschalk, a white concert pianist and composer (there are conflicting reports as to whether he had some African blood), may in fact have been inspired by the folk-dance rhythms of the Caribbean rather than by the early black syncopations of the southern states. (A composition by him from 1857 is entitled *Souvenir de Porto Rico*.) And by the 1890s both black and white composers had used Caribbean folk strains in composite pieces closely akin in form to the popular quadrilles and marches of the day. These were the rags. "Ragtime is essentially a late nineteenth-century American musical phenomenon that has influenced virtually every popular idiom in American music. Ragtime's unique syncopation has developed far beyond mere piano solos, and its range extends vividly and spectacularly from country blues to jazz . . . Ragtime developed from native American folk forms [and was] fostered in bars and brothels where it was played on banjos and pianos . . . it was as comfortable played by 'professors' in houses of ill-repute as it was by families at home."[3] This passage, from Lawrence Cohn's notes to the recorded anthology *Maple Leaf Rag: Ragtime in Rural America*, gets the facts right, and in the right order. Of particular importance is Cohn's statement that ragtime ranges from country blues to jazz.

Ragtime was, in the history of Black music in America, a form precariously balanced between rural folk traditions and sophisticated urban musical forms. It bridged a gap between early, wholly oral traditions and later scored versions of jazz and dance music and it provided a clear example of a successful Black art. [Scott] Joplin, [James Sylvester] Scott and [Joseph Francis] Lamb forged a large body of finished and self-consistent works of art and transmitted them to a large audience.[4] This pattern was later recapitulated in the history of jazz, as musicians worked to assimilate and re-organize the folk-materials of jazz to create a new art form—culminating in the works of jazz composers like Jelly Roll Morton, Joe Oliver, James P. Johnson and Duke Ellington and their followers. The example of ragtime as an antecedent form directly influenced these composers. Thus any study of the formulation of the art of jazz must proceed from a knowledge of the art of ragtime.[5]

In January 1897 came the first publication as sheet music of a ragtime piece: *Mississippi Rag* by William H. Krell, a white composer and bandleader from Chicago. In December of the same year the first rag by a black composer was printed: *Harlem Rag* by Thomas Million "Tom" Turpin, a well-known pianist from St. Louis and a close friend and associate of Scott Joplin. The year 1899, when Ellington was born, saw the first publication of a work by Scott Joplin (*Original Rags*, in March), and the publication of his most successful work (*Maple Leaf Rag*, in September). Born in Texarkana, Texas, on 24 November 1868, Joplin was by this time already a reasonably well-known writer and performer of ragtime.

Ellington and Joplin had certain similarities: both men were black, both were pianists, both composed music (instrumental works as well as songs) which depended for its identity on common devices of syncopation, and both collaborated from time to time with other composers. Each took on extended composition when well into his career, which was considered innovative throughout the ragtime era and well into the 1940s in jazz. In 1911 Joplin wrote the libretto and music for a full-length opera in three acts, *Treemonisha*, the story of a black foundling child who grew up to lead her people and fight for freedom and equality through education. "Unlike the earlier *Guest of Honor* (1903, unpublished and the score lost), *Treemonisha* is not called a *ragtime* opera. Joplin attempted in the later work to combine ragtime and folk-music in more time-honored forms . . . If *The Green Pastures* was a picture of a God who was a Negro, and of a Heaven made for the dark of skin, then *Treemonisha* is the legend of a Negro Eden."[6] Joplin has come to be recognized as the king of ragtime. "He was the central figure and prime creative spirit of ragtime, a composer from whom a large segment of 20th Century American music derived its shape and spirit."[7]

In 1943 Ellington, equally outstanding as a jazz composer, completed his first important extended jazz work, the suite *Black, Brown and Beige*,[8] given its premiere at Carnegie Hall on 23 January of that year. Although Ellington followed Joplin's lead in waiting until his early forties to produce his first large-scale composition (and until he had sufficient technique and experience), this was as far as the similarity went. His suite is dominated by blues and folk elements, and includes many opportunities for improvisation. Further, his choice of subject matter is the very antithesis of that used by Joplin. "[*Black, Brown and Beige*] surveys the history of the Negro in North America—depicting first his importation as a slave, and later the rather freer life achieved by him in the aftermath of the Civil War. It is outspoken about the color bar, sometimes aggressively so."[9] The styles of Joplin and Ellington are comparable in that they both used compounded song structures and syncopated phrasing. But the two had completely different ideas about how their music should be performed:

> *Joplin*. We wish to say here that the "Joplin Ragtime" is destroyed by careless or imperfect rendering, and very often good players lose the effect entirely, by playing too fast. They are harmonized with the supposition that each note will be played as it is written, as it takes this, and also the proper time divisions, to complete the sense intended.[10]

> *Ellington*. The music is mostly written down because it saves time. It's written down if it's only a basis for change. There's no set "system." Sometimes I write it and the band and I elaborate on the arrangement. Sometimes Billy Strayhorn does the arrangement . . . When we're all working together, a guy may have an idea and he plays it on his horn. Another guy may add to it and make something of it. Someone may play a riff, and ask, "How do you like this?" There may be a difference of opinion as to what kind of mute to use. Someone may advocate extending a note, or cutting it off. The sax section may want to put an additional smear on it.[11]

It is clear from these statements that although Joplin preferred for his music to be played strictly as notated, Ellington was content to have the score tempered by collective experience. He of course respected the written notes, as is clear from the polish of the recordings from his mature period, but in contrast to Joplin he provided ample opportunity for improvisation in his works, and encouraged the paraphrasing of his written strains.

With their sheet music on sale, Joplin, Scott, and Lamb could reach the public more easily. Performance of their music was within reach of everyone who could play a piano and read music reasonably well. With Ellington's music this was difficult: his seemingly casual approach to performance masked a tough standard, in that his works were written for specific and unique musicians to perform in a bluesy, nonstandard, and extempore manner (see chapter 4).

Ellington's debt to ragtime is evident in three areas: (1) he used diatonic harmonies, based on tonic, dominant, and subdominant (as in the blues), as well as related dominants; (2) he used compounded song strains, eight, sixteen, or thirty-two bars long, with shorter introductions, vamps, and codas; and (3) syncopated phrasing is apparent in all his melodies and a fair number of his accompanying rhythms. Harmonically, Ellington's root sequences are not complex, being closely aligned with the I, IV, V, and chain-of-dominants patterning favored by the ragtimers. The harmony in his early work was fundamentally diatonic, as exemplified in his *Soda Fountain Rag* (1914) and *Jig Walk* (ca. 1923); these early influences persist in Ellington's mature scores of the early 1940s.

Ellington's orchestra began as a dance band, and in all practical senses continued as such: its jazz concerts, theater presentations, and sacred concerts were interspersed with numerous engagements to provide music to accompany dancing. It is hardly surprising that the form of Ellington's music should have followed the structures of ragtime, the basic four-bar and eight-bar phrases of which are entirely conducive to both stylized and extemporized movement. But there is early evidence that Ellington was not completely ruled by the lowest common denominator of the four-bar phrase. For example, he inserted a ten-bar strain into his earliest known work, *Soda Fountain Rag*, composed when he was fifteen years old.

A Definition of Syncopation

Syncopation is demonstrably the dominant element in black music —blues, ragtime, and jazz. It evolves out of a natural tendency toward rubato in performance, and perhaps from something even more basic: "As individuals we play and sing with an improvisatory freedom that attempts to over-ride the earth-pull of metre and harmony. Syncopation itself is an expression of this desire."[12] Syncopation may be defined as follows: (1) the momentary displacement by some precise degree of anticipation or delay of the regular or normal accent of a piece of music, into a position between the pulses; or (2) the occasion when a strong accent is brought in where a weak one is expected; or (3) a displacement, in the manner of a rhythmic contradiction, of either the beat or the normal accent of the musical phrase—although the underlying, original metric pulse of the music, as indicated by its time signature, remains recognizable.

There appear to be only three fundamental types of syncopation:[13] mid-beat (untied, referred to as type A in my analyses and examples), mid-bar (tied, type B), and cross-bar (tied, type C). The permutations that can be derived from these basic types are limited only by the resourcefulness of the composer or improviser.

Examples 4.1–4.3 illustrate the three types of syncopation. Type A is described as mid-beat because the strong accents appear between the basic pulses indicated by the time signature of the music, and as untied because the effect is contained within the first two beats of the bar, or the second two beats of the bar, or both (as in ex. 4.1). Syncopation of the type shown in ex. 4.2 occurs in mid-bar: the final eighth-note in the first half of the bar is tied to the first note in the second half of the bar. In ex. 4.3 the final eighth-note of one bar is tied across the barline to the first note of the following bar.

Example 4.1, Type A: Mid-beat (untied) syncopation

Example 4.2, Type B: Mid-bar (tied) syncopation

Example 4.3 Type C: Cross-bar (tied) syncopation

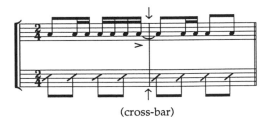

(cross-bar)

Secondary Ragtime

In 1938 Winthrop Sergeant described secondary ragtime as "the superimposition of a rhythm of different phrase-lengths, but of identical metric units upon the prevailing rhythm of the music. Usually the superimposed rhythm falls into phrases of three eighth-note units, which are set against a background of the normal four-quarter rhythm of [ragtime and] jazz."[14] In 1926 Don Knowlton had also defined this peculiarity, and I include his words because of their specific reference to the drum and banjo, the black musicians' primary rhythm instruments in the days before ragtime: "The imposition of a *one*, two, three element in rhythm, upon the one, two, three, four fundamental. This, I believe, is the only characteristic of jazz which is truly of American—or rather, of Afro-American—origin. A Negro guitar player once asked me, 'You know the difference between primary rag and *secondary* rag?' His primary rag was simply syncopation; his secondary rag was this superimposition of *one*, two, three, four . . . As it is a rhythmic rather than a melodic principle, it has found its exponents principally in the banjo and the drum" (italics in original).[15]

This rhythm is technically simple to execute with two sticks on a drum, and on the banjo as a down-and-up strum. Models of these instruments could be made cheaply at home (the woodblock and the cigar-box guitar, for instance), and this was important for the development of the syncopated style, which complemented the rhythmic emancipation of extempore blues. These basic technical points are illustrated in ex. 4.4, where two illustrations of secondary-ragtime grouping are also given.

Example 4.4

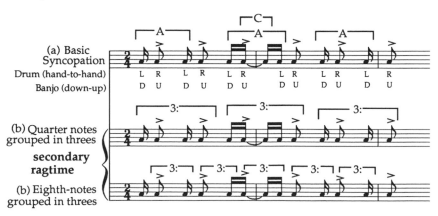

Example 4.5 Boogie Woogie Rhythm*

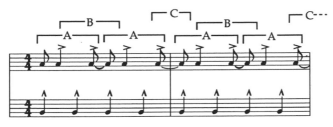

*incorporating syncopation types A,B, and C

The pounding, left-hand barrelhouse rhythm of ex. 4.5 had virtually been ignored by the conservative rag composers of the Joplin school, who were rarely inspired by the blues, but some acknowledgment of the barrelhouse genre had apparently been made as early as 1899, in the A strain of Eubie Blake's *Charleston Rag*. Blake (1883–1983), a fine pianist musically active well into his nineties and a prolific composer of rags and popular songs, first recorded this work in 1921, and did so again in 1971. The transcription in ex. 4.6 is based on the later recording.[16] Ellington made effective and tasteful use of this boogie-woogie rhythm (eight to the bar) in his composition *Subtle Slough*, which he recorded in 1941 with a small group under the name of the cornetist Rex Stewart.[17]

Joplin had definite ideas about syncopation. He had high ideals for performance and interpretation, and was particularly concerned that the syncopated rhythms in his own works should be accurately executed, as written, and played at relaxed tempos. Evidence of this concern survives in a booklet which he wrote and published in 1908, *The School of Ragtime: Six Exercises for Piano*, where instruction is offered regarding the phrasing of his syncopated strains, but no analysis given of the rhythms themselves. (*The School of Ragtime* cannot be regarded in any way as a system, but simply as a guide to performance.)

Ellington appeared on the scene when the reign of Joplin and his followers was drawing to its close. "The end came gradually, as the characteristics of ragtime were absorbed by jazz; for a while, the two terms were frequently interchanged. At last, supplanted by a newer wave of syncopation, ragtime ceased to be the emissary of American popular culture."[18] Ellington's career in jazz effectively began in 1914, when he composed his first attributable piece, *Soda Fountain Rag*. During the years leading to 1922 (when he traveled to New York for a short and unsuccessful stay with the Wilbur Sweatman Orchestra)

Example 4.6   *Charleston Rag* (1919), A Strain

he lost no opportunities to attend concerts given by visiting pianists in the black tradition, notably the great ragtime and stride pianist and composer James P. Johnson, whose work Ellington adored (he made many allusions to it in his own work in later years). In 1923 Ellington returned to New York to form a small band for an engagement at Barron's Club, a Harlem nightclub, on the recommendation of Thomas "Fats" Waller, whom Ellington had also met in Washington. Ellington worked in New York continuously until 1931: he spent 1923 at Barron's, then moved to the Kentucky Club, where he remained until 1927, then worked for five years at the Cotton Club. This engagement gave Ellington both security of employment and opportunity for experiment (see chapter 3). While Ellington worked in New York three other distinguished black musicians worked in clubs and theaters there as well: James P. Johnson (1891–1955), Willie "the Lion" Smith (1897–1973), and Waller (1904–43), all pianists, composers, and improvisers. After this time a wider recognition of his talents enabled Ellington and his men to tour, setting the pattern for the rest of their professional lives.

Ellington frequently expressed his admiration for Johnson's piano rag *The Carolina Shout*, a happy, tuneful, and buoyantly rhythmic piece. Of its composer he once said, "James, for me, was more than the beginning. He went right up to the top . . . There never was another." [19] He was similarly demonstrative in reminiscing about Smith: "The Lion . . . what a wealth of subject tingle. [I] got all dressed up and went down to the Capitol Palace [in 1923]. My first impression of the Lion . . . was the thing I felt as I walked down those steps. A strange thing . . . everything and everybody seemed to be doing what they were doing in the tempo that the Lion's group was laying down. The walls and furniture seemed to lean understandingly—one of the strangest and greatest sensations I ever had. The Lion has been the greatest influence . . . his fire, his harmonic lavishness and his stride . . . and of course I swam in it. Most of it still clings—agreeably." [20]

Waller, more a writer of tunes than a composer in the strict sense, was responsible for Ellington's return to New York. Ellington recalled: "Fats Waller came to Washington in the Spring of 1923 . . . in a burlesque show at the Gaiety Theatre . . . I had gotten to know him well when we [Ellington, the alto saxophonist Toby Hardwick, and the drummer Sonny Greer] were in New York with Sweatman [briefly in 1922], so now we had a chummy exchange. 'I'm quitting next week,' Fats said, 'Why don't you all come up to New York and take the job [at Barron's Club]? I'll tell them about you.' We jumped at the opportunity and were all on edge until the time came to go." [21] Ellington recalled one gladiatorial recital of improvised music involving all three men: "Mexico's [in Harlem] was the scene of many battles of music in the late 20s . . . Willie 'The Lion' played there, so it was a natural place for all piano-players to hang out. I shall never forget the night Fats Waller, James P. Johnson and The Lion tangled there. Too bad there were no tape recorders in those days." [22] It is interesting that the young Fats Waller had also been intrigued by James P. Johnson's *Carolina Shout*: "Fats discovered some James P. Johnson Q.R.S. [piano] rolls . . . and with the roll in place before him . . . he gave the pedals a slight pump and a new chord was struck on the piano. [Russell Brookes, a friend of Fats, asked:] 'What were you playing there?' '*Carolina Shout*,' said Fats . . . 'I wanna learn it, just like it's on here.'" [23]

Another important black pianist-composer who achieved recognition in the 1920s was Jelly Roll Morton, a Creole musician from New Orleans. I can find no evidence that Ellington had any partiality toward the music of Morton or was influenced by it. Morton, not overburdened with modesty, claimed to be "the originator of jazz and The World's Greatest Hot Tune Writer." That Ellington was unimpressed is borne out by this uncharacteristically dismissive remark of his which has survived in print: "[Morton] played piano like one of those high-school teachers in Washington; as a matter of fact, high-school teachers played better jazz."[24] It is hard to understand why Ellington should have taken such a tough stand. Morton's solo style apart (it is to this that Ellington referred), the recordings Morton made with his Red Hot Peppers during five sessions between 1926 and 1928 are a thoughtful, deft dovetailing of the devices of blues and ragtime.[25] There is a similarity between Ellington's and Morton's methods: both gave their creative soloists generous opportunity for improvisation, both were expert orchestrators, and for the most part both wrote their own material.

A stylistic revolution was taking place in black music at precisely the time when the young Ellington was ready to enter the music profession. Frank Tirro has defined classic ragtime as "a style, popular in the first two decades of the 20th Century, characterized by a non-syncopated bass in duple meter underlying a syncopated treble melody; functional, diatonic harmonies stressing tonic, dominant and sub-dominants in major keys; and compounded song-form structures with 16- or 32-bar periods and shorter introductions and codas."[26] By 1917, when Ellington had begun to work as a part-time bandleader in his home town of Washington, important changes were taking place in ragtime piano. These developments were noticeable in the left-hand parts, which had previously been relegated to an accompanying role, and which were generally unrelated rhythmically to the offbeat figurations of the right hand. The new developments, displaying more dynamic breadth and increased rhythmic and melodic integration with the treble, became a component of the more propulsive and aggressive style later known as stride, "a piano style characterized by using the left hand in a down-beat, up-beat pattern (oom-pah, oom-pah rhythm) in which beats one and three (in $\frac{2}{4}$ or $\frac{4}{4}$) are heavily accented single notes, octaves or tenths, and beats two and four are unaccented triads."[27] When the oom-pah pattern of accents and dynamics in the left hand is followed to the letter in performance, the result is a strong implication of augmented syncopation (a one-to-one relationship with the basic beat of $\frac{2}{4}$ or $\frac{4}{4}$). The rhythmic and melodic integration of the two hands was further exploited by the striders by alternating syncopated phrases between them.

An example of this latter device occurs in the fifth (E) strain of James P. Johnson's *Carolina Shout*; the alternation falls under the bracket marked "X" in ex. 4.7. In recalling the work of the prominent striders Johnson and Smith (both active well before his own professional debut) and Waller (almost an exact contemporary), Ellington remarked on the predominantly improvisational content of their public performances. In their historical study *Rags and Ragtime*, David Jasen and Trebor Tichenor also comment on this divergence from the formalities of classic ragtime: "[The New Yorkers] viewed their rags,

Example 4.7

not as polished compositions, but as special material for their exclusive use as performers . . . Stride ragtime was a framework upon which they could make changes as various ideas and tricks came to them in the immediacy of performance." [28]

The improvisatory aspects of black music inherent in folk blues and before, temporarily relegated to the wings by the ragtime classicists in the popular music of the period, were once more at center stage. Johnson, who played in and around New York during most of his career but toured extensively during the First World War, remembered those days: " 'I was getting around town and hearing everybody. If they had something I didn't have, I stole it . . . I was born with absolute pitch and could catch a key that a player was using and copy it.' And so it was that this giant of the New York scene, James P. Johnson, developed the stride sound and became the major influence of the great jazz pianists (Willie 'The Lion' Smith, *Duke Ellington*, Count Basie, Fats Waller, Teddy Weatherford, Cliff Jackson, Joe Sullivan, Ralph Sutton, Dick Wellstood and Thelonious Monk) through his many piano rolls, recordings and live performances" (italics added). [29]

Johnson recorded his stride-ragtime composition *The Carolina Shout* on a piano roll in 1918, and this performance profoundly affected the young Ellington: "My first encounter with James was through the piano rolls, the QRS rolls. Percy Johnson, a drummer in Washington, who told me about them, took me home with him and played me *Carolina Shout*. He said I ought to learn it. So how was I going to do it, I wanted to know. He showed me the way. We slowed the machine, and then I could follow the keys going down. I learned it! And how I learned it! I nursed it, rehearsed it . . . Yes, this was the most solid foundation for me. I got hold of some of his other rolls and they helped me with styling, but *Carolina Shout* became my party piece." [30]

Table 1

Section	Score Reference	Structural Element	Number of bars
Introduction	Introduction	Tempo-setting lead-in (in G major)	4
A	A	Strain A	32 (16 bars, repeated)
	B	Strain B	32 (16 bars, repeated)
	C	Strain C	32 (16 bars, repeated)
B	D	Strain D (trio, C major)	16
	E	Strain E	16
		Strain D (modified)	16
Coda	Coda	Optional break	4

Analysis of *The Carolina Shout*

Johnson's composition is a masterwork. It offers evidence of the strong reciprocal influence exerted by black and white music. The complete piano score on which I have based my examination of the piece is a copy of the original sheet music published in 1925.[31] The piano roll which the young Ellington industriously committed to memory was issued by the Quality Real Service Company (QRS) in 1918.[32] By this time the vitality and spontaneity of live improvisation could be captured quite satisfactorily on player-piano rolls and phonograph records, and predictably there is some variation in phrasing and melody between the sheet music and the roll, which bears out Johnson's predilection for improvisation. Harmonically the two versions are almost identical.

In form the piano roll version is followed to the letter by the sheet music published in 1925, which is quoted in exx. 4.8 and 4.10–4.12. Its five principal strains, the types of syncopation employed, and the construction and voicing of the right- and left-hand parts evidence minimal departure from the original concept only, enough to confirm Johnson's improvisatory leanings. The form of *The Carolina Shout* in its simplest terms is as follows:

Introduction // A // B // Coda

Example 4.8   *The Carolina Shout*

(from the opening strain)

A contains three different strains and B two, arranged in three sections, in A–B–A pattern (strain D, strain E, and again strain D). Table 1 is the detailed plan of the piece. The work has retained the form of the classic rags: modulation into the subdominant from the trio onward, and sixteen-bar strains with a shorter introduction and coda.

Example 4.8, an extract from the published sheet music (the first eight bars of the opening strain A), confirms the jaunty tunefulness and ebullient stride-rag style of the rest of the work.

The element of improvisation in black music was vehemently played down by the Joplin school, but it is clear from Ellington's published recollections that the spontaneity of the striders in New York had deeply impressed him. It therefore comes as no great surprise that Ellington granted so much opportunity for individual and collective freedom in his own music (after recognizing and recruiting the right musicians). The New Yorkers' tradition of improvisation is vividly demonstrated in Johnson's performance from 1918 of *The*

Example 4.9

(a)

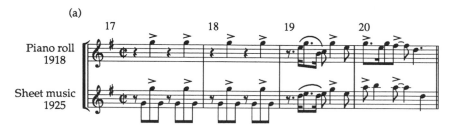

(b)

Carolina Shout. Comparison of this piano roll with the sheet music arrangement of 1925 reveals a rhythmic and melodic variation (ex. 4.9). The fluidity essential to jazz is typified by the difference between the roll (executed on the instant, with spontaneous decoration and rhythmic variation) and the sheet music (transcribed and edited later, with time spent on it).

Examples 4.10–4.12 are from the published sheet music. Each illustrates the influence of a particular musical style predating jazz and ragtime: the "ring shout," an antiphonal call-and-response pattern that is the forerunner of the jazz riff;[33] the blues, characterized by blue notes (appoggiatura, simulating glissandi, portamenti, nontempered pitching); and the boogie-woogie bass (eight to the bar), used in barrelhouse and fast western styles.

Examples 4.13–4.17 show developments from classic ragtime: the stride bass; the oom-pah bass (stride bass emphasized); secondary-ragtime grouping; alternating syncopation (between left and right hands); and cross-bar syncopation (here extended over six beats), which also implies the eight-to-the-bar rhythm of the boogie-woogie style.

To understand how all this may be seen to relate to Ellington's approach to jazz composition, one must answer the following three questions. First,

Example 4.10   Strain C, bars 33 to 36

Example 4.11   Introduction, bars A and B

Example 4.12   Strain E, bar 80

Example 4.13   Strain A, bars 1 and 2

Example 4.14   Strain B, bars 17 and 18

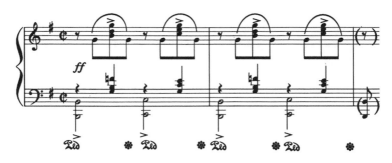

Example 4.15   Strain B, bars 19 and 20

Example 4.16   Strain E, bars 71 and 72

Example 4.17   Strain E, bars 76 and 77

what makes this rag so outstanding in itself? The five principal strains (A to E) are catchy, tuneful, and without exception phrased in a powerfully rhythmic manner. In form the composition is neat and rounded, well within the march and quadrille traditions of classic ragtime. There is a lively swing about the piece, generated by the ingenious permutation of the types of syncopation already identified, and including examples of secondary ragtime and alternating syncopation in both treble and bass.

Second, what made the rag so interesting to Ellington? I am convinced that Ellington was attracted primarily by the blackness of Johnson's music. This quality is revealed in quirks of style: the bluesy grace notes and obsessive use of the archaic ring shout (precursor of the riff). Johnson's deployment of both hands, polyrhythmically and antiphonally, is imaginative and exciting. This complementary bouncing of material between treble and bass seems related to Ellington's later facility in scoring for independent subgroups within his orchestra. As for the melodic content of the rag, its tunefulness was something Ellington emulated throughout his career.

Finally, how did the principles embodied in *The Carolina Shout* influence Ellington? The influence of ragtime on Ellington's early efforts as a composer and performer may be seen in two examples of his early piano rag style: *Soda Fountain Rag* (1914; the earliest published version dates from 1973) and *Jig Walk* (1923), originally written as a song for a revue and later arranged in rag style and committed to a piano roll.

In his autobiography Ellington recalled the composition of *Soda Fountain Rag*: "When I was confined to the house for a couple of weeks with a cold, I started fiddling around on the piano, using what was left over from my piano lessons—mostly the fingering—and I came up with a piece I called *Soda Fountain Rag*, because I had been working as a soda jerk at the Poodle Dog Café [in Washington]. I started playing this around and it attracted quite a lot of attention."[34] He did not get around to copyrighting the piece until 1958,[35] and the issue of the sheet music by his own publishing house, Tempo Music, was delayed until 1973. It is not surprising that *Soda Fountain Rag* should not have been published around the time of its composition, for Ellington during his teens was completely unknown outside Washington. It is however unfortunate that he did not see fit to include the piece in the recordings made by his group the Washingtonians during the mid-1920s, or indeed on any organized commercial session of later years.

The piano score of *Soda Fountain Rag* is reproduced in exx. 4.18 and 4.20. Ellington has employed all three types of syncopation—A, mid-beat; B, midbar; and C, cross-bar—and these are identified on the score.

The style of Ellington's composition is rag. The left hand is a classic, unsyncopated ragtime accompaniment—the first and third beats are single notes,

Example 4.18 *Soda Fountain Rag*

octaves, or tenths, the second and fourth beats triads or four-part chords; mid-beat syncopation (type A) is used throughout this strain. The form of the rag is basically A–B–A, as shown in table 2.

The introduction (bars 1 to 8) consists of two four-bar phrases that are almost identical. In bar 1 Ellington introduces the principal motif of the piece, made up of a quarter note and a triplet of eighth-notes, marked (a), followed by a mid-beat syncopation (type A) decorating the simple chromatic half-step

Table 2

Section	Score Reference	Bars	Structural Elements	Number of Bars
	Introduction (D minor)	1–8	Introduction and principal motif	8
A	Strain A (D minor)	9–16	8-bar melody	8
		9–14	Same, repeated	6
		17–18	Second ending	2
B	Strain B (F major)	19–28	10-bar phrase, highly syncopated	10
A	Strain A (D minor)	9–16	8-bar melody	8
		9–14	Same, repeated	6
		17	First of two second-ending bars, repeated	1
	Coda	29	Coda	1

phrase over the remaining two beats. Bar 2 is a repeat of bar 1 in all aspects save one: the sustained bass triad is now rooted on the minor seventh above the tonic. This means that the dissonance at (b) is now created by the interval of a minor ninth above the root C-natural.

Bar 3 is full of the blues. The underlying, sustained harmony here is the B-flat seventh (diminished as written). I find three instances of blues inflection in this bar: E-natural, marked (c)—the flattened fifth of the dominant seventh on B-flat is a familiar area for nontempered pitching within the blues scale;[36] C-sharp, marked (d)—the augmented ninth above the dominant seventh on B-flat is also subject to microtonal adjustment in blues performance; and G-sharp (grace note), marked (e)—rising to the A-natural of the melody and imitating the smear or portamento in blues playing or singing. In bar 4 Ellington has used cross-bar syncopation (type C) to connect the mid-beat phrase over the last two beats of the preceding bar with the identical construction which appears over the first two beats of this one. The left-hand chord is an A seventh (diminished as written). Bars 5–7 are a repeat of bars 1–3. Bar 8 repeats the mid-beat phrasing of bar 4, but here the A seventh chord is extended over a rich three-octave voicing (f) to lead into strain A.

In strain A (bars 9–16; when repeated, bars 9–14 and 17–18) Ellington has employed a straight, unsyncopated classic ragtime accompaniment in the left hand. With the exception of the first beats of bars 9, 10, 11, 12, and 13 (which

Example 4.19

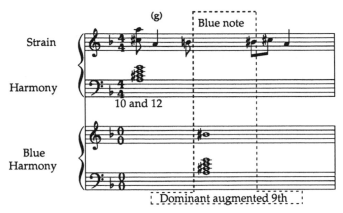

are triads voiced over a tenth—tonics in root position, dominants diminished as written), he has written single notes on the first and third beats of each bar, alternating variously with triads and four-part chords on the second and fourth beats. In the treble of bar 9 the principal two-bar motif (an obsessive "hook," as in popular song), already stated in the introduction, is elongated by the addition of the dominant, A-natural, marked (f), thus employing mid-beat syncopation (type A) in its pure form, and leading by an upward leap of one octave into the next bar, based on the dominant. The underlying harmony throughout bar 10 is the A seventh. A blues inflection is created here by the appearance of the C-natural (as written) in the treble strain; it is emphasized by its position on the strong third beat of the bar.

If this note is regarded as a B-sharp, then there is a momentary appearance of the blues-tinged chord of the dominant augmented ninth.[37] This is a clear, classic instance of a dissonant blue note (in nontempered vocal or instrumental performance it would waver around the major seventh above its identifying mediant, to be resolved by intuitive "correction," either upward or downward), but now moving upward to the stable third of the dominant seventh chord, marked (g) in ex. 4.19.

After bars 11 and 12, which correspond to bars 9 and 10, the principal motif of the rag is repeated in bars 13 and 14, but Ellington has anticipated the harmony in bar 14 by tying his final melody note (B-flat) across the barline. On the printed sheet music the harmony is allotted the chord symbol "E minor seventh/flatted fifth," but if the notes are retained and the chord reassessed as a G minor with added major sixth, marked (h), then a bluesy, pivotal change of I–VI is incorporated into the progression.

Except for the descending octaves on the first and third beats in the bass,

Example 4.20

bars 15 and 16 are identical. In bar 15, marked (i), the melody begins on an off-chord G-sharp against the A-natural on the first beat of the bass accompaniment, but ascends by a half-step to A-natural within the beat. The same license is taken over the first two beats of bar 16, again marked (i), but here it is ameliorated by the bass having moved to F-natural. At (j) in both bars, where the treble chord implied is the A-dominant seventh/minor thirteenth, the descent of the melody from F-natural, seeking the tonic (and eventually finding it in bar 18), suggests downward "correction" from the familiar nontempered third degree of the blues scale. Bar 17 is the first of two bars played when strain A is repeated, and is the same as bar 15. In bar 18, the second of the two, the underlying harmony is D minor, and from here Ellington modulates over bars 19 and 20 to F major in bar 21.

Strain B is ten bars long (bars 19–28), which is unusual in ragtime and jazz. It is interesting to note that a quarter-century later, in 1940, Ellington constructed the A strain of *Concerto for Cootie* (written for Cootie Williams) over the same number of bars.[38] Overall, the B strain is noteworthy for its rhythmic drive, generated by the ingenious interfacing of all three types of syncopation (all marked on score). The swing of the episode owes much to cross-bar syncopation (type C), which abounds. Over the eleven bars comprising strain B and the lead-in bar, 18, from strain A, there are seven instances of cross-bar syncopation (type C). A most impressive rhythmic construction resulting from the incorporation of cross-bar tied syncopation is sustained continuously over five bars (22 to 26), suggesting the mature Ellington. In bar 22 the treble A-flat, marked (k), which should be a G-sharp, appears momentarily as a disagreement with the A-natural in the bass accompaniment. The sheet music indicates a reprise from bar 28 back to the beginning of strain A in bar 9. After this strain is repeated, there is a one-bar coda (bar 29) after bar 17. The coda includes a finger glissando between the two D minor chords, concluding the piece on a pause.

There has been no attempt to incorporate a smooth modulation for the reprise from the dominant-seventh chord in the key of F major into the first D minor bar of strain A (bar 9). The score seems incomplete here. Should there have been a more euphonious transition, perhaps through the chord of the A-dominant seventh, or even by adding extra bars to make the length of strain B more typical of ragtime (and usually of jazz)?

Ellington's potential is hinted at in this early composition, written when he was by his own admission only a student. The tune of strain A is catchy, and there is a dynamic swing throughout the work which seems to reach its optimum in excitement in the consistently syncopated, anticipatory phrasing of the right-hand figures in strain B.

But is *Soda Fountain Rag* really a rag? The A–B–A form of its sheet music version is not typical of the classic ragtime in vogue when the piece was written. Can the sheet music be trusted, or has the piece been edited to limit the score to two pages? In either event, the significance of this work lies more in its originality than in its adoption of fundamental elements of the ragtime style (the unsyncopated left hand, the skillful use of all three types of syncopation).

The following anecdote concerning an early performance of the rag appears in Barry Ulanov's biography of Ellington:

> One day, the heavy-drinking pianist at one of the cafés [in Washington], a "whiz" of a pianist but even more brilliant a drinker, drank so much he knocked himself right out. Duke sprang to his place . . . and without a moment's hesitation to clear away the prostrate form of the overcome piano shouter, he jumped into the opening bars of *Soda Fountain Rag*. He played it as a one-step, two-step, waltz, and as a fox-trot, slow, middle-tempo and up. "They never knew it was the same piece," and "I was established. Not only did I write my own music, but I had a repertory!" . . . Washington was almost the gayest city of American cities in the years 1916 to 1919 when Duke was coming up. And his piano, even at its rag-giest, noisiest, most rhythmically confusing, was a welcome condiment to jaded diners looking for new seasoning.[39]

The overtly repetitive melody in strain A, which is assembled from four segments of two bars each, does lend itself because of this fundamental structuring to straightforward superimposition over the several dance rhythms referred to above. Latin American rhythms (tango, rhumba, bossa nova, cha-cha), similarly dependent on two-, four-, and eight-bar phrases, could be effectively and simply accommodated.

An example of Ellington's piano writing of the early 1920s survives in the form of a player-piano roll.[40] Its connection with ragtime is clearly established by its title: "jig" was the name given to the style of music which preceded classic ragtime: jigtime became ragtime, jig piano became ragtime piano, and a jig band was the forerunner of the ragtime band. *Jig Walk* was originally a song, with words by Jo Trent: "[In] 1923 . . . Duke wrote his first complete score for a show, *Chocolate Kiddies* with [the lyricist] Jo [Joseph] Trent. They completed it in one evening. 'I didn't know composers had to take to the hills and talk to the muses for a few months to get out a show,' Ellington later observed, ironically. His life's pattern was being set . . . The show, featuring [the singer] Adelaide Hall and [the dancer] Josephine Baker ran for two years, in Berlin."[41] Three songs from the show, *Jig Walk*, *Jim Dandy*, and *With You*, were copyrighted in 1925 (they are fourth, fifth, and sixth on the chronological list of Ellington's copyrighted works).[42] *Jig Walk* (listed as *Jig Walk Charleston* in the catalogue of Ellington's pieces issued by Tempo Music in 1981) was arranged as a piano rag and perhaps even committed to a piano roll by Ellington himself, though this is speculation.[43] The transcription which follows is based on a low-definition recording of this pianola version, the quality patently eroded by successive acetate dubbings or tape transfers. There does not seem to be any verifiable record of precisely when the original roll was issued, but the year has been reasonably narrowed down to either 1923 or 1924, and the roll would seem to be the earliest surviving recording of Ellington's piano style.

The initial exposition of Ellington's material follows its original form (A–A1–B–A), which is the conventional structure of the popular song. The plan of his rag arrangement, given in broad outline below, may be seen to conform materially to the pattern A–B–A of the earlier *Soda Fountain Rag*:

A = one A–A1–B–A pattern
B = middle section, developed from the "middle-eight" (B) section of A above
A = the original pattern A–A1–B–A
A = the original pattern A–A1–B–A, repeated, ending on a two-bar "tag" coda

There is no introduction; the recording starts abruptly after three and a half beats of the first bar of strain A. This may have been the result of a careless initial transcription to disc, or, more likely, the roll used for the rerecording may have been damaged at its start. For whatever reason, if there was an introduction to the piece it has been lost. The arrangement is laid out in detail in table 3. The three-page transcription of the original piano roll is reproduced beginning with ex. 4.21.[44]

Of the 114 bars in this arrangement of *Jig Walk*, 79 bars of the melody are phrased with mid-beat syncopation (type B), the principal rhythm employed in works written during the dance craze. There are only two instances of mid-beat syncopation (type A), in bars 19 and 14, and the cross-bar device (type C) is not used at all. Ellington's harmony is the straightforward succession of tonic, subdominant, and dominant (and related dominants) characteristic of classic ragtime.

Every bar of the jaunty, descending melodic line in strain A (score reference A, bars 1–8) is phrased in the Charleston beat (a modified mid-bar syncopation, type B); bars 5 and 6 are particularly good examples of this style. The melody at this point is held on a G-natural in both bars while the harmony beneath moves from the F-dominant ninth to the B-flat-dominant thirteenth. But it is in the bass where echoes of Johnson's stride style reverberate more audibly. In bars 1–3 are two instances where Ellington has clearly assimilated Johnson's oeuvre, especially *The Carolina Shout*: (1) in bars 2 and 3, the type of melodic phrase (so marked on the score) ascending chromatically from F-natural through F-sharp and on to the third degree of the tonic scale in bar 3 appears frequently in *The Carolina Shout*, notably in the ring shout passage already described; (2) Ellington's grouping of the bass accompaniment over the twelve beats of bars 1 to 3 in this strain (3: 3: 3: 3), repeated in bars 9–11 of section B and bars 25–27 of section D, is a prime example of secondary-

Table 3

Section	Form	Score Reference	Bars	Structural Element	Number of Bars
A	A–A1–B–A (popular-song form)	A	1–8	Strain A (E-flat major)	8[a]
		B	9–13	Strain A1	5
			14–16	New material, varied from 6–8 above	3
		C	17–24	Strain B (middle 8), four bars each of C minor, F major	8
		D	25–31	Strain A (E-flat major)	7
			32	Modulation (as in bar 16)	1
B	Middle section of developed material	E	33–40	New melodic material on harmonies of section C (middle eight)	8
		F	41–48	Strain C; new melodic and harmonic sequence	8
A	A–A1–B–A (as above)	—	1–31, 49	Repeat of sections A–D	32
A	A–A1–B–A (as above)	—	1–31, 50	Same	32
Coda	Coda		51–52	"Tag" coda	2

[a] Section A is assumed to have eight bars; the recording begins late.

ragtime grouping, and also a feature of Johnson's stride rag. The grouping is illustrated in ex. 4.22.

In strain B (score reference B, bars 9–16), bars 9 to 13 are a repeat of bars 1 to 5 in strain A. The remaining three bars of this section (14–16) progress through the dominant sevenths on F, B-flat, and G to modulate into the relative minor key at the commencement of strain C. In bars 15 and 16 sustained tremolos in the right hand descend from B-flat major against reiterated dominant-seventh triads in the middle register of the piano, suggesting an unsyncopated banjo strum.

In bars 17 and 18 of strain C (score reference C, bars 17–24), the Charleston motif is executed by both hands. Fortunately the recording here is quite well

Example 4.21

Example 4.22

Example 4.23 *Jig Walk* (Ellington)

(a)

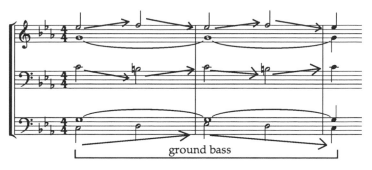

Kitten on the Keys (Confrey)

(b)

separated, and the strictly written four-part lines can be clearly identified. The lowest bass line here, a shuttling cancrizans which moves from tonic through supertonic to the minor third degree and back again (extending into bar 19), recalls a style of ground bass which had already been used to good rhythmic purpose by Zez Confrey in the opening bars of his novelty piano rag *Kitten on the Keys* (1921). The points observed above may be compared in ex. 4.23. The example from Ellington was taken from the transcription score (and also incorporates the simple counterpoint written into the arrangement); that from Confrey was taken from the published sheet music.[45]

Mid-beat syncopation (type A) occurs for the first time in this arrangement over the last two beats of bar 19, where the strum bass also reappears; this continues into bar 20. At the third and fourth beats of bar 20 I have suggested three notes from a G-diminished seventh chord (the recording is muffled and inconclusive at this point).

Bars 21–23 (ex. 4.24) are simply a transposition into F minor of bars 17–19, and therefore the points illustrated in ex. 4.21 also apply here. The first two beats of bar 24 contain the second and final example of mid-beat syncopation (type A), and in the second half of this bar the diminished seventh on E-flat leads into the F-minor seventh harmony at the commencement of strain D.

Strain D (score reference D, bars 25–32). Bars 25 to 31 repeat bars 1 to 7 of strain A, and bar 32 leads through a C-dominant seventh chord into a variation on strain C (the middle eight of the song form A–A1–B–A used in this work).

Strain E (score reference E, bars 33–40). Materially, the first four bars of this strain (33–36) are a straight transposition of the last four bars, which are in F minor. With regard to the structuring of this variation, the comments on the original exposition (strain C, bars 17–24) apply equally here. The left hand (in bars 33–35 and 37–39) moves closer to the more familiar boogie formula of eight to the bar, and the strum style in the bass of the original statement has been transferred to the right hand. Bar 40, however, eschews the diminished seventh on E-flat used in bar 24 and moves to F minor, continuing through the F-minor seventh harmony in the opening bar of strain F.

Bars 41–48 (ex. 4.25) present new melodic material over a new harmonic sequence. In the bass the melodic passing phrase (F-natural to F-sharp to G-natural), which has already appeared in bars 2–3, 10–11, and 26–27, is used again in bars 42 and 43 (marked on the score). On the first and third beats of bars 45 and 46 there is a similarly constructed line, this time descending in parallel with the treble melody, voiced two octaves and a major third or minor third above. In bar 47 the bluesy figuration in the right hand is supported over the first three beats by the chord of G-flat dominant seventh, the whole construction moving en bloc through a semitone to F-dominant seventh before

Example 4.24   *Jig Walk* (continued)

Example 4.25

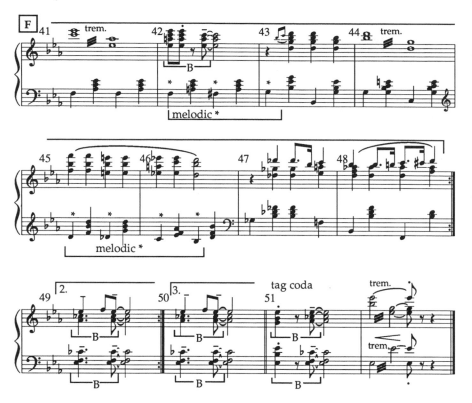

passing to the B-flat seventh in bar 48. Then there are two repetitions with no variation of the basic thirty-two-bar popular-song format A–A1–B–A, out of which this arrangement has been assembled, and finally a plagal cadence in the tag coda in bars 51 and 52.[46]

Certain passages on this low-fidelity, much-transferred rerecording of the original piano roll have prompted some researchers and discographers to assume that the performance was accompanied by drums. This is not physically possible, unless a drummer performed to a playback of the piano roll and the whole was then rerecorded on disc. It is more likely that some percussion accompaniment, delivered by a mechanical drum device,[47] was punched onto the roll. The result is a cold and inhumanly precise crush roll—a forerunner of the soulless rhythm effects of present-day electronic keyboard instruments.

Soda Fountain Rag and Jig Walk Compared

The recording of *Jig Walk* is particularly valuable, for it is a genuine example of Ellington's early style. The influence of classic rag is revealed in the straight, unsyncopated style of the left hand, and in the harmony of tonic, subdominant, and related dominants. The blues influence, so immediately noticeable in the introduction and strain A of *Soda Fountain Rag*, is by comparison minimal in *Jig Walk*.

Formally the two compositions depart from the conventions of classic ragtime, in the length of their sections as well as in their changes. Both approach classic rag, however, in that they have syncopated strains and predominantly unsyncopated accompaniment, although the influence of the stride school is more apparent in the parallel syncopations and strumming triads in the left hand of *Jig Walk*. In *Soda Fountain Rag* the key change which occurs at strain B is into the relative major, not into the subdominant which is more common in classic ragtime, and the form of the composition is a simple A–B–A.

Jig Walk is planned over a sequence of A–A1–B–A, in this way approaching the form of the earlier work. It must be remembered, however, that this piece was not originally a rag, but a revue number in the format of a popular song. There are no key changes in this surviving recording, perhaps because the roll data were duplicated mechanically.

THE INFLUENCE OF

TIN PAN ALLEY

QUESTION. *Where's the melody?, or, to put it more crudely;*
What are those musicians doing [on the bandstand]?
ANSWER. *The melody is the one the players are making. Hear it*
well, for it probably will not occur again. And it may well be
extraordinary.
—Martin Williams

Tin Pan Alley is the home of popular song, a genre which accounts for almost one-third of the items in Ellington's catalogue of copyrighted works.[1] Ellington and his collaborators produced more than three hundred songs between 1923 and 1973. The period 1938 to 1947 was exceptionally productive (119 songs were copyrighted) and roughly coincides with what I consider Ellington's summit as a composer.

Tin Pan Alley was already a successful and expanding commercial enterprise by the time Ellington launched his career. Centered almost exclusively on urban traveling theater and vaudeville, the promotions of Tin Pan Alley could be more easily assimilated and sold than either the blues or ragtime. Ragtime, written principally for solo piano, did enjoy a twenty-year boom, but this was effectively over by the beginning of the 1920s.

It is entirely fitting that Ellington should have become involved in Tin Pan Alley. By allowing the shrewd publishers and entrepreneurs of Tin Pan Alley to distribute his work, he ensured some regular income for himself in the form of royalties from the sale of recordings and sheet music. And Ellington was more of a composer than any other jazzman of his time. Not only were his melodic gifts unsurpassed, but his skill at editing his own material—at selecting, polishing, and writing down improvised motifs—made him ideally suited to the demands of the popular-song form. It was this ability that made his innovations accessible to a wide audience: the average listener, concerned only with being entertained, would hear his works and be intrigued by their unusual timbres and insistent rhythms.

Ellington and Popular-Song Form

"No songless people has ever been discovered . . . song, then, seems to be intuitive amongst human beings. Possibly the origins of organised human song may be looked for in a combination of the sense of rhythm, which seems to be likewise universal amongst men, . . . and the inflexions of speech . . . the development of speech rhythms into metrical verse forms sufficiently accounts for all types of traditional, unaccompanied unisonous song—folk song, that is."[2] A song is a concise, fully developed, and self-contained musical form, evolving out of unaccompanied folk singing or chanting, and achieving the satisfactory union of words with rhythmically compatible melody. In the purview of Tin Pan Alley and other forms of "popular" song, the chief concern of the listeners is entertainment, and of the purveyors, profit.

Popular song has usually been in simple binary or ternary form, or in combinations of the two, usually in four-, eight-, or even sixteen-bar episodes (and occasionally others, say by adding two bars to a sequence). The classic ternary form (A–B–A) was at first most common, but the binary (A–A–B–A or A–B–A–B) became more so in the late nineteenth century and the early twentieth.[3] For the first half of the twentieth century A–A–B–A was the form most often used, at much the same time as the binary twelve-bar form became the standard in rural blues—probably for similar considerations of metric, melodic, and harmonic order.[4]

An examination of thirty-eight songs by Ellington (some written with collaborators) contained in three albums of piano arrangements reveals the following scheme:[5]

	Number of songs
A–A–B–A	28
A–A1–B–A	1
A–A–B–A–C	1
A–B	2
A–B–A	1
A–B–A–B	1
A–B–C–A–B	1

A–B–C–B   1
A–B–C–D   2

These songs span thirty years of Ellington's middle career, including his artistic peak. I have selected for special attention two of these pieces, the piano scores of which are reproduced below, accompanied by brief analyses based on my discussions of the blues and ragtime.

Given that Ellington had a unique gift for melody, what criteria did he employ in crafting a tune? The composers of Tin Pan Alley wrote innumerable songs, most of which could be appreciated and retained by the average listener. The essential quality in a good tune, whether or not it has lyrics, is that of being memorable. In *Music Ho!* (1933), Constant Lambert stressed the importance to musical composition of memorable melody:

> During the Impressionist Period (of Debussy, Delius and Ravel, effectively from 1890 to 1930), the excitement advanced by the new world of color that had been opened up led to an almost complete neglect of the possibilities of line, and melody, through its traditional association with sentiment was tarred with the same brush as sentimentality. Melody came to be regarded merely as one of the elements in music, whereas it is not only the most important element but an all-embracing one. Harmony without melody is only an aural tickling, and rhythm without melody is not even rhythm—it is only metre, and can have at the most a vaguely mumbo-jumbo appeal, with no true musical significance.[6]

I cannot comprehend how Lambert dismissively denigrates the musicality of solo rhythm (presumably percussion), even though he is not discussing jazz (which has its origins in African drum culture). His next observations appear in some measure to contradict his earlier statements: "A composer may have a rudimentary harmonic sense or a rudimentary rhythmic sense and yet remain a great composer on the strength of his line alone. To a composer gifted with melodic genius there may be problems of technique but there can be no problems of style, for a vital melody not only has intrinsic value but carries with it the implications of its harmonic, rhythmic and contrapuntal treatment."[7] Lambert also says that facility in melodic invention does not necessarily ensue from traditional scholarship: "Melody cannot be learnt like counterpoint, nor is it capable of either dissection or synthetic manufacture. One cannot create a creature of flesh and blood out of fossil fragments."[8] And he concludes with his definition of a good tune: "The essence of classical melody is continuity of line, contrast and balance of phrases."[9]

On the subject of intuition, George Gershwin offered observations parallel to those of Lambert in his introduction to Isaac Goldberg's study of American popular songs *Tin Pan Alley* (1930), but he expressed reservations on whether a composer may progress further without some schooling: "For some song writers it is not even absolutely necessary that they know anything about music. Many of the popular composers with the greatest number of successes to their credit can't read a note of music. What they have is an innate sense of melody and rhythm; all they seek is to write a simple tune that the public can easily remember. In order to write longer compositions, the study of musical technique is indispensable. Many people say that too much study kills spontaneity in music, but although study may kill a small talent, it must develop a big one. In other words, if study kills a musical endowment, that endowment deserves to be killed." [10] Ellington clearly would not have agreed with this assessment. [11]

From a purely commercial standpoint, Ellington and Gershwin were equally welcome in Tin Pan Alley, but their ideas were poles apart. Gershwin was a composer of popular music who consciously and brilliantly took the idiosyncratic intervals of folk-blues and froze them into many of his melodies; Ellington was a jazz composer who chose technically accomplished musicians and sought to preserve the ethnic roots of his music. That the two were of different races and from different backgrounds is not relevant: both men were supremely gifted writers of good tunes.

In his television documentary *Duke Ellington and His Famous Orchestra* (1983), Russell Davies, then the television critic for the *Sunday Times*, discussed Ellington's fortunes as he approached the peak of his career: "Compositions like *Mood Indigo, Sophisticated Lady, Solitude* and *In A Sentimental Mood* were already entering the classic repertoire of jazz, but their author was anxious to extend his range and reputation beyond the 3-minute pop tune.

"He began to acquaint himself with the works of modern orchestral composers and sometimes they came to get acquainted with him. When he met [the Australian composer and concert pianist] Percy Grainger, it was under the eye of the man who managed all Ellington's commercial transactions at this time, Irving Mills. With Mills promoting, the band was never likely to be undersold." [12] Davies added this observation on the fickle nature of the music profession: "The future of the big band industry was pretty uncertain too. By 1948, many leaders had given up, and Duke himself came close to calling it a day." [13] According to Ed Anderson, a friend of the family and a lyricist, "Duke kept the band going at times when economically it was very unfeasible. But he kept that band together by using his ASCAP [American Society of Composers, Authors and Publishers] royalties. He kept the band together all the time, and the band was his joy." [14]

It seems clear that Ellington was quite purposeful and not at all reluctant to play popular songs. He felt that much of his work should be capable of being

Example 5.1   *Mood Indigo*

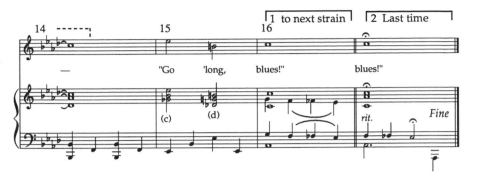

performed by orchestras other than his own, by musicians of adequate skill but not great creativity, even by nonmusicians. He also felt that memorable tunes belonged in the repertory of a band which in the generally accepted sense did not always play tunes at all.

Two Typical Songs

The sheet music arrangements for piano of two of Ellington's best-known songs are reproduced in their entirety in the next few pages. Each score is accompanied by a brief analysis in four sections dealing with the following topics: form (chord progressions typical of Ellington's style); blues elements (instances of major-minor implication, the imprint of the blue note phenomenon on Ellington's melodic lines and harmonies); ragtime elements (rhythms from early ragtime, the three basic types of syncopation); and motive—the principal melodic or rhythmic idea of a piece (that is, the "hook").

Ellington's original title for *Mood Indigo* (ex. 5.1), *Dreamy Blues*, evokes its nocturnal mood and bluesy style. His collaborators were Barney Bigard (then a solo clarinetist with his orchestra) and Irving Mills (Ellington's publisher and business manager at the time); exactly how much they contributed to the final product has never been firmly established.

Strain 1 is not in the standard pattern of four eight-bar sections, A–A–B–A; the piece consists of two distinct sixteen-bar strains, and each has four sections of four bars, A–A1–B–A. In bar 7 is a harmonization frequently encountered in Ellington's music, based on the flattened sixth degree of the tonic scale (here notated as based on the augmented fifth). To cite one example, he uses this as the startling final chord of his recording of *Hot Feet* (1929; see ex. 5.2).[15] In bar 8 the chord returns to the V-dominant seventh by means of a parallel shift downward through a semitone. Ellington's progression in bars 9 to 12 is

Example 5.2

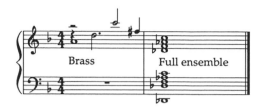

Brass   Full ensemble

overtly based on the blues: I-dominant seventh to IV^6 to IV-dominant seventh of IV, then back to the tonic in bar 13.

There are other blues elements as well in this arrangement. At bar 1 (a) the major-minor flexibility of classic blues around the third degree of the underlying scale is implied by the A-flat minor chord, which reverts immediately to the major at (b). But in his orchestral arrangements of the piece, Ellington invariably harmonized this chord either as I-diminished seventh (as notated in the scrap of manuscript in his own hand reproduced in ex. 5.3 in B-flat major, from a flyleaf in his autobiography),[16] or, in the sheet-music key of A-flat major, as G major, the middle element in a straight parallel chording of A-flat, G, A-flat. Strain 1 in the original version was arranged for a wind trio of muted trumpet, clarinet, and muted trombone; the actual voicing was quite unusual. Ellington's original mix is shown in ex. 5.4.

In its technically undemanding middle register, the trumpet provides the required whisper of sound. In contrast, the trombone enters in its high register, yet is not allowed to obliterate the delicate trumpet lead. Finally, the clarinet in its extreme low register moves in parallel major thirteenths to the trumpet before alighting in bar 3 on the identifying major third from the underlying II-dominant ninth harmony. Here is early proof of Ellington's ear for unusual tonal effect. A less imaginative composer might have settled merely for triads within the octave (as in Ellington's own sketch reproduced in ex. 5.3), or perhaps for the more spread out permutation in ex. 5.5. These alternatives may be pleasant enough, but their uniform middle-register voicings give them a blandness which was conspicuously absent from Ellington's original scoring; the high-register, pent-up trombone sound contributed the essential ingredients of passion and warmth which made this fragment so arresting. And surely it is a foretaste of the tonal and textural virtuosity to come. Clearly Ellington's wind trio of the day (Arthur Whetsol, trumpet; Barney Bigard, clarinet; Joe "Tricky Sam" Nanton, trombone) must have had a highly developed sense of internal orchestral balance to have brought off the effect with such finesse. At bar 3 (c) the V-minor chord logically follows the II-dominant ninth of the preceding bar, but the immediate shift to V-dominant seventh/augmented

Example 5.3

In Ellington's own hand (key B♭):

Sheet music (key A♭):

Example 5.4

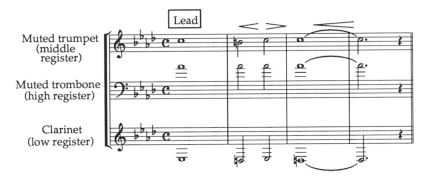

Muted trumpet (middle register)

Muted trombone (high register)

Clarinet (low register)

Example 5.5

Muted trumpet

Clarinet

Muted trombone

fifth at (d), setting up the two false relations noted earlier, creates a very blue impression.

The standard syncopation types A (mid-beat), B (mid-bar), and C (cross-bar) are marked on the sheet music in ex. 5.1. There is a suggestion of augmented syncopation in bars 9 and 10, by the implied stress occasioned by the phrasing of the melody, on the second and fourth beats of each bar (marked with an asterisk on the sheet music). The hook of this strain appears to be rhythmically stated in bar 1; this phrasing is in essence reversed in bar 7.

Example 5.6

In bars 18 to 20 Ellington has used a brief segment from the circle-of-fourths progression of related dominants, a pattern which frequently appears in his music. The sequence in bars 25 to 27 is in substance a repeat of bars 9 to 11 in strain 1, but the extension of the IV-dominant seventh into bar 28 appears to me to create an even bluer atmosphere than before. There are constant blue notes on the strong beats of the melody in bars 27 and 28, marked (e) and (f) on the music. Bars 25 to 28 evidence secondary-ragtime groupings, and the syncopated displacement is extended over the whole of bar 28, and into bar 29 with the implication of a cross-bar tie. The second harmony part on the treble staff at bar 17 restates the melody of the hook of strain 1, which may be extended without any disagreement through bar 18 (the harmonies being substantially the same).

Serenade to Sweden (ex. 5.7) was composed after a successful thirty-four-day tour of the Continent in spring 1939, of which three weeks (12 April to 1 May) had been spent in Scandinavia. Ellington celebrated his fortieth birthday, 29 April, in Stockholm, where a reception was arranged in his honor at the Crown-Prinz Cafe. Earlier in the day Ellington had given a short interview on Radio Stockholm, in which he discoursed on his own definitions of

Example 5.7   *Serenade to Sweden*

jazz and swing. "When the band returned to New York, at early recording sessions, Duke made permanent some of his strong sentiments about the trip . . . *Serenade to Sweden* was just that, a lovely melody which expressed Duke's thankful feeling for the country and its people." [17]

The form of the piece is A–A–B–A, with a four-bar extended ending making thirty-six bars in all. Throughout, Ellington's harmonization of the piece is neatly chromatic (exx. 5.7, 5.8). In the A sections, after the first bars (1, 9, and 25, where the harmony descends in parallel chords from I-dominant seventh to VII-dominant seventh), the progression is typical of his style: a chain of unresolving dominants through a segment of the circle of fifths (bar 2: VII seventh, III seventh; bars 3 and 4: VI seventh/augmented ninth; bar 5: II eleventh/minor ninth, thirteenth; bar 6: V eleventh, seventh). The extended ending to the piece offers further evidence of this root progression: the chain of unresolving dominants starts in bar 31, where Ellington's three-part chord of F major on the first beat has descended by a half-tone to the parallel chord of E major on the third beat. From that point, the chain of dominants may with minimal chordal reidentification be traced through to the tonic at the commencement of bar 35. The scheme is identified on the music, as shown below:

Bar 31 (e) root E-natural
            (f) A-natural
Bar 32   (g) D-natural
Bar 33   (h) G-natural
Bar 34 (i) C-natural: two beats C-dominant eleventh (implied), two beats
                       C-dominant seventh/augmented fifth/flat fifth/flat
                       ninth (written as G-flat dominant seventh/ninth)
Bars 35–36   (j) F-natural

In essence, section B (the middle eight) follows a root sequence of I–IV–II–V, a standard functional progression frequently slotted into the B section of a typical popular song of the form A–A–B–A. A striking example of the influences which the wayward idiosyncrasies of archaic blues exerted on Ellington's harmonic and melodic thinking occurs in bars 3 and 4 (repeated in bars 11–12 and 27–28), marked (d) on the example. Taking the harmony first, this bitonal construction (F major over D-dominant seventh, written out as D-dominant seventh/ninth augmented) includes the consonant blue note at the minor seventh (C-natural), and similarly the dissonant blue note at the augmented ninth (notated here as F-natural). This freezes the major-minor ambiguity of free blues into the underlying accompanying harmony of VI-dominant seventh; this is a common and expected occurrence in vocal or instrumental

Example 5.8

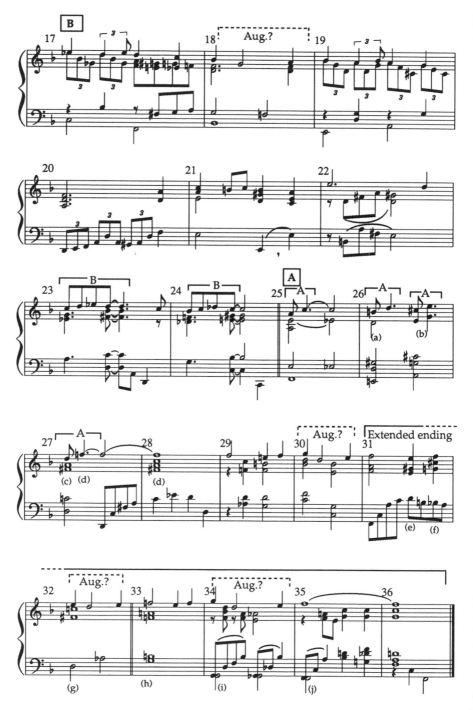

extempore blues performance against a basically inflexible chordal accompaniment. Ellington's debt to the blues could hardly have been expressed more conclusively; he has sustained this solo augmented ninth for a relentlessly dissonant seven and a half beats against the accompaniment.

Ellington's incorporation of off-beat phrasing into this work is sparing and basic. He uses only two types of syncopation, both in their "pure" form: mid-beat during the first three bars of each A section (bars 1–3, 9–11, and 25–27), and mid-bar during bars 23 and 24. The phrasing of the melody in bars 6, 8, 14, 18, 30, 32, and 34 may hint at augmented syncopation (marked "aug ?" on the score), but the moderato tempo indication on the printed music may not entirely support this possibility. The melodic ascent over the first three bars of each A section is ingeniously and thoughtfully assembled. After the first bar, based in the tonic, the tune alternates between leaps of a minor third and steps of a minor second, and moves up and across the three-link chain of related dominants:

> Second bar (a) fifth and minor seventh of the VII-dominant seventh harmony
> (b) third and fifth of the III-dominant seventh harmony
> Third bar (c) root and augmented ninth, in extension of the VI-dominant seventh harmony beneath

Effective use of phrase repetition has been made over the last four bars of each of the A sections, where the two-bar motif of bars 5 and 6 appears again in bars 7 and 8 (again, bars 29–30 are rhythmically identical with bars 31–32, bar 32 being melodically varied to allow for the harmonic regression to V-dominant seventh/ninth in preparation for the extended ending). Ellington's final attack in bar 8 has however been varied, and descends to the dominant of the home scale (instead of ascending to the upper tonic through the leading-note, as it did two bars earlier); this is preparatory to the reprise of the A section from bar 9 onward. In section B, substantially similar rhythms and melodic construction have been written into bars 17, 19, and 21.

Toward the end of his career Ellington was wont to conclude his concerts with a "finger-snapping" patter routine, the band playing very quietly behind him. This monologue was recorded in England in November 1969 and issued as the final item of the double album *70th Birthday Concert*.[18] I include my transcript of his whimsical speech as a memento of the purely show business side of his career and character, so much in evidence during his work in Tin Pan Alley:

> Thank you very much, ladies and gentlemen; you're very beautiful, very sweet, very gracious, very generous. This is *Satin Doll* [the band plays the

song behind him, very quietly]. We use it for the purpose of giving background to this finger-snapping bit, and you are cordially invited to join in the finger-snapping. [Ellington pauses to allow the audience to begin, then continues.] Crazy, I see I don't have to tell you; one never snaps one's fingers *on* the beat, it's considered aggressive. Don't push it, just let it fall. And if you would like to be conservatively hip and at the same time tilt the left ear-lobe *on* the beat and snap one's fingers on the *after-beat* . . . And so, by routing one's finger-snapping and choreographing one's ear-lobe tilting, one discovers that one *can* become as cool as one wishes to be. With that, we certainly want to thank you for the wonderful way you've inspired us, and remind you that we do love you madly.

THE MUSIC OF

THE MATURE PERIOD,

1939 TO 1941

From the beginning of Ellington's musical career in the early 1920s, his style was shaped by a variety of influences, by his gift as a melodist, and by his flair for choosing sympathetic musicians; these all had a powerful effect on his music. Ellington's style was polished and firmly fixed by 1939. Performances of his works recorded between 1939 and 1941 profited immensely from his having a stable ensemble, which included the trumpeters Ray Nance, Rex Stewart, and Cootie Williams, the trombonists Lawrence Brown, Joe "Tricky Sam" Nanton, and Juan Tizol, the saxophonists Harry Carney, Johnny Hodges, and Ben Webster, the clarinetist Barney Bigard, the pianist Billy Strayhorn (in addition to Ellington himself), and the double bass player Jimmy Blanton. Also performing dependably during this time were the lead trumpeter Wallace Jones, the alto saxophonist Otto Hardwick, the guitarist Fred Guy, the drummer Sonny Greer, and the double bass player Alvin Raglin, Jr. (substituting for Blanton during his illness).

During the period ending in 1943 these musicians stayed with Ellington for an average of ten years—a relatively long time in which to assimilate his style. Ellington's output increased markedly after 1938,[1] although there was a quite understandable fall-off in 1968 and 1969, the two years immediately following the death in 1967 of Strayhorn, who had provided the knowledge of an academically trained musician, as well as technical brilliance, unflagging industry, constructive criticism, imagination, and loyalty.

In the following chapters five compositions by Ellington from 1939–41 are transcribed in full score from the original 78 rpm records.[2] All parts are notated at sounding pitch. The first two works analyzed, *Ko Ko* and *Mr. J. B. Blues*, display the strong influence of ragtime and especially of the twelve-bar blues. The last three, *Concerto for Cootie*, *Junior Hop*, and *Subtle Slough*, are examples of how Ellington's sound was shaped by the interpretive skills of his soloists.

Each of the analyses includes an introduction to the work; the full score; an analysis of the harmony, form, voicings, tempo, and other elements; and conclusions drawn from the analysis (such as comments on influences or individual performances).

KO KO

Ko Ko is a composition drawn from the unfinished score of Ellington's proposed opera *Boola*, a work which he had planned to "tell the story of his race." Sketches for the opera had been drafted at intervals during the ten years preceding the appearance of *Ko Ko* in 1940. Although the opera was never finished, much of the thematic material which Ellington had notated and set aside for it was saved. In addition to *Ko Ko*, his suite *Black, Brown and Beige* (1943) was assembled in part from sketches from the *Boola* notebooks.[1] Owing to the chaotic state of Ellington's filing systems, there is no way of knowing precisely to what extent *Ko Ko* and *Black, Brown and Beige* benefited from the original drafts for the opera. In 1939 *Ko Ko* was scored as an independent, free-standing work, and has come to be hailed as one of Ellington's masterpieces. It is a crystallization of his "jungle style," which had developed during his band's engagement from 1927 to 1932 at the Cotton Club in New York, where Ellington provided musical backing for innumerable revues featuring black performers, including exotic dance routines. The jungle style complemented the club's decor, which depicted in stylized fashion the African jungle.

During most of his stay at the Cotton Club, Ellington's jungle style was stamped on his music largely by two men: Bubber Miley, who played his trumpet with a plunger mute in a manner often savage and always inspired by the blues, and the trombonist Tricky Sam Nanton, whose playing evoked the sound of the human voice but was no less violent than Miley's. The sound effects produced by the two were by turns guttural, raucous, and animalistic. Miley, installed as the first trumpeter and principal trumpet soloist in autumn 1924, exercised a profound influence on Ellington's thinking and style, as evidenced by his collaborations with Ellington on such works as *East St. Louis Toodle-oo* (1926), *The Blues I Love to Sing* (1927), *Black and Tan Fan-*

tasy (1927), *Goin' to Town* (1928), and *Doin' the Voom-voom* (1929). *East St. Louis Toodle-oo*, a vehicle for Miley's growling solo style, was Ellington's signature tune from 1926 until 1941, when it was supplanted by Billy Strayhorn's *Take the "A" Train*. By the time *Ko Ko* was molded into its final shape and recorded, Miley was long gone: he had died in 1932. But his influence on Ellington's music and choice of musicians was still apparent in 1940; in *Ko Ko* it is particularly evident in the work of Nanton.

Whether *Ko Ko*, in its embryonic, sketchbook state, was originally intended as a jungle piece may only be the subject of speculation, the original manuscripts seemingly having gone the way of most of Ellington's paper. The original title of the piece was *Kalina*.[2]

Ko Ko is strongly atmospheric. Ellington evoked the sounds of Africa by blending blues elements, jazz rhythms, and the conventions of European instrumentation and harmony. The analysis which follows is based on a recording made in Chicago on 6 March 1940.

The harmonic sequence used by Ellington throughout the piece is that of a conventional twelve-bar blues, repeated seven times with little variance except in the introduction and coda. Three simple ideas contribute to the continuity of the work: (1) jungle drums are evoked through tom-toms (or timpani), but only in the introduction and coda—the device could soon become wearisome if overused; (2) no modulation occurs—the work remains in the somber key of E-flat minor throughout; (3) a dominating ostinato rhythm is woven into the phrasing in every section of the piece: (written as ⟪♩♩♩⟫, played as ⟪♩♩♩⟫).

These ideas, somewhat primitive in a compositional sense, further electrify the highly charged jungle atmosphere created by the instrumental voicing and extempore passages. There are only two substantial solo improvisations: twenty-four shouting, anguished bars from Nanton, and twelve from Ellington himself. Blanton's double bass later shares a chase chorus with the scored ensemble; his brief solos give him little opportunity to display his skill as an improviser, for they are simply an extension of his function to provide a rhythmic bass line.

Ko Ko is written in a transposed Aeolian mode. The work's principal motif is a rhythm written in the score as ⟪♩♩♩⟫ but in performance phrased like this: ⟪♩♩♩⟫. The seven sections of twelve-bar blues (letters A to G in the score) are based on transformations of this motif. Wherever this dominating ostinato rhythm occurs, the score has been marked with an "X" for both the pure form and its derivatives (I will refer to it from now on as the X motif). The motif is a two-bar unit, repeated in most instances as in ex. 6.1. There is however one passage (section D, bars 37 to 46) where the X motif is compressed into one bar, as shown in ex. 6.2. There are several examples of

Example 6.1

Example 6.2

Example 6.3   Beethoven, Symphony No. 5

Example 6.4   *When the Saints Go Marching In*

Example 6.5   *Boogie-woogie*

Example 6.6   *Jumping at the Woodside*

Example 6.7   Ko Ko

earlier uses of this rhythm: in Beethoven's Fifth Symphony (ex. 6.3); in the traditional New Orleans tune *When the Saints Go Marching In* (ex. 6.4); in Lester Young's *Boogie Woogie* (1936), recorded by the Count Basie Quintet (ex. 6.5); and in the recording made by Count Basie and his orchestra in 1938 of *Jumping at the Woodside* (ex. 6.6).[4]

The X motif is stated initially by the tom-tom lead-in (ex. 6.7), then echoed by the baritone saxophone playing a sustained tonic pedal on its lowest E-flat. In bars A and B a trombone trio plays parallel triads; the progression starts on G-flat major (a), making a minor seventh against the E-flat tonic pedal in the bass. This relates to the mode of the whole piece (transposed Aeolian on E-flat). The piece descends through F major (b), F-flat major (c), and on to the E-flat minor root position triad at (d). Bars C and D feature major and minor first inversions, following the same chromatic progression as in bars A and B: E-flat minor (e), G-flat major (f), F major (g), F-flat major (h), ending on the tonic first inversion at (i).

In bars E and F (ex. 6.8) the phrasing of bars A and B is repeated, but Ellington has structured his chording for the trombone trio on the V of E-flat minor, and his bass part is a simple V and V of V. The E-flat tonic pedal is sustained throughout. The dominant-based trombone chords appear as: (a) B-flat eleventh/ninth, flat, (b) B-flat fifth, augmented, and (c) B-flat seventh. The B-flat seventh chord at (c) sets up the perfect cadence which resolves on to the tonic minor seventh appearing at (d) in bar G. The root position triads in bars G and H are a repeat of the opening two measures of the introduction, before the valve trombone leads into section A of the score.

The valve trombone plays the underpinning line here (ex. 6.9). Ellington has taken advantage of Tizol's valve mechanism: in the X-motif lead-in, the first two notes, B-flat and C-flat, would have demanded on a slide trombone a shift from closed position to seventh position (awkward at this tempo). That Ellington occasionally lapsed by assigning unplayable parts to the slide trombone after Tizol left his orchestra is attested by the complaint of one of his trombonists, who is often quoted anonymously: "Man, this thing ain't got no keys on it, you know!"[5]

The theme stated by the saxophone quartet answers the solo trombone's X motif antiphonally, in a ritualistic, gospellike seesaw of calls and responses. The basic rhythm remains on the chord of E-flat minor sixth throughout, and the decorated tonic pedal is continued on Tizol's trombone. In the pair of identical two-bar phrases here, the saxophone quartet is however harmonized into a series of alternating minor and major chords (beginning and ending on the minor), centered on perfect cadences between (a)–(b) and (c)–(d). Bluesy dissonances are created by the B-flat seventh/augmented ninth chords at (a) and the B-flat seventh/minor ninth chords at (c). These constructions are ex-

Example 6.8   2

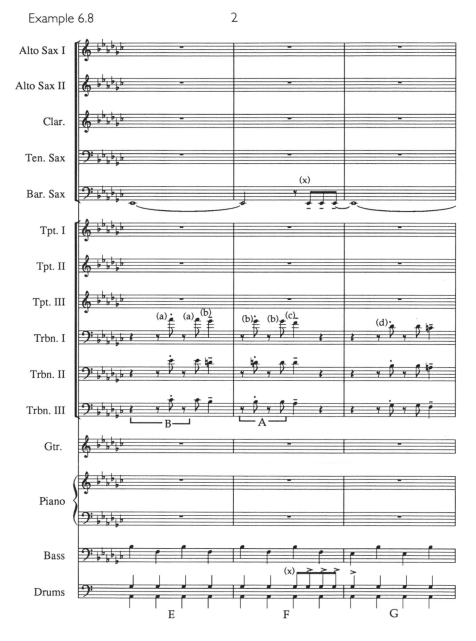

Example 6.9   3

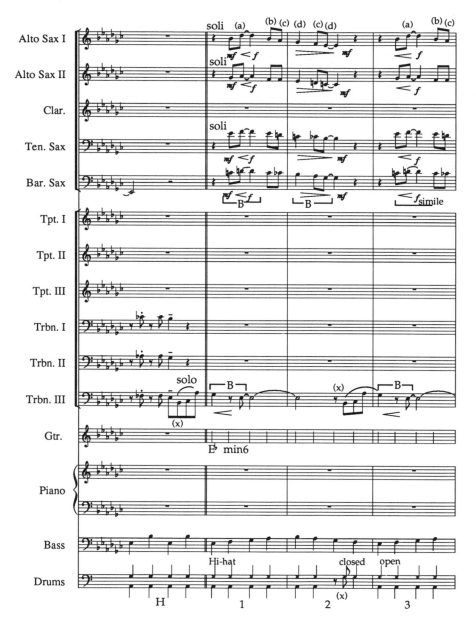

Example 6.10   4

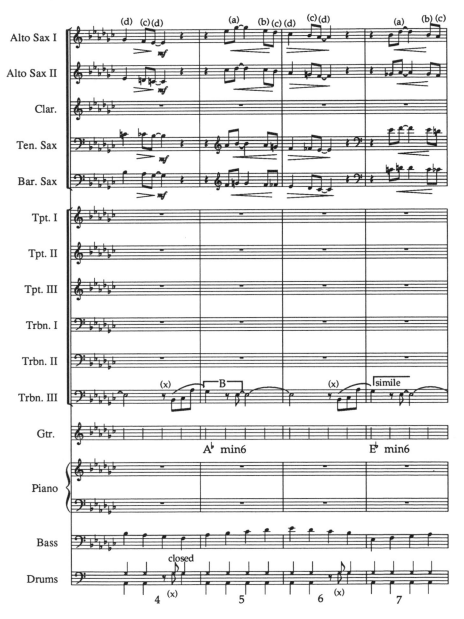

amples of "frozen" blue note chords.[6] Throughout, the tonic major sixth is added to the E-flat minor chords, and Greer's choked cymbal provides extra impulse to the recurring X motif.

During bars 5 and 6 (ex. 6.10) the tonality shifts to IV of E-flat minor (following the basic twelve-bar blues sequence), and the saxophone quartet is harmonized exactly as in bars 1 and 2 in section A (the third page of the score). This voicing is repeated, this time back on E-flat as the root, in bars 7 and 8. Ellington's fondness for the blues-inspired dominant augmented ninth and minor ninth chords is by now quite apparent.

In the two identical bars 9 and 10 (ex. 6.11), the saxophone quartet is voiced for one and a half beats on the third inversion of the dominant major ninth of B (a), and descends by half-step to the same inversion on B-flat (b) for the rest of the bar. The rhythm guitar plays a foursquare accompaniment: two beats each of B ninth and B-flat ninth. It seems, however, that Ellington's intention is to preserve the B-flat tonality through the two bars, because apart from the A-natural at (c)—which is a chromatic passing note—the bass in bar 9 follows with A-flat, G-flat (F-sharp), and F; these three notes, marked (d), are clearly the minor seventh, augmented fifth, and dominant of B-flat. In bar 10, marked (e), the reiterated B-flats and the D-natural clearly identify the root as B-flat, the whole four bars being in effect one perfect cadence. This is in spite of the temporary elevations to B major by the saxophones and guitar. These latter devices echo Ellington's use of parallel chromatic triads and first inversions in the introduction to the piece (bars A to B, first page of the score). In bars 11 (ex. 6.11) and 12 (ex. 6.12) the saxophones are as in their original entry into this episode. Throughout this four-bar phrase, Ellington's piano emerges on an offbeat dominant pedal (avoiding the B major variations) to point up the entries made by the X motif in Tizol's statement of the decorated tonic pedal.

The next twenty-four bars (sections B and C; exx. 6.12 to 6.18) contain an ad lib solo by Tricky Sam Nanton backed by the full ensemble, excepting the first trumpet and the valve (third) trombone. Throughout episode B (bars 13 to 24) and episode C (bars 25 to 36) the orchestra is deployed as follows. Saxophones, in true unison, simply state the X motif in an unvarying ostinato every two bars, for the whole of the twenty-four-bar sequence; there is a lead-in of three eighth-notes on the notes of the root triad to a sustained drone on the subdominant, with well-placed eighth-rests for breathing before each lead-in. The brass (two trumpets, one trombone) play hurried $\frac{6}{3}$, $\frac{5}{3}$, $\frac{6}{4}$, and $\frac{6}{3}$ chords antiphonally against the reeds on the traditional blues changes throughout. The chords are staccato and urgent, the plungers alternately open and closed. In the rhythm section, guitar, double bass, and drums play straight-ahead accompaniment, the piano supporting the X motif entries of the reeds. This

Example 6.11   5

Example 6.12   6

Example 6.13

formulates the pattern over the next twenty-four bars of the score. And Nanton plays his solo with force and conviction, never descending from his top register. He manipulates his plunger cup to produce three of his vocalizations within the first four bars of the solo. There are only seven attacks, the first on subdominant rising to dominant, which he plays five times, ending on the subdominant, which is approached with an upward smear.

There are three "ya-ya" mouthings (ex. 6.13), as before. A chord on IV now forms the basis of the rhythm and orchestral accompaniment for two bars. Nanton's three high B-flats at (a) are now a major ninth away from the tonic. On the actual recordings these notes, transcribed as B-flats, sound sharp, siting them somewhere between B-flat and C-flat—an instance of the nonstandard intervals encountered in a blues performance, and an occasion where conventional notation cannot accurately accommodate the actual pitching. Bars 19 and 20 revert to E-flat minor. Nanton's final phrase, in bar 20, descends through a partially smeared triplet on to a snatched couplet on the minor seventh.

Bars 21–24 are even simpler in construction: the same three vocal sounds, all on the IV in E-flat minor, are heard against two bars of the dominant seventh/minor ninth chord, resolving into the final two bars (23 and 24) on the tonic (exx. 6.14 and 6.15). Ellington's piano chord of E-flat minor with the major sixth added, struck hard after two and a half beats of bar 24, rhythmically points up the entry of the X motif played by the saxophones.

The second twelve bars of Nanton's improvisation begin with two identically phrased two-bar constructions on the chord of the tonic minor seventh (ex. 6.15). Therefore, if harmony in this extract is viewed as consisting of the major chord of G-flat, making a minor seventh against the E-flat in the bass, then Nanton's solo is fashioned entirely out of the degrees of the pentatonic scale on G-flat. Bar A, the first of the introduction to this work, is harmonically identical in construction. The plunger mute is tightly closed against the bell of the horn, thus strangling the violently attacked notes and increasing the dramatic impact of the passage.

In construction, this phrase (with the exception of the upturned step in bar 31) is a swung version of the preceding four bars (ex. 6.16). A peak of drama is attained as Nanton compresses his phrasing when entering and leaving bar 30; at the same time he releases the constrictions on his output by opening wah-wah movements of the plunger cup. Bars 31 and 32 (ex. 6.17) are completely free from the plunger, and the purely straight-muted and abrasive tone emerges.

The solo ends abruptly on the tonic in bar 35 (ex. 6.17), after two vocalizations on the minor seventh of V—the first is smothered as soon as spoken, the

Example 6.14   8

Example 6.15   9

Example 6.16 10

Example 6.17

Example 6.18   12

second stentorian. Nanton's economy of notes is striking against the ostinato patterns in the orchestral accompaniment.

The whole twenty-four-bar solo can be seen to be constructed from only five notes: E-flat, G-flat, A-flat, B-flat, and D-flat, and therefore pentatonic, at least on paper. In fact this is not so, for the many bends, smears, and glissandi in the recorded performance impart a microtonal chromaticism not accommodated by the twelve-note system, much less the pentatonic scale. This observation generally holds true for transcriptions of jazz performances inspired by the blues, other than those given on instruments of fixed pitch (such as the piano) or indeterminate pitch (such as untuned percussion).

Section D (bars 37 to 48) contains Ellington's extemporized piano solo, performed over the ensemble (exx. 6.18 and 6.19). First the orchestral plan is traced, as in Nanton's solo. Saxophones in unison are allotted the unvarying X motif, which is now compressed into the space of one bar, with the lead-in rising by step this time, from subdominant to minor ninth. The ostinato figure is not modified in any way to heed the blues changes followed by the guitar and bass (I, IV, V, I). The brass (two trumpets, one trombone, still played with plunger mutes) punctuate the saxophone line as before, implicitly following the basic blues changes ($\frac{5}{3}$, $\frac{6}{4}$, $\frac{5}{3}$, $\frac{7}{5}$, $\frac{5}{3}$). In bar 48 the root position triad of D-flat is substituted for the E-flat minor indicated by the rhythm section (guitar and double bass). This variation prepares for Ellington's tenth in the right hand (between B-flat and D-flat in his solo; see the analysis which follows), and may have motivated it.

The first four bars of Ellington's solo are revealing. At (a), in bars 37, 39, and 40, a bitonal chord (in the right hand, G-flat $\frac{7}{5}$ flat; in the left, root position E-flat minor triad) is assembled in two stages, treble chord followed by bass chord, fused together by the sustaining pedal. The treble chord (a), encompassing four whole tones and decorating the low tonic triad of E-flat minor in the left hand, presages the whole-tone sixteenth-note sprays which follow at (b) in bars 37 and 38. Devices (a) and (b), examined in the preceding section, are repeated in bars 41–44 (exx. 6.19 and 6.20).

Throughout his extemporization, Ellington has maintained some harmonic contact with the basic progression through the triads of E-flat minor and A-flat minor in the bass, over the first eight bars (exx. 6.18 to 6.20). Bars 45 to 48 feature an offbeat percussive exchange between hands, on the dominant seventh chord in E-flat minor at (a), but at (b) the sound quality of the recording is poor: there could be an E-flat minor seventh chord, except that the A-natural seems to be there, as notated above. There follow the tonic minor seventh at (c) and the root harmony at (d), with bell-like open tenths during bars 47 and 48. In bar 48 the trumpets in unison, their brilliance dimmed by half-open, stationary plunger cups, state the X motif (the version just heard,

Example 6.19

Example 6.20   14

Example 6.21   15

but here commencing a major third higher), which leads into the next section of the work.

The X motif lead-in, just mentioned, guides the trumpets on to a sustained ninth over the root (ex. 6.21). Ellington has varied the three-note lead-in. The lead-ins, beginning in bar 48 (p. 15 of the score), start on C-natural, B-flat (bar 50), A-flat (bars 52 and 54), B-flat (bar 56), and finally A-flat (bar 58), reaching the plateau of the major ninth by these varied steps. Above all this, saxophones led by the clarinet contribute to the eighth-note flow of the passage with their own, identically constructed phrases over every two bars. For the first time in this work the baritone saxophone is voiced over the tenor saxophone. Carney's baritone saxophone is also allotted a sixteenth-note ornamentation, preceding the hint of the X-motif lead-in phrasing. At the same time, trombones fill any remaining gaps in the continuity of eighth-notes by interpolating emphatically attacked offbeat chords. Ellington, having rejoined the rhythm section, is silent until bar 52, when he resumes his rhythmic support of the trumpets' X-motif lead-in.

Bars 53–56 (exx. 6.22 and 6.23) closely resemble the four preceding bars. Ellington adds his offbeat chords in bars 54 and 56.

In bars 57–60 (ex. 6.23) the raglike eighth-note repartee between reeds and chorus continues (ex. 6.24). At (a), where the basic rhythm chord is B-flat seventh/minor ninth, the reeds, widely spaced between clarinet on lead and first alto saxophone, are closely voiced in a cluster (A-flat, B-flat, C-flat) for second alto, tenor, and baritone saxophones. The chord of B-flat seventh/augmented ninth/minor emerges, and this ninth overlaps the trombone trio on the flattened fifth, minor seventh, and minor ninth of B-flat. The overlapping construction has been extracted in ex. 6.25. This chordal edifice could also be regarded as two superimposed harmonies; the extended B-flat dominant seventh over the root triad of F-flat major.

Trombones in bars 57 and 58 vary the basic rhythm section chord of B-flat seventh/minor ninth by employing these substitutions in succession— marked (b):

> B-flat eleventh/minor ninth
> B-flat seventh/minor ninth/diminished fifth
> B-flat eleventh/minor ninth
> B-flat seventh/minor ninth/diminished fifth

The saxophones enter (ex. 6.26), joined in turn by trombones and trumpets, the whole topped by the clarinet which glides in over all on a long upward glissando—in effect a further entry. The form of this assembly is a contrapuntal imitation based on the X motif. The ensemble remains tacet to allow Jimmy Blanton on double bass to take a solo on two conservatively constructed bars

Example 6.22

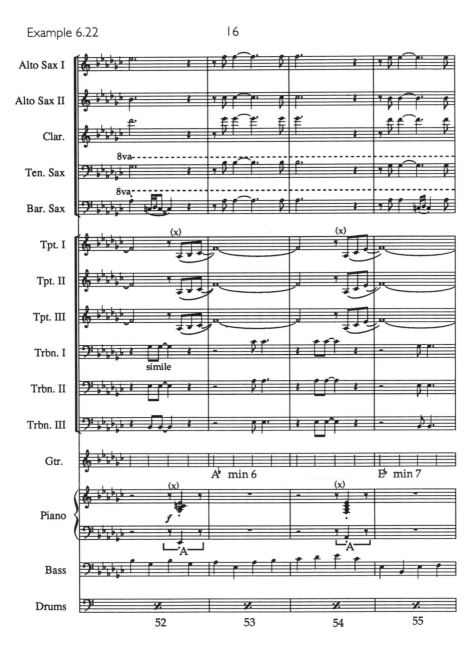

Example 6.23   17

Example 6.24

Example 6.25

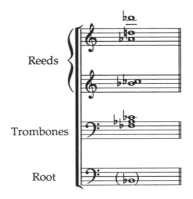

Reeds

Trombones

Root

(the A-natural in bar 64 is the only surprise, being out of mode). This brief sidestep has a distinct air of the blues about it, as it achieves the home tonic through the minor-mediant and supertonic. The notes making up this brief, bluesy phrase are marked (a). The saxophone quartet now takes up the X-motif lead-in in four-part harmony to prepare for the buildup to the orchestral tutti in the next two bars.

Bars 65 and 66 (ex. 6.27) reuse the imitative device from the preceding section, though the brass are given fresh material. A feature of this construction is the closely voiced four-part block scoring of clarinet leading the three trumpets. Blanton's solo bars (67 and 68) are simply a modest melodic variation within the mode. Bars 69–72 (ex. 6.28) follow the pattern of the sections just examined, except that Ellington has reversed the order of entry for the trumpet and trombone sections.

Brass led by clarinet, in a loud, sustained E-flat minor seventh chord spread over two and a half octaves, anticipate the first beat of bar 73 (ex. 6.29). The saxophone quartet plays in unison a descending eighth-note and sixteenth-note figure starting on the supertonic, through bars 73 and 74. With the exception of the baritone saxophone ornamentation first appearing in bar 49 (p. 15 of the score), which resembles an upper mordent, this is the first real sign of subdivision into sixteenth-notes. Bars 75 and 76, (b)–(c), accommodate a climb back to the supertonic, F-natural, at the end of the phrase by means of the $^6_4$ construction marked (b) in bar 75.

Example 6.26   18

Example 6.27 19

Example 6.28   20

Example 6.29   21

Example 6.30   22

Example 6.31   23

The deployment of the ensemble in bars 77–80 (ex. 6.30) follows the plan of the preceding section. Here saxophones again play predominantly scalar constructions in two V-shaped phrases, the second of which is bounded by a highest note of A-flat and a lowest of E-flat (the tonic). In range this second phrase is pitched one whole-tone higher than the first; the phrases are marked (a) and (b) on the score. Phrase (b) in bar 79 is the same as phrase (a) in bar 73 (on p. 21 of the score), except that the first note (A-flat) is additional.

Whereas the rhythm section's harmony in bars 81 and 82 is B-flat seventh/augmented fifth (ex. 6.31), Ellington has commenced his descending unison saxophone run on the flattened fifth (a). During bar 81 he makes melodic capital out of the minor ninth (C-flat) of the B-flat dominant seventh chord, and emphasizes the root by means of half-step ornamentation, in a manner recalling Bach, on the last three notes of the bar, before resuming the octave run down to the lower F-flat through the four whole-tones in bar 82. Bars 83 and 84, marked (c), are a reprise of bars 73 and 74, which began this episode (see p. 21 of the score). Throughout, Ellington's offbeat piano chords have steadfastly plugged away, as before, in support of the X motif ostinato rhythm which pervades the whole score.

The coda in bars 85–88 (ex. 6.32) is a repeat of bars A–D of the introduction, and bars 89–92 (ex. 6.33) are a repeat of bars E–H of the introduction. In bars 93–96 (ex. 6.34) an extra four-bar tag is attached to the introduction. The X motif forms the basis for a gradual buildup from an ensemble consisting only of rhythm section and baritone saxophone to the full, final band chord led by the clarinet of Barney Bigard during bars 95 and 96. Ellington's succinct mention within this short span of four bars of all the components of his composition is skillful. Cemented together by the long, low E-flat of the baritone saxophone, the final four bars of the coda are a potent distillation of his central ideas:

1. The double bass on the chord of E-flat minor and the tom-toms on supporting eighth-notes reiterate the X motif throughout the ending.
2. The trombones recall their initial statement in the introduction.
3. The first and second alto saxophones, tenor saxophone, and clarinet enter on the X motif to construct the chord of E-flat minor seventh. The trumpet trio plays the second inversion ($^6_4$) of the F minor chord, trombones the root E-flat minor triad.

The final tutti reveals the assembled bitonal chord illustrated in ex. 6.35 (E-flat minor plus F minor). This means that every note of the E-flat minor scale is present, plus the flattened seventh, and the overall construction therefore falls within the mode in which the piece is written (transposed Aeolian).

There are two other ways of looking at this final chord—as an amalgam of

Example 6.32   24

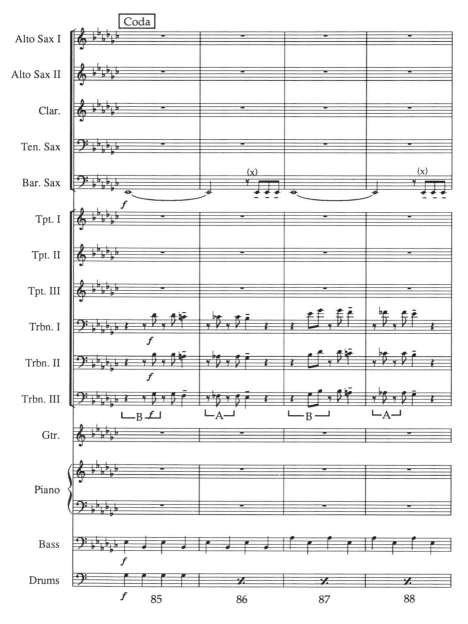

Example 6.33

Example 6.34   26

Example 6.35

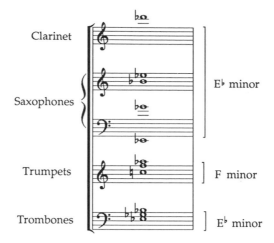

Example 6.36

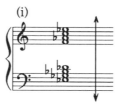

Example 6.37

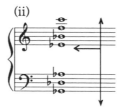

superimposed major and minor thirds (in ex. 6.36 doubled notes have been omitted, except for the tonic on top), or as a tower of fifths (symmetrical outward from E-flat; ex. 6.37).

Conclusions Drawn from the Analysis

Ko Ko clearly shows Ellington to have been a genuine composer rather than simply an arranger. He had the technique and depth to create large structures from small components—in this case by constantly including and reworking a dominating ostinato rhythm, the X motif. He was also able to hold the attention of his audience without resorting to singable tunes: the hook of *Ko Ko* is surely the relatively mundane X motif, and after the introduction and first twelve bars of tuneful antiphony there is little in the way of catchy melody to stir a first-time audience. *Ko Ko*, once a new composition, has passed into the standard repertoire owing to its energy and atmospheric quality.

Ellington planted the easy, flowing twelve-bar blues in E-flat minor (an unfamiliar key for much of jazz), which invokes a somber, sable mood. And he used his trombone soloist well: Nanton's bizarre, primitivistic style is employed in moderation, as is the obvious ploy of the tom-tom drum. The only other solo of consequence, by Ellington himself, is a mélange of brittle dissonance and whole-tone rootlessness, adding just enough sinister malevolence to the jungle atmosphere. His use of bitonal clashes and whole-tone flurries, bound together by the sustaining pedal, may be an evocation of Debussy— perhaps an unconscious one.

Ko Ko is an evocative piece that summons visions of violence. In it a well-worn rhythmic device is ingeniously transformed into a substantial one. The piece exemplifies Ellington's synthesis of blues and ragtime elements, and his ability to recognize and integrate the idiosyncratic talents of his musicians. My own reaction to this work has not changed over the forty years since I first heard it: it still strikes me as tough, gruff, and bellicose.

Martin Williams's chapter on Ellington in his book *The Jazz Tradition*, entitled "Form beyond Form," includes the following observations:

> *Ko Ko* is in a sense opposite to Concerto for Cootie [see chapter 8]. Its point of departure is simple, a succession of twelve-bar choruses; however its handling is not so simple, particularly harmonically. In these two performances, Ellington and his Orchestra pass two aesthetic tests: in the *Concerto* of undertaking a variety of material in a brief performance, and in *Ko Ko* of undertaking a simplicity of material without letting the results seem monotonous. *Ko Ko* begins with an Introduction . . . Then come solos by two of the orchestra's trombonists, Juan Tizol's valve instrument (one chorus) and Joe Nanton's plunger-muted horn (two choruses). The secondary theme of *Ko Ko* is explored largely by the orchestra in four choruses, but using exchanges with Ellington's piano in the first, and with Jimmy Blanton's bass in the third. An excellent touch is that the transition from the primary to the secondary theme of *Ko Ko* is made easier by a brass figure which accompanies Nanton's solo and which is carried over, in modified form, to the first exposition of the secondary theme. The

performance ends with a balancing restatement of the opening chorus.

In *Ko Ko* Ellington's talent again reaches full expression. The piece provides exceptional primary and secondary themes, both of which are projections of basically simple, traditional blues ideas. He handles them with appropriate robustness and continuity. And his sophistication is used to enhance the themes and to enhance the work of his soloists. Finally, he develops the second theme orchestrally in a manner otherwise unknown in jazz.[7]

In his essay on form, content, and symbol in music, Gunther Schuller numbers *Ko Ko* among an eclectic list of masterpieces:

> In the great masterpieces of music—whether a superb Bach fugue or chorale, Handel's *Messiah*, Mozart's *Marriage of Figaro*, Beethoven's *Eroica*, Duke Ellington's *Ko Ko* . . . Stravinsky's *Rite of Spring*, Schoenberg's *Erwartung*, or Babbitt's *Composition for Twelve Instruments*— show us that ultimately technique and form/structure at their most sublime levels *are* equivalent to the content; they produce the content. One can also revise that statement, with content as the subject: content = form/structure/technique. For the truth is that content and form occur, at least in the highest creative hands, simultaneously and concurrently. It is the confluence of *both* aspects in a moment of inspiration . . . that produces what we listeners and appreciators see as monuments of perfection and beauty. (italics in original)[8]

MR. J. B. BLUES

The idea of the jazz duo was not new when Ellington and the double bass player Jimmy Blanton recorded *Mr. J. B. Blues* in Chicago on 1 October 1940 (along with three other duets).[1] In 1928 the guitarists Eddie Lang and Lonnie Johnson recorded their "blue guitars" duets, notably *Midnight Call Blues*,[2] and Louis Armstrong and Earl Hines recorded *Weather Bird*.[3] Both duos were well rehearsed, and their exchanges included a large number of extempore solos. The rhythmic drive and swing were remarkably unimpaired in both cases by the absence of the full rhythm teams often deemed indispensable. In 1940 Blanton brought the duo to a high level of sophistication.

Blanton joined Ellington's band at the Coronado Hotel in St. Louis in December 1939 and remained with him until he was forced by illness to retire from playing in October 1941; he died of tuberculosis on 30 July 1942.[4] During his three years with Ellington, Blanton virtually redefined jazz double bass playing, freeing it from the necessary but prosaic task of underpinning the harmonic changes with a steady beat (say, four beats to the bar, or two beats in traditional jazz). He brought the double bass out of the shadows and took his place alongside the front-line performers.

I chose to transcribe and analyze *Mr. J. B. Blues* because it offered me these opportunities: to appraise a substantial, extended example of Ellington's mature piano style, both in a solo capacity and as a member of a jazz rhythm section; to comment on Blanton's dexterity and musicianship, both as an ensemble and rhythm player and as an improviser; and to identify instances of Ellington's permutation of the basic three-chord harmony of the blues (tonic, subdominant, and dominant).

Mr. J. B. Blues adheres to a plan of A–B–C–B. Strain A, an eight-bar construction on the tonic major harmony, is played twice. It is followed by two choruses of twelve-bar blues (B), then a sixteen-bar section written and extemporized over blues-related cadences (C). The work concludes after five consecutive choruses of the twelve-bar blues (B).

General Observations

When I first heard this duet for piano and double bass, in 1942, I formed an impression which has remained with me: that the performance was largely a well-rehearsed exercise in extended improvisation, and that there would have been the sketchiest of written scores—perhaps a roughly prepared aide-mémoire outlining the sequence and duration of solos, and any agreed modifications to the harmony.

This impression is perhaps borne out by an analysis of the work. In the first sixteen bars (pp. 1 and 2 of the score, sections A and B), Ellington and Blanton play an obsessive, antiphonal two-bar riff (suggesting that they were reading written parts, or at least well-rehearsed parts). The strains which emerge later are fragmentary, rarely developed to fill a complete section. There are two exceptions: in section D (p. 3 of the score, bars 29–37), Ellington's piano interpolations in bars 29, 31, 33, 35, and 37 follow the classic cadences of the twelve-bar blues and are phrased on a Charleston motif (syncopation type B), which figured so prominently in his early composition *Jig Walk* (1923);[5] section G (pp. 5–6 of the score, bars 69–80) repeats the Charleston motif and blues chording, as in section D. Ellington varies the sequence over bars 79–80 by playing a D-dominant thirteenth to modulate back to G major in section H.

Overall, Blanton's contribution sounds improvised, except for the initial riffing in sections A and B (bars 1–16) and his phrasing of Ellington's stop-time Charleston motifs in section D (bars 29, 31, 35, and 37). His decorations, which are random but entirely apposite, are based on nontempered blues devices: appoggiaturas, smears, and glissandi.

Harmonically, Ellington has arranged his composition over ten episodes, seven of which conform to the classic root progression of the twelve-bar blues: I–IV–I–V–I. In the three remaining sections the sequences have been varied. In sections A and B (bars 1–16), Ellington's harmony is based exclusively in the tonic (unless the single D's in the piano's left hand and the double bass imply the dominant). The introductory sections of his small-group composition *Subtle Slough* (see chapter 10), recorded during the following year, are similarly static.[6] When the chord sequence of section E (bars 41–56) is presented as in ex. 7.1, it seems clearly to follow the normal changes of the

Example 7.1   Section E, bars 41 - 56

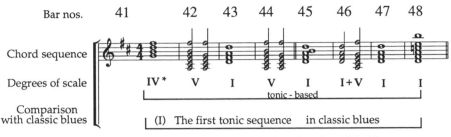

*Exceptionally IV, dictated by bass line; bar 45 (with same melody) reverts to I.

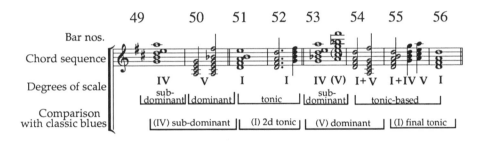

archaic twelve-bar blues, and is therefore in complete stylistic accord with the adjoining sections of the piece.

One may look at section E in another way, again referring to ex. 7.1. If one regards as a "vamp-till-ready" Ellington's first four bars (41–44—a repeated two-bar melodic motif based in IV in bar 41, and in I in bar 43), then the remainder of the episode (bars 45–56) presents one complete and conventional twelve-bar sequence, albeit with some passing harmonies added.

As for the phrasing adopted by the performers, they play the many couplets (consisting of a dotted eighth-note and a sixteenth-note) strictly as notated. This is a characteristic of ragtime, not of most jazz performances from this period and later, in which the dotted rhythm is rounded and the meter made to sound less like $\frac{4}{4}$ than $\frac{12}{8}$.[7]

Ellington does not adhere slavishly to the conventional three-chord progression of classic blues. In strain A (score references A and B, bars 1–16, exx. 7.2 and 7.3), except for a shift to an implied V-dominant thirteenth on the last beat of bars 2, 4, 6, 10, 12, and 14, in the phrases marked (a) on the score, the underlying harmony is the tonic, G major; this is confirmed by

Example 7.2 *Mr. J. B. Blues* (Ellington)

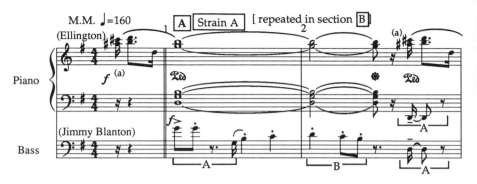

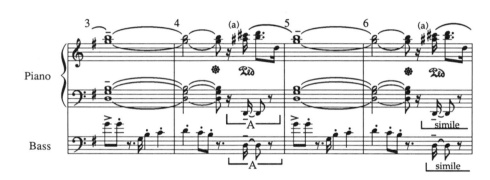

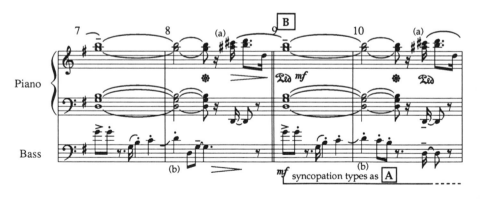

the sustained piano chords over Blanton's two-bar riff. And the final bars of the two identical sections, 8 and 16, remain on the tonic.

Ellington's lead-in phrase to bar 1 is repeated every second bar through the whole of this strain. On the phrases marked (a) referred to above, the parallel chromatic minor thirds (A-sharp–C-sharp), which slide into the two-part chords of B-natural–D-natural at the center of each phrase, are reminiscent because of their strict interpretation as sixteenth-notes of the smears in untempered blues. Blanton's full-toned, incisive attack is pitched for the most part in the "cello" register of the double bass. At the points marked (b), in bars 8, 10, 12, and 16 (these last two bars are on p. 2 of the score), he attains his D-naturals by means of a brief but definite portamento—more evidence of a blues influence on his style.

Strain B (score reference C, bars 17 to 28, exx. 7.3 and 7.4) introduces to the work the conventional twelve-bar blues progression. It commences with a brilliant-toned piano lead on a descending four-bar strain, in which the material used in the first six beats is repeated one octave lower in the six succeeding beats; the phrases, marked (a) in the example, are voiced in major and minor thirds, with a single tonic or dominant note on every fifth attack during bars 17 to 19. There is an example of secondary-ragtime phrasing in bars 17 to 19, evolving from the imitations remarked on above (see ex. 7.4).

During bars 24 to 27 Ellington interpolates four percussive, staccato phrases, constructed on a V-dominant seventh and on ninth/thirteenth chords, concluding with the tonic major sixth at the commencement of bar 27. Blanton gives rhythmic support to the piano strain in bars 17 to 19 before leading in at (b) (bar 20) to his first improvisatory contribution over the remainder of section C. The heavy emphasis which he places on the second sixteenth-note of each couplet in bar 21, and into the first beat of bar 22, implies the introduction of mid-beat syncopation into the passage; this is marked (bb) and bracketed in broken lines on the example. During bars 22 to 26 Blanton's line is well thought-out, both harmonically (it implicitly follows without decoration the guidelines of Ellington's dominant ninth, eleventh, and thirteenth chords) and rhythmically (the boogie ostinato is well sustained throughout the four-bar phrase).

Ellington's final staccato major sixth chord on the first beat of bar 27 activates Blanton's explosive two-bar solo break, which concludes section C of the score. This break is rhythmically the high point of the piece so far. Delivered with confidence and verve, it incorporates two stylistic traits stemming directly from vocal blues: the blue minor sevenths, marked (c), and the pronounced upward smear into the top G-natural, marked (d). Blanton may have been pleased with the effect, for he repeats it in substance over bars 87 and 88 in section H (p. 7 of the score).

Example 7.3

Example 7.4   Secondary Ragtime

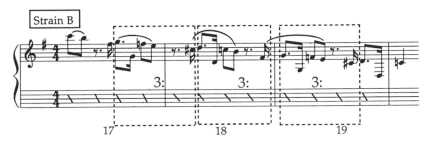

During the first ten bars of strain C (score reference D, bars 29–40, ex. 7.6) there is little of melodic interest in the piano part. Ellington has adopted the archaic two-bar ring shout sequence (call and response), which is such a prominent feature of James P. Johnson's stride rag *The Carolina Shout*.[8] The piano part's calls are represented by the phrases with mid-bar syncopation (the Charleston motif) which occur in the first bar of each two-bar unit, all marked (e) on the score. They are harmonized according to the sequence I–IV–I–V–I of the classic twelve-bar blues. Excepting the phrase in bar 33, the "melody" note at the start of each phrase is approached by means of a grace note from the semitone below, in simulation of the variable third degree of the blues scale. Ellington varies this pattern in the last two bars (39 and 40) by sustaining the chord of the tonic triad over seven and a half beats, above Blanton's propulsive, syncopated solo figurations.

Throughout this section, Blanton either phrases with Ellington's Charleston motifs or complements them rhythmically. In bars 29 to 30 the call consists of his phrasing with the piano while sustaining his B-natural almost to the end of bar 29; the response is his transition from B-natural to C-natural, accomplished with an almost unbroken smear (notated here strictly as played). The call in bars 31 to 32 occurs when Blanton joins Ellington's chord after a delay of half a beat, marked (f): this leads into his response, after a leap of a tritone from G-natural to D-flat. Bar 32 and the lead-in on the last beat of bar 31 are interesting and important. In only five beats they offer an example of all the nonstandard properties which give the blues its distinctive black flavor (for a discussion of the wayward idiosyncrasies of the style see chapter 3).[9] In ex. 7.5, I have analyzed this passage, using the method adopted in ex. 3.4.[10] Blue notes are marked *; Blanton's part is transposed two octaves above sounding pitch to facilitate comparisons.

The blueness of the descending phrase in bar 32 is intensified by Blanton's glissandi between C-natural and B-flat, then F-natural and D-natural. From bar 33 to bar 35 and in bars 36 to 40 (which complete section D), Blanton's

Example 7.5

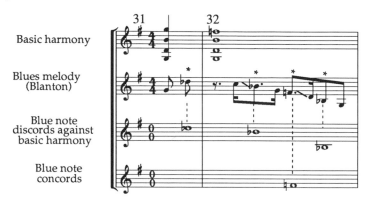

solo, although still influenced rhythmically by the Charleston phrasing in
bars 35 and 37, is thoughtfully constructed; it is developed from a reworking of ideas first stated and then imitated in each of the two four-bar phrases
making up the sequence. The phrase bracketed at X in bars 33 and 34 is
closely imitated, both rhythmically and melodically, by the phrase bracketed
Y in bars 35 and 36 (ex. 7.6). And the rhythmic patterning during bars 37
and 38 (ex. 7.6) is substantially repeated in bars 39 and 40, by means of the
continuous alternation of syncopation types C and B, as marked.

Bars 33, 34, and 35 (ex. 7.6) each contain an example of melodic freedom in the variable pitching around the third degrees of the scale. At (g) the
flattened third degree of the scale of C major, against Ellington's G-seventh, is
approached by the grace note on D-natural. At (h) is the same note—here
Blanton climbs to the E-flat with a well-defined glissando from the tonic, C-
natural. (Actually his top note is pitched between E-flat and E-natural; on the
score the E-natural is marked to be played one quarter-tone flat.) At (i) the
third degree of the tonic major scale is approached from an appoggiatura on
A-sharp, as in bars 29 and 31.

In strain D (score reference E, bars 41 to 45, ex. 7.7, and bar 56) the modulation from the old key of G major to the new key of D major is achieved
through a plagal IV–I cadence into a sixteen-bar chord progression that shows
a blues influence. Ellington's part in this episode, after his first, vamplike
four-bar statement, is in a chordal accompanying style, heavily accented and
highly syncopated. The close voicing of his four- and five-part chords in treble
and bass, and his use of the sustaining pedal (indicated by long accents), provide for an orchestral sound and style, which with ease and minimal revoicing
could have been transferred to full instrumental sections.

After four bars of straight rhythm below Ellington's opening statement,

Example 7.6   3

Example 7.7   4

Example 7.8

Blanton plays a stanza of improvised blues (bars 45 to 56). At (a) the flattened fifth of the tonic scale (G-sharp as notated) rises to the major sixth by means of a glissando; there follows a tritone descent to (b), where the flattened third degree is briefly but confidently stated. Both the G-sharp and the E-sharp are delivered against Ellington's sustained F-sharp in his left hand, which implies that the underlying harmony remains D major.

Blanton's constructions in bars 47 and 49 do not stray far from the harmony as laid down by Ellington's accompanying chords. There are brief variances in bar 48, at (c), where the chromatic passing note C-sharp is played, and in bar 49, at (d), where there is a minor seventh in the chord of G-dominant seventh (the chord normally played at this point in a twelve-bar progression), against Ellington's clear and confident chord of G major with an added major sixth and ninth.

The bluesy descending phrase, bracketed (e) in bar 50, dovetails directly into Ellington's chording: two beats of A-dominant seventh/flattened ninth, one and a half beats of A-thirteenth/flattened ninth. A secondary-ragtime construction appears in bars 52, 53, and 54, marked (f) on the music. I have converted the quotation into even eighth-notes to focus on what is essentially the $\frac{3}{8}$ grouping of this passage (in ex. 7.8).

In bar 53 Blanton's rolling, chromatic, step-by-step improvisation ploughs through Ellington's sustained chording, which is based on the implied dominant. At (g) in bar 54 is a bluesy clash between Blanton's F-natural and Ellington's F-sharp in the accompanying chord of A-dominant thirteenth.

Strain E (score reference F, bars 57 to 68, ex. 7.9) presents a further variation on the classic blues progression: a simplification of the archaic progression I–IV–I–V–I, from which Ellington has retained only I and IV. In ex. 7.10 the traditional cadential plan is compared with the decorated sequence which Ellington has used.

The new strain, stated by the piano, consists of three four-bar sections which are identically phrased (with the exception of the cross-bar tie leading into bar 57). Ellington's offbeat strain (comprising the three syncopation types A, B, and C, as shown in the example) extends over nine beats in each section.

Example 7.9   5

The voicing is two-part (except for sustained triads in bars 59–60, 63–64, and 67–68); the intervals are major sevenths, marked (a) in bars 57 and 58 and substantially the same in the remaining two sections of the strain, and minor sixths, marked (b) and likewise repeated in the remaining two sections. A strong blues effect is created by the parallel major seventh (between the minor seventh and the major thirteenth of the implied, underlying dominant harmony). Ellington executes the complete strain with an incisive, percussive touch and a full, chiming, almost metallic tone. Blanton, apart from three rhythmic fill-in phrases under Ellington's triads (described above), plays the roots of the substantially unrelated piano harmonies. His final, improvised, offbeat fill-in in bars 67 and 68 is an inventive chromatic exploration of the underlying dominant seventh harmony. The augmentation and diminution of the basic intervals of the chord have been extracted in ex. 7.11.

In complete contrast to the foregoing sections, Ellington's role in strain F (score reference G, bars 69 to 80) is now subservient to Blanton's. Ellington plays four- and five-part chords over every two-bar harmony change, beginning each segment on a mid-bar Charleston motif. There is no real melody line here: the top line of Ellington's chords merely alternate between the fifth and sixth degrees of the tonic scale. Harmonically this is a traditional twelve-bar blues sequence, varied only in bars 79 and 80 (ex. 7.12) when Ellington plays a D-ninth/thirteenth to modulate into G major for the next section of the piece.

After three bars of straight rhythm (69 to 71), during which Blanton selects notes which impart a strongly dominant flavor to his line (bar 70), he improvises the next three bars (72 to 74) in an eight-to-the-bar rhythm consisting of a dotted eighth-note and a sixteenth-note; there is no decoration or extension of the underlying chordal structure. In bar 75 Blanton delivers a powerfully rhythmic arpeggio figure which builds in volume through a cross-bar tie in bar 76 (ex. 7.12), where it peaks and then subsides. By this time the phrase has a completely pentatonic construction.

Blanton's solo moves over bars 77 to 80 (ex. 7.12) in a series of alternating mid-bar and cross-bar syncopations to end on a firmly expressed mid-beat phrase on the tonic, D (V of the new key in section H). There are two blue accidentals in bar 78: the minor ninth, marked (a), and the flattened fifth, marked (b); these are played against Ellington's accompanying dominant-thirteenth chord. It was rare in improvised jazz of the early 1940s to move a semitone down to the tonic (D) from the flattened fifth of the dominant scale (A) over a perfect V–I cadence, here marked (b) and (c). From bar 81 to the end of the performance, Blanton plays arco.

Strain G (score reference H, bars 81 to 92) begins with a figure which Ellington used at (d) one octave higher to begin the lead-in to section A and

Example 7.10

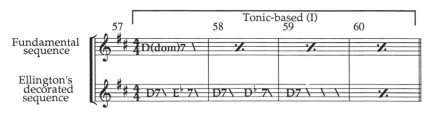

set the tempo for it. Over bars 81 to 84 his lead is reminiscent of the reiterated four-bar motif in strains A and B (bars 1 to 16); he continues afterward with a fragmented accompaniment to Blanton's solo, based on the traditional blues sequence. Blanton has not improved his performance in any way by taking up the bow at this point. His delivery is scratchily sul ponticello, and he is uncomfortably out of tune in the higher passages. A certain drive and dynamism have been sacrificed to novelty for its own sake; the pizzicato should have been retained to the end. The antiphonal exchanges between Ellington and Blanton, marked (e) in bar 81 and (f) in bar 82, are constructed solely from the degrees of the pentatonic scale in G major. After two unremarkable bars (83 and 84), Blanton reverts in bars 85 and 86 to a predominantly pentatonic construction; the ascending phrase is marked (g) to (g), but there is a chromatic decoration at (h). This phrase reworks the material transcribed in bars 33 to 36 (p. 3 of the score). Further evidence of the recycling of favorite

Example 7.11

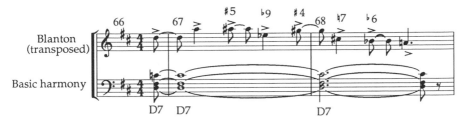

rhythmic devices occurs in bars 87 and 88 (ex. 7.13), which are reminiscent dynamically and melodically of bars 27 and 28 (p. 3 of the score).

The next two bars, 89 and 90, offer evidence that parts had been sketched out, or at least that precise agreement had been reached on phrasing and harmony. The first four of Ellington's five offbeat attacks are extensions of the dominant seventh on V: the ninth/thirteenth, thirteenth, ninth/eleventh/thirteenth, and ninth. The fifth attack resolves to the tonic major harmony with an added major sixth and ninth. Blanton resumes his solo over bars 91 and 92, where he executes with agility a series of triplets. At this tempo, forty bars to the minute, arco may offer a slight advantage over pizzicato, at least from a technical standpoint. Blue notes appear, marked (j), against the implied G major harmony in bar 91, and there are explicit blue clusters if one includes the minor third at (k) in Ellington's right-hand part.

Bars 93 to 104 (score reference I) have no recognizable theme; the phrasing of the piano part has no cogent form either rhythmically or melodically. During the first three bars of the section, Ellington sets the pattern for the whole sequence (completed on p. 8 of the score). He supports Blanton's extemporizations by interpolating percussive, offbeat stop-time chords, pointing up each harmony change. The absence of a developed strain or rhythmic pattern seems to indicate that section I was wholly improvised. Blanton's solo begins in bars 93 and 94, where he plays in a raglike eight-to-the-bar rhythm with short strokes of the bow. The passage is harmonically unadventurous, offering only one chromatic passing note, marked (l) in bar 94. Bar 96 (ex. 7.13), approached through the ascending scalar phrase in bar 95 on the preceding page of the score, presents a brief instance of augmented syncopation, a rhythmic displacement created when the E-natural, marked (a), is barely sounded at all, the heavy emphasis being placed on the concordant blue F-natural, tied over two beats, at the center of the phrase.

In bar 97 the mid-beat syncopation, marked (b), achieves the same offbeat rhythm as was delivered in the preceding bar, but in half the time. The syn-

Example 7.12   6

Example 7.13   7

copation introduces two bars of offbeat phrasing extending over eight beats and including all three syncopation types (as marked on the score). At (c) and (d) in bar 98, Blanton interpolates into his extemporization a minor ninth and flattened fifth over the underlying V-dominant seventh. This chromatic embellishment of a simple perfect cadence was quite innovative in jazz, as noted above.

Bars 99 to 100, and 101 to 102 (ex. 7.14), contain the only instance during this solo of imitation in phrasing. The two halves, bracketed in broken lines and marked (e) (e) and (f) (f), are rhythmically at one. Blanton's extemporization in bars 101 and 102, bracketed (g) on the music, appears to be in G-sharp major, and to adjust quickly to a harmony based on the dominant on the third beat of bar 102. In bar 103 the solo climbs, following Ellington's harmonic lead, to the high G-natural in bar 104. This phrase is substantially repeated in bar 111 (ex. 7.15; the triplets are omitted but a stronger syncopation is marked by accents).

Strain H (score reference J, bars 105 to 116) begins with a descent in the piano over bars 105 to 108 that is melodically and harmonically in imitation of strain B (p. 2 of the score, bars 17 to 20). But the attractive secondary-ragtime grouping of the earlier passage has been omitted from this latter variation, which is rhythmically less complex. During bars 113 and 114 Ellington interpolates supporting offbeat chords, then phrases with Blanton for a neat finish in bar 116. Blanton's solo extends over the first ten of the twelve bars in this final section, and is the longest single construction in the whole work. I do not find it as melodically inventive or as blue as much of the foregoing improvisation: the concordant minor seventh degrees of each underlying scale, marked (h) throughout the passage, appear repeatedly, and there is no valid example of a blue third or fifth degree. Where such accidentals do occur, for example at (i), they are simply chromatic passing notes. Blanton's invention over bars 113 and 114, bracketed (k), is solidly assembled around its pivotal A-natural, which occurs four times within the phrase. The descent from B-natural to D-natural at the end of the phrase (through a glissando) is a singularly strong melodic twist. On the other hand, the chromatic ascending phrase from dominant to tonic over bars 115 and 116, bracketed (i), was a lightweight and overused phrase in jazz even in 1941. The piece ends on the fourth beat of bar 116 on a long pause on the tonic, with an octave unison in the extreme bass register.

Example 7.14 8

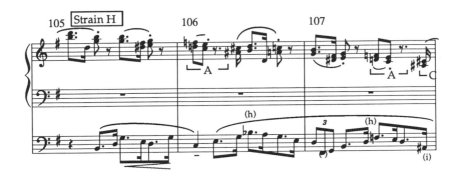

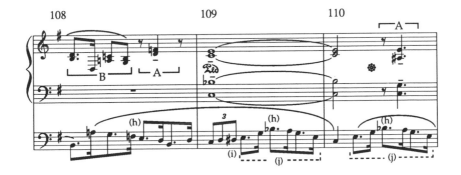

Example 7.15   9

Conclusions Drawn from the Analysis

It is an acknowledgment of the highly developed sense of rhythm of Ellington and Blanton that the rhythmic surge and swing of *Mr. J. B. Blues* are in no way diminished by the absence of drums and guitar. Around the time *Mr. J. B. Blues* was recorded these were normally played by Sonny Greer and Fred Guy, who underpinned Ellington's performances with a simple, unsyncopated, foursquare pulse. Blanton seldom plays or directly implies four straight beats to the bar: even when he plays an eight-to-the-bar boogie rhythm and uses the raglike figure of a dotted eighth-note and a sixteenth-note, there are instances where syncopation is implied by the placing of offbeat accents on the sixteenth-note of each couplet.

My experience as a solo jazz performer convinced me long ago that a jazz band is only as fine as its rhythm section. That Ellington felt the same way is clear from his choice of Blanton to be his accompanist. The rhythmic subtlety of *Mr. J. B. Blues*, in which an insistent beat of $\frac{4}{4}$ is implied rather than overtly stated, is evidence of a major break with the oom-pah rhythms which had fairly tyrannized ragtime and stride piano.

I have already speculated that some sections of *Mr. J. B. Blues* were scored (or roughly sketched, or at least evolved through repeated rehearsal) and that others were improvised in the studio. In the best traditions of immediate "composition" in jazz, the piece seems to have been in a state of flux.[11] The take which was issued differs substantially from the one which was not (for instance, in the alternative take Blanton does not use the bow). I am sure that most of Ellington's compositions began with relaxed, sketchy improvisation at the piano, or with the scribbling of fragments of melody on odd scraps of manuscript. This is confirmed by the way Ellington distributes his accompanying chords between the left and right hands. These three-, four- and five-part chords have an orchestral texture: wide intervals in the left hand, narrower ones in the right, and spans exceeding an octave. This approach to scoring for the keyboard has come to be called "arranger's piano" over the last forty years, as the left hand has gradually been relieved of its responsibilities to provide an explicit four beats to the bar, as it had in ragtime and stride piano.

Mr. J. B. Blues offers a clear insight into Ellington's compositional processes; it could well have been the model for a later piece for a larger ensemble. This is an impressive work: it has a wide-ranging and vibrant jazz sound despite a minimum of instrumental resources; it demonstrates Ellington's powerful rhythm-section playing, powerful yet unobtrusive; and it offers a fine example of Blanton's virtuosity at playing pizzicato (which I do not feel was matched by his playing with the bow), his relaxed but powerful swing, and his gift for melodic invention. In addition the performance is entertaining; it has a happy surface sound which belies the subtleties of the blues inflections in the playing of both men.

CONCERTO FOR COOTIE

Ellington wrote *Concerto for Cootie* for one of his most distinctive soloists, the trumpeter Charles Melvin "Cootie" Williams, whose first long tenure in the Ellington Orchestra lasted from 1929 to November 1940. He was a master of both the plunger-mute technique and the brilliant open horn, and the *Concerto* was designed to display his wide range of techniques. The plunger solo became one of the trademarks of the Ellington Orchestra. From late 1925 James "Bubber" Miley specialized in the emotional "growl" solo. On Miley's departure from the band in early 1929, Ellington engaged Williams to take his place. Until then Williams had apparently ignored the plunger-growl technique in his solos and it seems Ellington never actually instructed him to play like his established "growlers." But by sitting next to Tricky Sam Nanton in the brass section he soon mastered the growl and developed it into a personal and recognizable style. His second term with the orchestra began in September 1962 and ended with the death of Ellington in May 1973.

Concerto for Cootie is characterized by Williams's adroit handling of the plunger mute (he produces for the most part a softly growling timbre in the middle and lower registers of the trumpet), and by his beautiful, broad-toned playing of high notes with the open horn, phrased with a simple, majestic lyricism reminiscent of Louis Armstrong. To my ear Williams did not explore the outer limits of nonstandard timbre as deeply as did the cornetist Rex Stewart, who joined Ellington five years later than Williams did. (For a discussion of Stewart's style see the analysis of *Subtle Slough* in chapter 10.)

A noticeable characteristic of *Concerto for Cootie* is the fluent, uninterrupted dialogue between the soloist, Cootie Williams, and the orchestral accompaniment. This continuity of line is all the more impressive when it is remembered that Ellington's piano is absent from the rhythm section: this could normally be counted on to provide the ensemble with a rhythmic

Rex Stewart (cornet)

Sonny Greer (drums)

Ben Webster
(tenor saxophone)

Johnny Hodges
(alto saxophone)

Barney Bigard (clarinet)

Cat Anderson (trumpet)

Ray Nance (trumpet)
with Ellington

Lawrence Brown (trombone)

Fred Guy (guitar)

Cootie Williams (trumpet)

Duke Ellington and His Famous Orchestra, 1939. From left: Ellington (piano),
Sonny Greer (drums), Tricky Sam Nanton (trombone), Harry Carney (baritone
saxophone), Otto Hardwick (alto saxophone), Fred Guy (guitar), Juan Tizol
(valve trombone), Rex Stewart (cornet), Barney Bigard (tenor saxophone),
Lawrence Brown (trombone), Cootie Williams (trumpet), Johnny Hodges (alto
saxophone), Wallace Jones (trumpet), Jimmy Blanton (double bass)

Ellington at the piano

Rex Stewart and Johnny Hodges leaving Copenhagen for Malmö, 1939

Johnny Hodges, Juan Tizol, Barney Bigard, and Sonny Greer leaving
Copenhagen for Malmö, 1939

Ellington and Rex Stewart on the ferry from Copenhagen to Malmö, 1939

chordal backing. The principal melodic motif from which the composition is developed, the X motif, is presented with all its variants in ex. 8.1.

The X motif consists of seven eighth-notes and moves within the interval of a perfect fourth. The last three notes of the phrase—C-natural, B-flat, G-sharp/A-flat—are in a whole-tone relationship, and yield after a rise of a half-step to the third degree (A-natural) of the tonic. There appears to be no genuine improvisation in the solo trumpet part—the closely woven antiphony in the work leaves little opportunity for embroidery of the themes—and Wil-

Example 8.1   The X motif

The X motif, either in the form above or with some variation, appears in the following positions in the score:

Example 8.1 (continued)

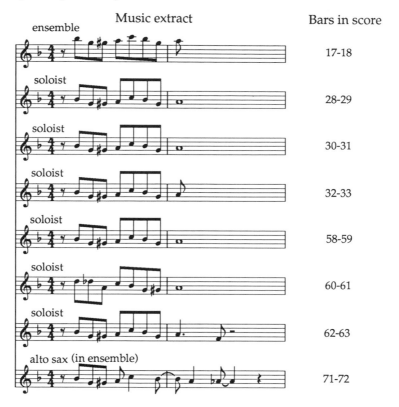

	Music extract	Bars in score
ensemble		17–18
soloist		28–29
soloist		30–31
soloist		32–33
soloist		58–59
soloist		60–61
soloist		62–63
alto sax (in ensemble)		71–72

liams could take no more initiative than simply to paraphrase. In the full score reproduced below, variations by paraphrase may be recognized in bars A–B, 2–3, and 3–4, and in the almost completely transformed construction in bar 60. The variations in bars 14 to 16 would seem to be Ellington's own written extension of the hook of the motif. His harmonizations of the X motif, where he has woven it contrapuntally into a succession of parallel, chromatic dominant sevenths, ninths, and thirteenths for the accompanying ensemble, strongly recall the parallelism so common in the popular music of the 1920s and 1930s.

Parallel, vertical block-scoring, which is pianistic in origin, is prominent in *Concerto for Cootie*, where it is predominantly chromatic. Other examples of this style may be found in the works of two of Ellington's important contemporaries: George Gershwin and Bix Beiderbecke,[1] the outstandingly lyrical improviser on both trumpet and piano.

In bars 9–10 of *In a Mist* (1928; ex. 8.2),[2] repeated in bars 11–12, Beiderbecke has employed parallel dominant ninths, beginning with F, then de-

Example 8.2   from *In a Mist* (Bix Beiderbecke, 1928)

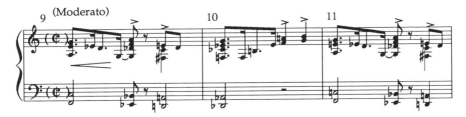

scending chromatically through E-flat, D, and D-flat. Ellington used this pattern of harmonization repeatedly, with some inconsequential modifications, in his orchestration of *Concerto for Cootie*. This obsession of the 1920s with parallel chording shows again in the highly chromatic passage of bars 13–14 and into bar 15.

In *Nice Work If You Can Get It* (from *Damsel in Distress*, 1937), the circle-of-fourths progression of related dominants[3] used by Gershwin (which was also much used by Ellington) is reharmonized in the first two beats of bars 1 and 3 (ex. 8.3). An uninterrupted sequence of chromatic, parallel dominant ninths is created in the accompanying harmony, as shown in ex. 8.4. This has entailed the substitution of only one note in each chord.

In *Concerto for Cootie*, I have identified four passages where Ellington has introduced extended similar motion (exx. 8.5–8.8). In the first three examples, he follows a rigid pattern of parallel dominant seventh, ninth, and thirteenth chords (with some instances of diminution or augmentation), descending in semitones above or below the X motif whenever this is stated by the soloist or

Example 8.3   *Nice Work If You Can Get It* (Gershwin)

(a)

Copyright © 1937 by George Gershwin Publishing Corporation. Copyright renewed, Assigned to Chappell & Co., Inc. International Copyright Secured. ALL RIGHTS RESERVED. Printed in the U.S.A. Unauthorized copying, arranging, adapting, recording, or public performance is an infringement of copyright. Infringers are liable under the law.

Example 8.4

(b)

ensemble leads; this device is written contrapuntally against the rigid succession of parallels by the trumpet soloist, or as an inner voice in the ensemble.
In exx. 8.5–8.7 these instances are referred to as the "Y harmonizations," and
the descending dominants begin successively on G-flat, B-flat, and A-flat.

The version of *Concerto for Cootie* analyzed in the following pages was
recorded in Chicago on 15 March 1940. Ellington has turned the technical as-
suredness of two of his talented sidemen to practical advantage throughout this
work by writing prominent melodic parts for both. The flexibility and puissant
natural legato made possible by Juan Tizol's valve trombone have been combined with Jimmy Blanton's perky pizzicato to give the lower-pitched voices
of the ensemble more muscle and an improved sonority. Throughout, Sonny
Greer's gentle and unobtrusive work with wire brushes provides a steady $\frac{4}{4}$ pulse
beneath the constantly syncopated movement of solo and ensemble parts. The
plan of the work is shown in table 4.

The introduction to the work (bars A to H, exx. 8.9, 8.11, and 8.12) extends

Table 4

Section	Form	Score Reference	Bars	Structural Element	Number of Bars
—	Introduction	—	A–H	Material based on strain A (F major)	8
A	A–A1–B–A2	A	1–10	Strain A	10
	(popular-	B	11–20	Strain A1	10
	song form,	C	21–28	Strain B	8
	but in ten-	D	29–40	Strain A2 and bridge passage	8
	bar units)			Modulation	4
B	A–A1 strain pattern	E	41–56	Strain C (D-flat major)	16
—	—	F	57–58	Modulation and lead-in	2
A	—	G	59–68	Strain A (modified F major)	10
—	Coda	Coda	69–74	Material developed from strain A	6

over pp. 1 to 3 of the score. Cootie Williams, delivering a quiet, purring sound behind the closed plunger and playing completely solo, sets the tempo for the performance (bar A) with a straight statement of the hook of the A strain's principal motif (the X motif). This is varied only by a full-value quarter note on the first beat of the bar in place of an eighth-note after a single eighth-rest. The clarinet, leading the orchestral ensemble, echoes the hook one octave higher in bars C and E (marked X on the score). From bar H onward, however, the hook has been subjected to a change in rhythmic emphasis, from being the lead phrase to the secondary lead-in phrase, introducing strain A in section A of the score.

Bars C and D feature the first of Ellington's chromatic harmonizations of the X motif (marked Y on the score). Jimmy Blanton's bass sounds one octave below Harry Carney's baritone saxophone, on the roots of the descending dominants. I consider bar D (the valve trombone's lead-in over sustained harmony from the reeds) to offer evidence of Ellington's facility in constructing chromatic melodic material. In ex. 8.10 I have renotated the bar in its actual

Example 8.5

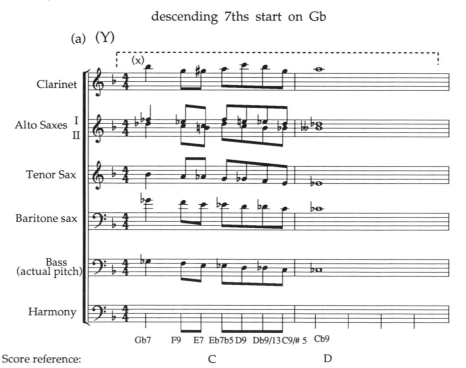

descending 7ths start on Gb

condensed to basic dominant 7ths
in accompaniment

C   D

Example 8.6

descending 7ths start on Bb

(b) (YY)

Example 8.7

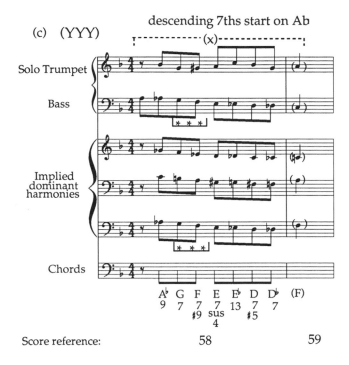

Score reference: 58   59

key of C-flat, voiced the sustained dominant-ninth harmony above the sounding pitch of Blanton's reiterated C-flats, and indicated the augmentations and
diminutions of the intervals of the underlying dominant-ninth chord which
have been written into Tizol's ascending solo line.

Ellington's harmonization, which omits the fifth and doubles the minor
seventh, permits euphonious progress in the melody line. Only one chordal
disagreement occurs against the ensemble voicing: D-natural, marked (a), a
classic blue note third degree, is sounded against the sustained mediant in the
reeds' harmony. The following note, marked (b), occupies the next nearest,
traditionally nontempered area in the blues scale, although here, with the fifth
omitted from the ensemble chord, the blue effect is not so pronounced.

Tizol's ascending lead-in is extended over two more bars (E and F) in variations on the hook of the X motif, interpolated as a contrapuntal voice into
the chromatically descending parallel dominants written for four saxophones
and the first and third trumpets (in the YY harmonization already analyzed).
The double bass remains in octave unison with the baritone saxophone, in
a simple doubling device which contributes a rich sonority to the ensemble.

Example 8.8

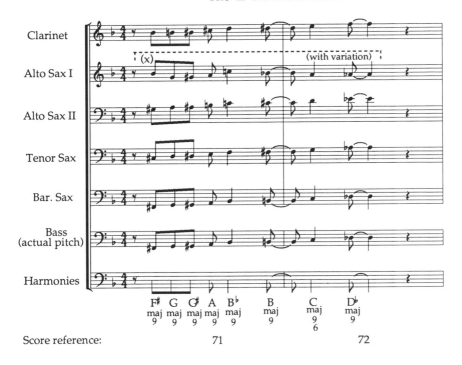

The Z Harmonization

Score reference: 71   72

The chromatically descending phrase in bar E has been marked with "straight" eighth-notes at the beginning and "swung" eighths over the final two beats to acknowledge this nuance in the interpretation. During the first six beats, the notes are given full value and equal emphasis with no vibrato—features uncharacteristic in jazz of this period. The last four bars of the passage lean toward a $\frac{12}{8}$ style of phrasing (that is, a triplet rhythm consisting of a quarter note followed by an eighth-note), although this is not pronounced enough to be precisely notated as such. Ellington may have directed his men to phrase in this way (or, just as likely, they did so naturally), to prepare for the jazzy mid-beat and mid-bar syncopations in the last tutti in bar 6. In bar H Williams, playing completely solo, picks up the X motif to lead into strain A in section A of the score.

Strains A and A1 of sections A and B (pp. 3 to 8 of the score, exx. 8.12 and 8.14 to 8.18) are assembled in ten-bar phrases, a grouping seldom encountered in formalized jazz composition in 1940. (But this idea was not new to Ellington: in his arrangement for piano from 1973 of his earliest accredited composition, *Soda Fountain Rag*, an arrangement presumed to be faithful to

Example 8.9   *Concerto for Cootie*

Ellington has retained the central idea of parallel chromatic block scoring, but here the chords are in ascending order.

the original version dating from 1914, the B strain is also ten bars long). At first glance Ellington's ten-bar strains A and A1 appear to be conventional eight-bar strains with two-bar orchestral afterthoughts. Closer scrutiny, and comparison of the two variants, reveals in addition a subtle shift in the rhythmic emphasis placed within the melodies themselves, which renders unreasonable such an arbitrary division of the sequence into eight- and two-bar segments. This may

Example 8.10

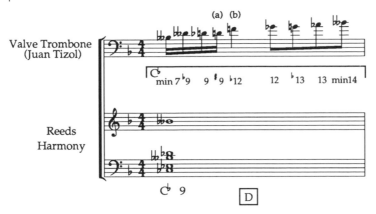

be seen in ex. 8.14, where the end of strain A, marked X in bar 6, arrives one bar sooner than is common practice in jazz (in the sixth bar of the notional eight-bar section).

In strain A1, however, the final note is delayed until the customary seventh bar of the section (marked Y in bar 17). This elongation of the strain has been achieved simply by inserting an extra bar of developed thematic material in bar 15 (indicated by broken lines). For the purposes of clear differentiation, I have confined the extracts in ex. 8.13 to rhythmically straightforward expositions of the soloist's part alone.

That the X motif occupies the first four bars of strain A and the first five of strain A1 (either because of its return to the third degree of the tonic scale or because of movement around it) suggests that the underlying harmony should be based in the tonic, but in the writing of the orchestral figures which support these two themes there are departures from this principle. Ellington has returned here to the ring shout antiphony which figures so prominently in *The Carolina Shout*, by his mentor James P. Johnson. There are six appearances of this call-and-response device in the work (four in sections A and B on pp. 3 to 6 of the score, and two in section G on pp. 18 and 19). By their unique melodic and harmonic constructions (rhythmically they are identical) these six responses merit individual attention. They are labeled R I to R VI on the music.

Cootie Williams's exposition with closed plunger mute of strains A and A1 is restrained, his growl barely perceptible. The trill marked over the whole-notes in bars 1 and 3 (A-natural to B-flat) sounds like a genuine lip trill, and not an artificial one accomplished by rapidly oscillating the second valve. A real lip trill is not easily brought off in the middle to lower register of the

Example 8.11   2

trumpet. At (a) and (b) in bars 2 and 4, Williams offers two distinctly varied paraphrases of the hook of the strain.

During response I (bars 1 to 2) the trombone triads are approached by means of bluesy portamenti (this presents no problems for the slidemen, and is accomplished through half-valving by Tizol). Each phrase consists of four attacks, the first and last of which are harmonized on the tonic major triad. In

Example 8.12   3

bar 1 the triads set up a disagreement with Williams's sustained third degree, marked (c) on the score.

Response II (bars 3 to 4) is rhythmically identical to response I, and contains a blue E-flat in the dominant seventh at (d), where the soloist's A-natural is the thirteenth.

Williams concludes strain A on the rhythmically weak sixth bar of the ten-

Example 8.13

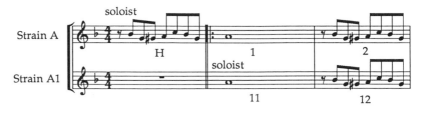

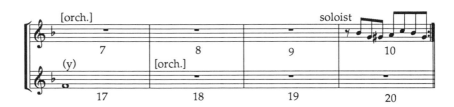

bar sequence (ex. 8.14). In bars 6 to 8 and 9 to 10 (p. 5 of the score), reeds led by the clarinet play parallel, block-scored harmonies, after the soloist states the theme. Depth is added to the ensemble sound by Tizol's valve trombone, doubling the clarinet lead, and Blanton's bass, phrased with the section on the roots of the parallel chords—except for the F-natural, marked (a) in bar 7, which remains as the fifth of the IV-ninth.

Williams restates the X motif in bar 10 (ex. 8.15), leading into strain A1 in section B of the score. This time he plays a straight-toned A-natural in bar 11, now omitting the lip trill, and there is no growling at all. In bar 9 the tutti played by reeds, valve trombone, and double bass on the II-diminished seventh chord returns to the V-dominant seventh through the cross-bar, syncopated stop-time phrase marked (a). In this figure, the texture of the parallel dominants on D-flat and C has been thickened by the tenor saxophone's insertion of the major second. Saxophones led by clarinet (with double bass, as before) make response III (bars 11 to 12). The melody lead is new, as is the underlying harmony.

The extra bar of melody has again been inserted in bar 15 (the motif from

Example 8.14

the last two beats of bar 14 is repeated twice; see ex. 8.16). Williams then reverts to the original melody from strain A. Response IV (bars 13 to 14) presents another new melody lead and a new harmonization. Jimmy Blanton's bass line, descending by half-steps in bars 15 and 16 (and anticipating the chromatic passage in eighth-notes which immediately follows), accompanies Williams's solo until the final two beats of bar 16, where consecutive major sevenths are created between the pairs of notes marked (a) and (b) (the double bass sounding one octave lower than written).

Example 8.15   5

Ellington repeats the Y harmonization (ex. 8.17), his device of parallel, chromatically descending sevenths which he had used in the introduction to his composition (pp. 1 and 2 of the score, bars C and D), but here he has extended it over three more semitones. On a bluesy progression of I–IV⁷– $II^{\text{minor }7}$–V, a sharply attacked syncopated phrase in bars 19 and 20 from the brass section (without Williams), ending on a V-dominant seventh, links the final sustained chord of the reeds with Williams's fierce, growling triplet lead-in to strain B in section C of the score.

Example 8.16   6

In matters of harmony, form, and sound, section C of the work (strain B, ex. 8.18) is pure blues, set in the eight-bar convention of the genre. The basic harmonic plan, I–IV⁷–I, incorporates the pivotal shift to subdominant harmony which is fundamental to the classic blues sequence. And the strain itself is assembled in ternary form: there are three self-contained two-bar stanzas (bars 21–22, 23–24, and 25–26), melodically and rhythmically similar, before the last two bars of the strain prepare and lead into the final complete exposition of the principal motifs making up the A strains.

Example 8.17   7

Williams's intensification of delivery, from gentle purr to savage growl, kin-
dles a dramatic highlight and provides a definitive example of the bluesy jungle
trumpet which had been a trademark of Ellington since Bubber Miley joined
the band in autumn 1924. His gritty timbre leads me to believe that in addition
to the throat growl he may have employed flutter tonguing on the longer notes
of his solo (this is accomplished by holding the tongue in the same position as
when one rolls a spoken ar).

Example 8.18   8

Section C (bars 21 to 28, pp. 8 to 10 of the score) has a dense antiphonal patterning, in which mid-bar syncopated phrases from the saxophones in bars 21 and 23, marked (a), are echoed by staccato offbeat chords from the five remaining brass in bars 22 and 24, marked (b). Ellington's figures in bars 22 and 24 for the unison saxophone trio create brief clusters at (c)—a flattened fifth from the saxophones against a perfect fifth from the first trombone—and at (d) in bar 24, where the saxophones play the major sixth of the underlying

Example 8.19   9

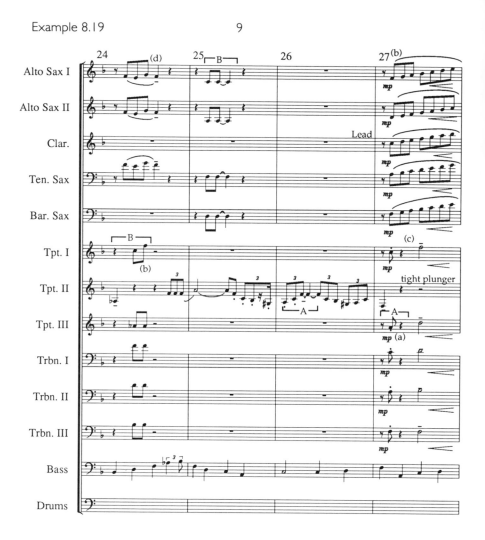

B-flat scale against the minor seventh written for the third trumpet (as part of the chord of the B-flat dominant ninth). In the rhythm section, Sonny Greer continues to play legato in $\frac{4}{4}$. Jimmy Blanton's rhythm is made up of three full-value quarter notes followed by a phrase consisting of a quarter note followed by an eighth, as in $\frac{12}{8}$, on the last beats of bars 21, 22, and 24; this rhythm reappears in *Subtle Slough*, recorded in 1941.[5]

Ellington's written strain concludes on the lowest F-natural, marked (a) in bar 27 (ex. 8.19). It is no problem to play this on the trumpet.[6] But as a trum-

Example 8.20   10

peter I recognize that such a clear, broad, bell-like tone, doubly obstructed in
this position by a straight (or pear) mute and a plunger cup, can be achieved
only by a player with the fattest and thickest tone. Ellington always appreciated Williams's beautiful sound on the open trumpet, fully exploited later in
this piece at strain C, bars 41 to 56 (pp. 13 to 17 of the score).

The ascending scalar passage for reeds, marked (b) in bars 27 to 28, is voiced
in parallel major and minor triads, with major and minor sixths added, against
a IV–I plagal cadence played by the brass. Except that Cootie Williams's solo

Example 8.21   II

is a straight statement of the X motif, without paraphrase and with little or no vibrato, bars 29–32 (exx. 8.20 and 8.21) are a repeat of bars 1 to 4 (pp. 1 and 2 of the score).

Bars 33 to 35 and the first two beats of bar 36 (exx. 8.21–8.22) are a repeat of bars 5 to 7 and the first two beats of bar 8 (p. 5 of the score). Underpinned by Greer's choke cymbal, the trombones and double bass at (a), sounding in octave unison, descend chromatically from the tonic to the minor seventh of the tonic scale. The minor seventh (E-flat) is tied across the barline into the first bar of the modulatory sequence on the next page of score.

Example 8.22   12

The soloist is tacet throughout bars 37–40 (exx. 8.22–8.23). (I suspect that
Ellington was thoughtfully giving his soloist a rest, to prepare him for the
rigorous top-register blowing to come.) The ensemble's playing substantially
follows the I–IV–I convention of classic blues. The actual modulation is in
bar 40, where anticipatory offbeat chords from the brass move in contrary
motion to the on-beat figure written for alto and tenor saxophones.

Until bar 41 (ex. 8.23) Cootie Williams has used three disparate methods
of tone production: plunger-muted (closely), with a pronounced vibrato frequently developed into a lip trill and a trace of growl (bar H and bars 1 to

Example 8.23   13

6, pp. 3 to 4 of the score); plunger-muted (closely), with almost no vibrato and with no throat growl (strain A1, bars 10 to 17, pp. 5 to 8 of the score); and plunger-muted, with the plunger cup now freely manipulated around the half-open position, and with a dramatic increase in volume, a savage growl, and exaggerated vibrato (strain B, bars 20 to 27, pp. 8 to 9 of the score). Strain A2 thus appears as a straight statement of the original strain A, without paraphrase. In this section Williams reverts to the quiet, cool, vibratoless delivery noted above.

The next solo, consisting of fifteen bars played with a superb tone on open

Example 8.24

trumpet, is pitched in the high and upper-middle registers of the trumpet. The principal motif of this new strain (C) occurs three times, in bars 41–42, 45–46 (p. 14 of the score), and 49–50 (p. 15), and it appears to have been varied in performance each time by paraphrase. In ex. 8.24 the three paraphrases are shown together for comparison, beneath my suggestion of the possible form of Ellington's original melody: straight and "unswung."

By means of a broad-toned, half-valved glissando, a device which he repeats to reach F-natural, marked (b) in bar 43 (ex. 8.25), Williams attains a majestic top B-flat; this is the trumpet's "top C," marked (a) in bar 43. This marks the first occasion in this work of a definite, extended glissando. In practice both glissandi are easy to execute, by tightening the lip while half-depressing two valves or all three, until the required pitch of the melody note has been attained. The D-flat, marked (c) in bar 43, is the augmented ninth. Sounded against the four-part VI-seventh chord from the reeds it is blue, and it falls by half-step to the ninth of the continuing VI-seventh harmony.

The basic root progression of bars 41 to 44 is simple: two bars on D-flat, two bars on B-flat. There are passing harmonies traced by the unison line written for alto and tenor saxophones, rising chromatically between the interval of the tenth sustained by Harry Carney's baritone saxophone and Barney Bigard's clarinet. The reeds continue with a V-seventh chord in which the minor seventh is doubled.[7]

Example 8.25   14

Williams executes his second paraphrase of the principal motif of strain C, now returning to the tonic in bar 47 (ex. 8.26). In the ensemble the pattern set in the four preceding bars is closely followed. Beneath the soloist, unison saxophones play a countermelody, this time a descending scalar line, additionally supported by triads from the trombones (B-flat minor, D-flat, E-flat ninth, and A-flat seventh). Reeds led by the clarinet play a descending phrase to link the first section of Williams's solo with the last one. Ellington has scored his reeds in parallel major sixth chords, marked (a) to (a), followed by a series of dominant sevenths and ninths. Except for the passing notes at (b) and (c) in

Example 8.26   15

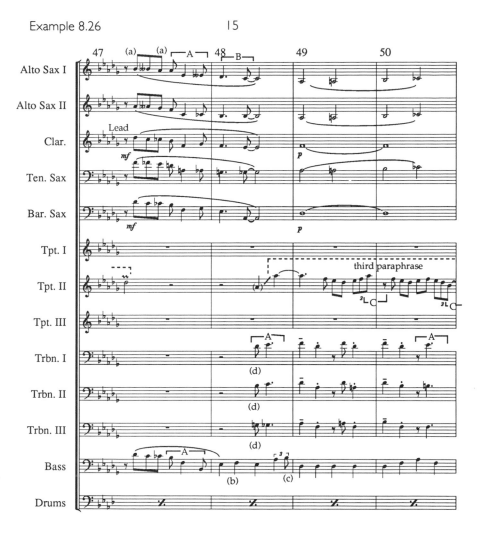

bar 48, Jimmy Blanton remains on the roots of the harmonies throughout this two-bar linking phrase.

In bar 48 the three trombones are added to the V-dominant ninth chord sustained by the reeds, entering through an appoggiatura, marked (d), which implies a passing harmony of II-dominant seventh (diminished as written).

Williams approaches his third and final paraphrase of the principal motif of strain C through a perfectly controlled slow glissando over an octave, starting on the third beat of bar 48 (p. 15 of the score) and tied to the A-flat at the beginning of bar 49 (ex. 8.26). He plays a glissando with a similarly full tone in

Example 8.27   16

bar 51, marked (a), until the F-natural at the commencement of the four-note phrase linking the change in underlying harmony. Bars 49 and 50 repeat the harmony and countermelody for reeds which had been used at the beginning of the episode (bars 41 and 42, p. 13 of the score), now additionally supported by triads from the trombone trio.

A countermelody of chromatic passing notes, marked (a) to (a) in ex. 8.27, is a partial cancrizans in form and moves freely within the intervals of the enveloping trombone triad. By means of the mid-beat figure in bar 55 (syn-

Example 8.28   17

copation type A), trombones then link with the ensemble V-dominant seventh chord which brings this section of the composition to a close. The stentorian sound of this chord has in fact masked the double bass over the last two beats of bar 56. (The two D-flats in my transcription represent an educated guess: they make some sense when considered against the more faithfully recorded bar which follows—bar 57, p. 17 of the score).

In Williams's assigned part, phrased on alternate mid-bar and cross-bar syncopations, there are two classic blue notes, both marked (b) in bar 53,

Example 8.29 |8

in disagreement with the underlying harmony. I consider this two-bar fragment, full of movement and attractive dissonance, to offer a fine example of
how blues practice can be smoothly integrated into the conventions of the
conservatory.

In the short bridge passage at score reference F (bars 57 to 58, ex. 8.28), the
first trumpet leads the ensemble through from the A-flat dominant seventh of
bar 56 and the F-major sixth in bar 57 to achieve a direct modulation back to
the original key of F major. This three-note, offbeat phrase, which descends

Example 8.30   19

through the $^6_4$ inversion of the F major triad, has already been used to vacate
the ensemble passage in bar 39 (p. 13 of the score).

Williams's restatement of the X motif in bars 62 and 63 (exs. 8.29 and 8.30)
is followed by a descent to the tonic through the phrase in bar 63, marked
(a), and further varied by the inclusion of the unusual snatched snap at (b)
in the following bar. Ellington's final response, indicated as R VI over bars
61 and 62, completes the series of six constructions which have decorated the
A strains of the composition, each melodically and harmonically unique but

Example 8.31   20

all rhythmically identical. A scurrying scalar ascent for ensemble sections in octave unison, played fortissimo, leads into the final four-bar section of this ten-bar episode.

In bars 65–68 (exx. 8.30–8.31) the full front line (except for Williams) delivers two rhythmically imitative, descending two-bar phrases at full power, scored in parallel five-part block harmony on the basic root progression IV–V–I–VI. Williams's high-note interpolation over the sustained ensemble dissonance in bar 66, marked (a), is strikingly dramatic in effect. In this curious

Example 8.32 21

grouping of five against three I have marked the notes "+o" on the score: this indicates that to produce the sounds Williams has fanned each attack by alternately opening and then closing the plunger cup against the bell of his horn. These top A-naturals, in this unusual context and with this unusual rhythm, may have been a master stroke of personal inspiration, or perhaps the result of Ellington's guidance.

The ensemble harmony, sustained over the first three beats of bar 66, is revealed as a simple IV-minor triad scored for first trombone (doubled by tenor saxophone), second trombone (doubled by second alto saxophone), and third trumpet (doubled by first alto saxophone). The texture is enlivened by the dissonant major seventh written for third trombone (doubled by baritone saxophone), first trumpet, and, one octave higher than the first trumpet, by the soloist.

In bars 69 and 70 (ex. 8.31), ensemble chords of IV-major with added major seventh and V-dominant ninth support Williams's curious snaps (first introduced on bar 64, p. 19 of the score), marked (a) in bar 69 and repeated rhythmically though less excitedly at (b) in bar 70. Williams holds his F-natural firmly throughout bar 71 against the series of parallel rising ninths (see the opening of this chapter).[8] The passage is enhanced by a variation on the X motif played by the first alto saxophone: a simple reversal of the last two notes of the hook, which has been stretched over seven beats (the original phrase was contained in one bar). It is played with just the right amount of emphasis by Johnny Hodges; the line is neatly inserted into the parallels scored for the rest of the reeds and the double bass. This offers further proof of Ellington's compositional ingenuity—it is an effective reworking of an important fragment of his original material.

The piece ends quietly (ex. 8.32). Williams's sustained tonic note, faintly growling and with a warm, wide vibrato, is allowed to develop full tone through the half-open plunger. Beneath, saxophones and trombones voiced over a range of an octave and a major seventh play the final cadence of the work, marked (a): the dominant seventh on the minor second of the tonic scale (G-flat seventh) resolving to the final chord of F major with added major sixth. By reason of its chromaticism, Ellington's chording here resolves in similar fashion to a neapolitan sixth at a full close.

Conclusions Drawn from the Analysis

This recording of *Concerto for Cootie* has been in my collection for more than forty years, during which I have listened to it with pleasure hundreds of times. Even before analyzing the work I enjoyed its technical, surface brilliance, and as a lifelong student of the technique of playing the jazz trumpet I found Williams's work affecting to the point where it influenced my own playing.

By virtue of the repetitive and compacted construction of the three main strains of *Concerto for Cootie*, there is no space set aside for extended solo improvisation in its literal sense (a rare situation in Ellington's works). There are, however, some exceptions:

1. Williams paraphrases the X motif in strain A (bars 2 and 4, pp. 2 and 3 of the score).
2. He varies the principal motif of strain C on each of the three occasions when it appears (paraphrases marked on pp. 13–16 of the score).
3. His variation in bar 60 (p. 18 of the score) is far removed from the original phrase which it has supplanted.
4. There is no evidence that Williams's notes in the *Concerto* were not wholly preconceived by Ellington. Apart from the several instances of paraphrase, an extempore feel is created by Williams's broad, varied spectrum of tone colors (which Ellington may have had a hand in choosing).

As for compositional devices, Ellington seems to have relied on only three central ideas:

1. The incorporation of pianistic, chromatically descending, and un-related dominants—these are the Y, YY, and YYY harmonizations marked on the score and extracted to exx. 8.5–8.7.
2. The use of chromatically ascending major ninths (the Z harmonization, extracted to ex. 8.8), closely related to the harmonizations mentioned in the preceding paragraph.
3. The rhythmically identical phrasing of the ensemble's responses to Williams's statements of all the A strains throughout the piece (marked on the score on pp. 3 to 10 and 18 to 20).

I agree completely with the opinions expressed by André Hodeir in his essay "A Masterpiece: Concerto for Cootie," which constitutes a chapter of his book *Jazz: Its Evolution and Essence:*[9]

All that remains is to place CONCERTO FOR COOTIE as jazz. Almost twenty years of experience were required before orchestral jazz produced, within a few days of each other, its two most important works. The first is KO KO.[10] It has less freshness and serenity, but perhaps more breadth and grandeur. The second is the CONCERTO. In the perfection of its form and the quality of its ideas, the CONCERTO, which combines classicism and innovation, stands head and shoulders above other pieces played by big bands. It has almost all the good features found in the best jazz, and others that are not generally found in Negro music. It makes up for the elements is doesn't use by the admirable way in which it exploits those that constitute its real substance. Isn't that exactly what a masterpiece is supposed to do?[11]

As a postscript, I note that material from *Concerto for Cootie* was used in

Do Nothin' 'till You Hear from Me, one of Ellington's most popular songs, which became much more famous than the original.[12] The song, with lyrics by Bob Russell, was published in 1943. It was assembled from the A strains of the *Concerto* adapted into conventional, more easily comprehended eight-bar phrases; its harmonies follow the sequence used in the commencement of section G (bars 59–63, pp. 18–19 of the score), and except for the initial modulation into D-flat major there is a completely new middle eight. The modifications are compared with the original in ex. 8.33.

Example 8.33   A *Concerto for Cootie* (1940)
                B *Do Nothin' Till You Hear From Me*

Strain A reduced from a 10-bar phrase to an 8- bar phrase

B   (two bars excised from song)

The final 8 bars of Strain C, rewritten as the release

(Implied key: Db major) -

- (reverts to F major) - - - -

- -

JUNIOR HOP

The alto and soprano saxophonist John Cornelius Hodges,[1] nicknamed "Rabbit" by his colleagues, was born in Cambridge, Massachusetts, on 25 July 1906 and died in New York in 1970. As Ellington recalled:

On May 11, 1970 I was thinking about how I could persuade [Hodges] to get his soprano saxophone out once more to play on A *Portrait of Sidney Bechet* in *The New Orleans Suite*.[2] The telephone rang and I was told that he had just died at his dentist's office. This is the eulogy I wrote that night, and it still captures my feelings about him:

Never the world's most highly animated showman or greatest stage personality, but a tone so beautiful it sometimes brought tears to the eyes—this was Johnny Hodges. This *is* Johnny Hodges . . . Because of this great loss, our band will never sound the same . . . Johnny Hodges sometimes sounded beautiful, sometimes romantic, and sometimes people spoke of his tone as being sensuous . . . With the exception of a year or so, almost his entire career was with us.[3] So far as our wonderful listening audience was concerned, there was a great feeling of expectancy when they looked up and saw Johnny Hodges sitting in the middle of the sax section, in the front row. I am glad and thankful that I had the privilege of presenting Johnny Hodges for forty years, night after night. I imagine I have been much envied.[4]
(italics in original)

I have already discussed Hodges's blues style in chapter 3. Hodges was equally comfortable when extemporizing a blues at a relaxed or moderate tempo,[5] and when playing a succession of written strains, as in *Junior Hop*. He had a rich, full tone, absolute technical command, impeccable intonation, a warm, expressive, perfectly disciplined vibrato, and a personal, instantly recognizable way of decorating a phrase, sometimes with glissando and portamento. It may be gathered from Ellington's recollections of Hodges that he valued his presence immensely.

General Observations

As in *Concerto for Cootie*, there is little extemporization, literally speaking, in the solo part of *Junior Hop*. The notes appear to be too closely knit with those of the accompanying ensemble horns to have been freely phrased. But there is room for self-expression and interpretation on the part of the soloist: just as Williams added his own blues inflections and atmospheric jungle timbres to *Concerto for Cootie*, Hodges enhanced the performance in *Junior Hop* of Ellington's written themes with bluesy glissandi and smears. (Unlike Williams, however, he did not resort to any brutalization of tone, no matter how apposite doing so might have seemed.)

Ellington's own piano interpolations in *Junior Hop* occur in sections F to I of the score (bars 41–72); Lawrence Brown's trombone solo is in section L (bars 89–96). Both contributions are revealed in analysis to be thoroughly disciplined rhythmically and melodically, and to be derived by all indications from thoughtfully assembled written parts, firm direction, and assiduous rehearsal.

In table 5, I have classified each eight-bar melodic sequence in *Junior Hop* as a substrain, using the same letter code with which I have identified the passages on the transcription score, and I have divided the piece into seven episodes. Excepting the two eight-bar sections which act as the introduction and coda and are almost identical (sections A, bars 1–8, and N, bars 101–08), all the remaining strains at the heart of the work have been grouped under the four-section format of popular song. But whereas the common order of strains in this genre is A–A–B–A, Ellington has composed a succession of no fewer than twelve individual melodic sequences (substrains A–L; substrain M is a repeat of the first four bars of substrain E). The pop-song pattern is reinforced by his use twice during the work of the same basic thirty-two-bar root sequence (episodes 2 and 3) and his repetition for a third time of its first twenty-eight bars (episodes 4, 5, and 6—the last four bars may have been cut because the disc was not long enough to accommodate them).

It would seem from the recording of 1940 that Ellington did not play at all during the first thirty-nine bars of the performance. His piano work after that point is well recorded and important to the development of the piece. In the examples which follow, I have used bracketed chord symbols in the unoccupied sections of the piano staves to indicate the harmonies which are

Table 5

Episode	Score Reference	Bars	Substrain	Structural Element
1 (Introduction)	A	1–8	A	Alto saxophone with ensemble support
2	B	9–16	B	Same
	C	17–24	C	Same
	D	25–32	D	Same
	E	33–40	E	Same
3	F	41–48	F	Tutti with piano interpolations
	G	49–56	G	Same
	H	57–64	H	Same
	I	65–72	I	Same
4	J	73–80	J	Ensemble and solo alto saxophone
	K	81–88	K	Same
5	L	89–96	L	Trombone solo with piano support
6	M	97–100	M	Alto saxophone with ensemble support (first four bars after score reference E only)
7 (Coda)	N	101–08	A	Alto saxophone with ensemble support

identifiable from the ensemble voicings or have been implied by the solo alto saxophone or double bass lines over the four beats of each bar. It may be observed that whereas Ellington has composed twelve substantially individual but structurally related substrains (A–L), he has used only six chord sequences in support.

Closer examination of the varied substrains which constitute the core of the composition (episodes 2 to 6) reveals that Ellington constructed both his melodic and rhythmic motifs to precise and persistent patterns. In the ex-

Form	Chord Sequences	Remarks	Number of Bars	
—	A	—	8	8
A	B		8	
B	C		8	32
C	D		8	
D	E		8	
A	B		8	
B	C		8	32
C	D		8	
D	I	New sequence, in lieu of E	8	
A	B		8	
B	C		8	
C	D		8	28
D	E		4	
—	A	—	8	8

amples which follow, the rhythmically and melodically related motifs appearing through the work have been sorted into five main categories:

1. the hook of the piece, in all its variants
2. rhythmically or melodically related constructions, first group
3. rhythmically or melodically related constructions, second group
4. rhythmically or melodically related constructions, third group
5. rhythmically or melodically related constructions, fourth group.

These groups account for ninety-five and a half bars of the 108 in the composition; the remaining twelve and a half bars contain the two passages noted below:

1. score reference H, bars 61–64, where the repeated note rhythm has been developed over the whole of the four bars
2. score reference L, bars 88 (beginning with the two-beat lead-in to the following bar) to bar 96, where Lawrence Brown's trombone solo has basically been conceived as two phrases of four bars each.

In the examples which follow (which do not include the two passages referred to above), I aim to identify the elements directing the development of the complete work, and to demonstrate that subgroups of similar structure are remarkably constant in application. The analysis suggests to me that the alto saxophone part—the substance of the piece—was largely prescored, and that the soloist did not engage in much melodic paraphrase or variation. What little freedom of interpretation was granted is accounted for by Hodges's interpolation of smears and glissandi—his instantly recognizable trademarks.

In the extracts from the score, melodic motifs of similar or identical derivation are referred to by bar number. As in ragtime, the strains are predominantly diatonic, laced with chromatic elements (these are also identified in the extracts). As in earlier analyses, syncopation types are labeled A (mid-beat), B (mid-bar), and C (cross-bar).

Apart from the common and pivotal use of cross-bar syncopation throughout the group of two-bar extracts in exx. 9.1–9.3, Ellington has employed four distinct variations in rhythm. The overall patterns which emerge from the shifts of rhythmic emphasis compared in ex. 9.4 suggest a Latin American influence (a predominating cha-cha rhythm). The strains in this group are laced with chromatic passing notes (marked X), all confined within the same interval of one whole tone (E-flat/D-sharp to D-flat/C-sharp).

The similarity in melodic construction noted between bars 21–22 (repeated in substance in bars 23–24 and 85–86) and bars 51–52 reveals an interesting volte-face in syncopation: the former contain mid-bar syncopation, the latter mid-beat syncopation (ex. 9.5). A comparison of the syncopated motifs from the whole work reveals a high degree of unity. The rhythms are consolidated in ex. 9.6.

From the transcription score in exx. 9.7, 9.8, 9.12, 9.13, 9.15, 9.16, and 9.20–9.22, I have extracted Johnny Hodges's solo passages to separate music examples.

In the introduction to the work (episode 1), Hodges's personal stamp is immediately impressed on the performance by his use of glissandi, marked (a) in bar 1 and repeated in bar 5. In bar 2 another characteristic touch occurs when

Example 9.1   The Hook

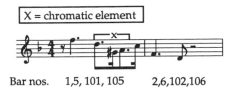

Bar nos.   1,5, 101, 105   2,6,102,106

25   26

27   28

29   30

73,81   74,82

Rhythms:

Example 9.2   Group I

Rhythms:

Example 9.3   Group 2

Rhythms:

Example 9.4   Group 3

Rhythms:

Example 9.5   Group 4

Rhythms:

he bends the F-natural, marked (b), in bars 2 and 6. (In ex. 9.9 the phrase is notated exactly as it sounds.) The reiterated, sharply tongued staccato F-naturals in bar 4 and continuing into bar 5 imply all three syncopation types within six beats.

The hook of the eight-bar substrain A, which is the introduction to the work and also the coda, is repeated with slight modification in substrains J and K (bars 73–74 and 81–82, pp. 10 and 11 of the score). Cootie Williams uses the plunger mute, with the cup held in half-open position and moving minimally; there is a faint throat growl in his tone. The trombonist Lawrence Brown seems to have been blowing into a metal "derby" (a device shaped like an inverted bowler hat, usually flock-lined, and mounted on a tripod stand), producing a sound similar to that of a french horn. Harry Carney plays the baritone saxophone with a soft tone throughout, in perfect match with the brass.

In another example of ring shout antiphony, the ensemble in section A (sub-strain A) responds gently in octave unison to the forthright level of Hodges's hook with the tuneful and raglike chromatic phrase in bar 3, constructed over II^7 and V^{13} harmonies and leading to the tonic in bar 4. This sequence (lasting four bars, not including Hodges's offbeat lead-in phrase in bar 4) is repeated in bars 5 to 8. Throughout the performance, Sonny Greer's use of wire brushes on the side drum is confined to an unobtrusive, gently swinging $\frac{4}{4}$ beat (until the final bar of the piece, when he phrases with the piano and double bass on a concluding mid-bar syncopation).

Blanton's double bass in bars 1 and 2 moves in contrary motion to the hook of the strain, and phrases with Hodges over the mid-bar syncopation (type B) in bar 2. He continues in bar 3 by phrasing with the ensemble over the first three beats, sounding an interval of a major sixth below the trombone and baritone saxophone. Blanton anticipates the ensemble unison on the tonic in bar 4 by a half-beat, at the note marked (c). This anticipation fits the solo saxophone pattern of bar 4 and of bar 5 (which is bar 1 repeated)—it is already "built in" as a sprung rhythm. The anticipation occurs again between bars 7 and 8, also marked (c).

I have been guided in my choice of II^7 and V^{13} chords in bars 3 and 7 by evidence which has been withheld until bars 106 and 107 at the end of the piece (p. 14 of the score). The trite descending chromatics played by Hodges and Ellington leave little room for doubt on the matter. In episode 2 the first two-bar phrase of substrain B, bracketed (a), reoccurs over the first two bars of substrain C (bars 17–18, similarly bracketed). And the phrases bracketed (b) in bars 12 and 13, repeated in substance over bars 14 and 15, commence with identical accompaniment motifs (see the discussion above) on a cross-bar syncopation.

Hodges's solo lead in bars 19 and 20 (ex. 9. 10) is constructed on an A-minor harmony (and its related V-dominant seventh), to bridge into the second half of substrain C. The phrase includes two full-toned glissandi which have been marked (c), in addition to being marked as to direction by oblique straight lines on the manuscript. (In later examples the glissandi are marked by oblique lines only.)

Throughout sections B, C, D, and E (bars 9 to 40, pp. 2 to 6 of the score),

Example 9.6

The Hook

Group 1

Group 2

Group 3

Group 4

The principal and unifying   rhythmic motif

└─A────┘└─C─┘└─A and B─┘

Example 9.7   *Junior Hop* (Ellington)

Example 9.8   2

Example 9.9

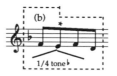

Example 9.10

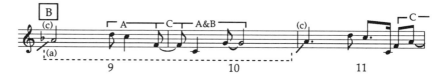

Williams's faintly acid-toned trumpet, played with plunger mute, leads the ensemble horns in sustained "organ" triads, in a series of offbeat, staccato, punctuative phrases behind and in the pauses of Hodges's extended melodic statements. The rhythmic relationship between soloist and ensemble (and section B on this page of music is representative of sections C, D, and E which follow) provides some evidence that there is little real improvisation in this piece.

At (d), bars 9 and 10, the soloist and accompanying ensemble phrase together on the cross-bar tie, in a further instance of anticipation. At (e), bar 12, the offbeat, plagally resolved interpolation by the ensemble horns is perfectly balanced between the rhythmically identical cross-bar motifs which enter and leave bar 12. The imitative rhythmic progression thus created is clearly depicted in ex. 9.12. This rhythmic exchange occurs repeatedly throughout the whole piece.

At (f), (g), and (h), bars 13, 14, and 15, are instances of tutti phrasing, matching soloist with ensemble. These remain closely integrated throughout the remainder of section C, also through the complete sections D and E (pp. 4 to 5 of the score).

In the rhythm section, Ellington remains silent until bar 40 (p. 6 of the score). Apart from the two passing notes on the sixth of the tonic major scale in bars 9 and 11, Jimmy Blanton's walking bass continues to be based on straight arpeggios.

On p. 3 of the music (ex. 9.11), the ensemble continues on sustained triads behind the soloist. Blanton progresses through the inversions of the underlying chords in a manner stolid and functional, yet swinging. There is no trace of decoration or syncopation in any bar. I view this economy of line and selectivity as being in altogether appropriate contrast with the quite fussy solo line.

The last four bars of substrain C (bars 21 to 24) remain centered on the key of A minor (exx. 9.11 and 9.13). There is a similarity in melodic construction between bars 21 and 23, bracketed (a) in ex. 9.14. Bar 21, however, is jauntily syncopated and raglike in style, whereas bar 23 is evenly paced and "un-swung." After the highest note is attained in each bar-long phrase, marked (X)—the minor sixth of the underlying E-dominant seventh chord— the melody descends in each case to the implied tonic of the next bar, in the convention of classic blues melody. A comparison of the two bars suggests that an element of improvisation may be present, for both rhythm and melody have been changed. The awkward tritone leap over the third beat of bar 21 has been supplanted by a straightforward octave jump over the same position in bar 23, with the reiterated minor sixth serving to accentuate the blueness of this final two-bar construction. Substrain D (bars 25 to 32), which reverts to

Example 9.11   3

Example 9.12

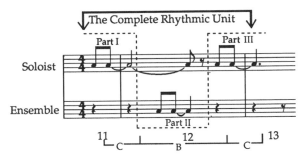

the original, F major tonality, has been developed in a similar style. Rhythmically bars 25, 27, and 29, bracketed (b) in the extract, are identical, and Ellington has further developed this idea of similarity by using identical motifs in bars 27 and 29. Each of these phrases is approached by one of Hodges's characteristic glissandi.

In substrain E (p. 5 of the score, ex. 9.15), the ensemble closely follows the pattern set in substrain B (bars 9–16, pp. 2–3 of the score). Blanton remains supportive, if a little stolidly. Over the first four bars of this substrain, Hodges plays two complementary two-bar phrases, bracketed (a) and (b) in bars 33–34 and 35–36 of ex. 9.17. These display considerable skill at balanced compositional development, with no trace of contrivance. Particularly outstanding is the poise created by the positioning of the two descending phrases: the first, bracketed (X) in bar 34 of the example, is a smooth glissando through a minor sixth; the second, bracketed (Y) in bar 36, is similarly enhanced and now extended through an octave. Chromatic embellishments are bracketed and marked Ø.

The last four bars of the substrain (37–40, ex. 9.18) are closely related both in harmony and in melody to the last four bars of substrain B. Ellington's elegantly crafted phrases in bars 33 to 36 are reminiscent of a bit of earlier music from a related genre (ex. 9.19). The similarity is probably a coincidence, but it is nonetheless striking.

In substrain F Ellington makes his first audible contribution to the recording, in bar 40 (9.16). His percussive phrase in the right hand sets the tone of his playing over the next thirty-two bars. He does not appear to have used his left hand at all in this sequence (unless he played some of the dense clusters in episode 3 with both hands). The first attack of his opening phrase involves the aptly named blue tritone, marked (a) on the score, where the flattened third degree of the tonic scale, notated G-sharp on the music, slides to the natural third above (as nearly as may be accomplished on a tempered keyboard). This note disagrees with the tonic triad expressed by the ensemble horns.

Episode 3 (bars 41 to 72, pp. 6 to 10 of the score) consists of four eight-bar substrains F, G, H, and I, constructed over four individual chord progressions. (In root progression the first three sections are a repeat of the sequences used under substrains B, C, and D, but the final eight-bar progression is used only this one time.) Throughout this third episode the ensemble is augmented to a quartet of horns by the addition of Johnny Hodges, who temporarily relinquishes the role of soloist. The descending scalar phrases which introduce the four substrains in episode 3 are voiced against the underlying tonic major and dominant-seventh harmonies over a succession of parallel major, minor, and diminished triads, with the melody doubling the mediants one octave higher. The playing is tight and tidy, with meticulously matched accenting (marked in full on the transcription).

Blanton's bass line appears more melodically inventive from this point in the work, which could mark an improvisatory leaning—an escape from the strictly triadic selection of notes most frequently employed until now. In bar 44 he allows himself to respond to the piano by playing a skipping figure consisting of a dotted eighth-note and a sixteenth, and a similar embellishment of the straight rhythm occurs in bar 64 on p. 9 of the score.

The pattern set throughout episode 3 is one of regular antiphonal exchange: a call by the ensemble followed by a response from Ellington over each successive two-bar unit. Ellington's touch is resoundingly percussive (and fortunately well recorded), producing a sharp, metallic tone—the ideal sound for the bluesy dissonances which abound in this section of the performance. The tidy dovetailing of ensemble, piano, and again ensemble belies the notion of pure improvisation, although Ellington's incisive attacks, reproduced with fine presence on the disc, retain a lively, extempore feel.

For the remainder of my analysis of episode 3, I concentrate on Ellington's piano. In bars 41–42 he uses blue tritones (b), and jarring dissonance set up between leading note and tonic in the final, hammered, three-part chord in bar 42 (c) extends the bluesy sound into the next bar. In bars 43–44 a grace note (d) is used as a smear into the fifth degree of the tonic scale. Over the last two eighth-notes (e), Ellington anticipates with a chromatic motif the ensemble entry in bar 45.

In bars 46 and 47 of episode 3 (pp. 6–7 of the score), a sixteenth-note embellishment at (a) in ex. 9.16 leads into the cross-bar syncopation marked (b). Ellington sustains a tonic first-inversion triad with added major sixth, preceded by the blue grace note marked (c). In substrain G (bars 49 and 50, ex. 9.20), a root position tonic triad with added natural seventh at (d) is again in accord with the ensemble harmony. A substantially pentatonic construction at (e), rising through bar 50, prepares through the implied cross-bar tie on the final

Example 9.13   4

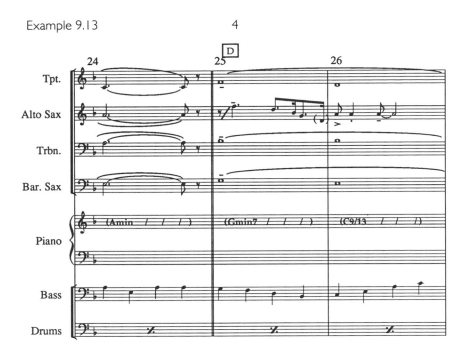

Example 9.14

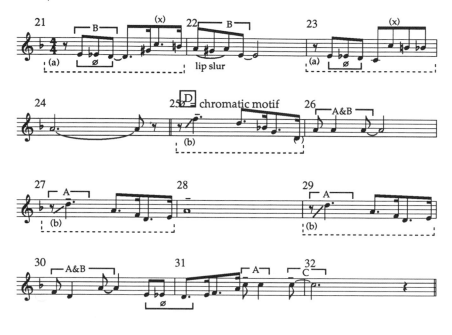

Example 9.15   5

Example 9.16 6

Example 9.16 (continued)

Example 9.17

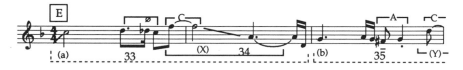

ø = chromatic motif

Example 9.18

X = chromatic motif

A-natural for the direct modulation to the A minor ensemble harmony over the next four bars. In bar 52 a simple A minor broken-chord figure, (f), ends on a mid-beat syncopation (type A).

From his final E-natural in bar 52, Ellington ascends by half-step to F-natural; this careful dovetailing must have been planned. At (g) is an extension (the minor ninth) of the underlying E-dominant seventh chord, and at (h) a ringing, sforzando A minor triad (with added major sixth) is superimposed, mid-beat, on the concerted descending glissando of the ensemble horns. Ellington's hard G-sharp anticipates at (i) by a half-beat the E-dominant seventh harmony in bar 55. In the strongly accented A-naturals at (j) in bar 56, approached by means of rapid, thirty-second-note, A minor arpeggios on the second and fourth beats of the bar, there is a strong implication of augmented syncopation. Ellington's final note at (k), B-flat, foreshadows the C-dominant seventh harmony in bar 57 on the next page of the music, in a hustling fashion similar to that of the phrasing marked (i) in bar 54.

In substrain H (p. 8 of the score), Ellington uses smears at bar 58 (ex. 9.21) to lead into the descending phrase marked (a); appoggiaturas in parallel major thirds lead into the implied V-dominant ninth chord. This device is repeated in substance at (b), but this time in minor thirds into the F major harmony. A straightforward A-dominant seventh arpeggio in bar 60, marked (c), leads into bar 61. Over the next three bars Ellington's contribution is minimal—reduced to one fleeting attack in each of bars 61 and 62 (exx. 9.21–9.22). The interest lies instead in the ensemble in bars 61 to 64. This is unique in this work, both harmonically and rhythmically. There is no "melody" as such, for Williams's trumpet lead is restricted to a repeated-note motif on A-natural, until the B-flat which ties over into bar 64. Blanton's bass line, performed in a sequence of four three-beat groups (as marked on the score—this is an instance of one-to-one secondary rag), is firmly rooted on the supertonic, and underpins the alternating II-dominant ninth and II-diminished seventh (with added ninth) ensemble chords which move beneath Williams's static lead.

Ellington's piano interpolation in bar 64 (p. 9 of the score), executed with almost spiteful belligerence, incorporates two blue clusters (as far as I can positively identify from the record), semitones simultaneously struck below the third and minor seventh degrees of the implied scale of C major. This takes in two of the three areas of indeterminate pitching encountered in the blues scale (the third surrounds the fifth degree of the scale). Ellington may have played this crowded chord with both hands, as shown in ex. 9.23 and marked (d) on the score.

In bar 66 of substrain I, Ellington's descending run of sixteenth-notes at (e), on F major with an added major sixth, ends on A-natural at (f), in disagreement with Blanton's F-sharp. Ellington adds a blue grace note to his final attack. The phrase marked (g) in bar 68 prepares for the dominant harmonies in bar 69 by reverting after the implied B-flat minor harmony over the first three beats to B-flat major at (h), on the final beat of the bar.

In episode 3 (p. 6 of the score), Ellington repeats in bar 70, at (a), the bluesy cluster which appeared in bar 64, at (d), against an implied V-dominant seventh harmony (see ex. 9.24). This second time, however, the identical construction is phrased with the ensemble, but the ensemble is now voiced on a tonic major seventh chord (incorporating E-natural, not E-flat as in Ellington's cluster). In bar 71 the implied V-dominant seventh harmony for ensemble at (b) is extended by Ellington's V-eleventh/thirteenth triad, also marked (b). The hustling phrase marked (c) to (c) in bar 72 includes all three syncopation types, and begins on a very blue cluster (a grace note on the flattened third of the F major scale, and also an abrasive minor second between leading note and tonic). This passes to the next strain through quirky leaps of an octave and a major sixth, in a rhythm which appears in substance in bar 4 of the introduction and is repeated in bar 104 of the coda.

In episode 4, the ensemble in bars 73 and 74 of substrain J (including Hodges) plays the hook of substrain A fortissimo. This is followed by two bars of new melody constructed on the tonic major harmony, and including the major seventh and major sixth degrees of the scale. The progression differs from the original of substrain A in the third and fourth bars (bar 3: two beats II-seventh, two beats V-thirteenth; bar 4: four beats I-sixth). The ensemble remains silent for the next four bars.

Example 9.19   A *Beautiful Dreamer* (Stephen Foster, 1864)
              B *Junior Hop* (1940)

Hodges's solo in bars 77 to 80 is developed from the motif which first appeared in bar 39 of substrain E (p. 6 of the score). The relevant bars are bracketed (X) in ex. 9.28.

In substrain K (p. 11 of the score), Hodges leaves the ensemble after the two-bar hook to prepare for his solo entry in bar 84 (ex. 9.25). The front-line horns repeat bars 73 to 76 of substrain J. When compared with the first four bars (73 to 76) of substrain J, Blanton's line in bars 81 to 84 appears less markedly melodic.

Johnny Hodges's solo entry emerges on the dominant of the underlying A minor harmony, on a slight crescendo, from between the octave unison of brass and baritone saxophone on A-natural (ex. 9.26). The next four-bar section (bars 85 to 88) follows the sequence of harmonies based in A minor used in bars 21 to 24 in the second half of substrain C (pp. 3–4 of the score). Hodges continues to play against double bass and drums only, and consequently has unrestricted space in which to move around. This four-bar sequence may have been entirely improvised, so dissimilar is it in construction to any of the thematic material which has preceded it—particularly the loping, descending phrase in bars 86 to 88. I have bracketed this phrase (a) in ex. 9.26, noting especially the unexpected fall of a minor seventh, marked (b) on the music.

In episode 5, substrain L (bars 89 to 92, ex. 9.27; and 93 to 96 on the next page of score, ex. 9.28), Lawrence Brown's trombone solo is joined from bar 91 onward by Ellington's monophonic piano line. The unanimity of phrasing in bars 91, 92, and 96 would seem to establish that this sequence had first been preconceived and then polished in rehearsal, if not written down.

In episode 6, substrain M (exx. 9.29 and 9.31), Hodges repeats the first four bars of substrain E (see p. 5 of the score and ex. 9.19). The playing of the ensemble and rhythm section departs from the original routines of substrain E

Example 9.20   7

Example 9.21 8

Example 9.22   9

Example 9.23

in several respects: the ensemble horns remain silent; they are replaced by Ellington's single-note contrapuntal line, decorated at (a), (b), and (c) in bars 97, 98, and 99 with blue grace notes, smeared at (a) and (c) into the third degrees of the underlying scales, in classic blues style; and Blanton's bass part is completely rearranged, which may suggest some improvisation.

In episode 7, substrain N (the coda), bars 101 to 105 (ex. 9.30) are a repeat of the first five bars of substrain A (p. 1 of the score). In bar 106 Hodges and Ellington initiate in unison the somewhat predictable, chromatically descending line which proceeds into bar 107. I have had to guess the pitch of the second half-note in the piano part in this bar, bracketed and marked (d) on the score: the recording of the piano is overshadowed by the sound of the unison ensemble horns and the alto saxophone of Johnny Hodges. The piece ends, in bar 108, on a tidy mid-bar syncopation (marked as type B) played by Ellington, Blanton, and Greer. Ellington moves during this figure from a I-diminished seventh to I-major against the sustained tonic in the ensemble, and has the last word by playing in the extreme bass register of the piano a quiet F-natural which is allowed to die away.

Conclusions Drawn from the Analysis

Except during his own contributions in episodes 3 and 5, Ellington has moved some distance away from the rawness of traditional blues and closer to the lenitive music of Tin Pan Alley. After the first bar of the hook of strain A (which contains a bluesy fall through a tritone from the sixth of the tonic scale to a flattened third, resolving upward in traditional fashion to the natural third), he has produced a succession of pretty, singable substrains — ideal material with which to exploit the tonal brilliance and relaxed delivery of Johnny Hodges. There is however little similarity between Ellington's thirty-two-bar episodes in this piece and the typical thirty-two-bar pop song from Tin Pan Alley, except that both consist of four eight-bar strains. Ellington has set up a pattern of A–B–C–D by writing four themes, whereas popular songs of comparable length invariably contain some repetition of strains (for example, the pattern A–A–B–A contains only two).

The rhythms written into *Junior Hop* are inventively varied; in each eight-bar section all three syncopation types have been included (mid-beat, mid-bar, and cross-bar).[6] And the rhythms are ingeniously developed from one seminal motif (see the introductory analyses above).[7] The work confirms Ellington's gifts as a writer of tuneful, extended strains: there are eleven eight-bar tunes in the piece, and one more if one includes Lawrence Brown's solo (score reference L), probably rehearsed as a duet with a single piano line. Ellington seems to have written in this melodic style expressly to exploit the talents of a musician whom he long admired, and whose singing tone and effortless delivery were ideally suited to the exposition of cantabile strains. Ellington obviated any blandness in the sound by interpolating crackling blues piano phrases into the heart of the composition, where Williams's gritty ensemble lead is also in accord with the temporary change of mood.

A stylistic allegiance closer to the tradition of the dance band than to that of the jazz band is suggested by the tunefulness of Ellington's themes in *Junior Hop*, and by the straightforward, basically unvarying rhythm accompaniment: Jimmy Blanton has some syncopation to play in the introduction and coda, but Sonny Greer maintains a metronomic beat until the final bar. In form and orchestration, Ellington's piece closely follows the all-purpose formula of the functional, technically undemanding stock arrangements of popular dance tunes used by publishers from the early 1920s onward. These invariably have an introduction (usually contrived from the hook of the work), followed by three choruses of the song: the vocal refrain, a two-staff, optionally repeatable chorus where the lead is transferred from one section of the band to another; a chorus in a different key, where the melody may be given to a soloist, to be played strictly as written; and the chorus or a part of it in yet another key, leading into a short coda. Clear statement of the melody is assured by the generally rudimentary embellishments in the arrangement. There are frequent tuttis and unisons supported either by sustained block harmonies or by offbeat chordal punctuations. Overall, the orchestral sections (trumpets, trombones, and reeds) are block-scored vertically, with much parallel chording. Ellington's composition evidences all these arranging devices, and the melody has priority throughout. There is little space set aside for improvisation, which is unusual in Ellington's works. There are only two passages where some freedom is implied: in Ellington's piano interpolations (and even these are subservient to a strongly recallable theme) and in Lawrence Brown's eight bars of trombone playing.

In his two long stays with Ellington (from 1928 to 1951 and from 1955 until his death in 1970), Johnny Hodges demonstrated great invention and a

Example 9.24   10

Examples 9.25   II

pronounced melodic quality in his improvisations. He was at his best at slow and medium tempi, given the space to develop his carefully crafted phrases and indulge his fancies in the blues. Nearly twenty years after *Junior Hop* was recorded, a remarkably successful recording session took place on which Hodges and Ellington performed with a fine pick-up group; in this relaxed environment Hodges was able to engage in the sort of spacious, unhurried improvisations for which he became famous.[8] Example 9.32 is from his solo in *Weary Blues*, composed in 1915 by Art Matthews, a twelve-bar melody based on the classic blues sequence.

In ex. 9.32 Hodges's predilection for the major-minor ambivalence of the blues shows in his emphasis on the minor third degree (F-flat) in bars 1 and 2 against the straight D-flat major harmony. Also noteworthy is his return in bars 5 and 6 to the phrasing he constructed in bars 1 and 2. The only significant departure from the classic blues sequence occurs in bars 9 and 10, where the performance substitutes the dominant-eleventh chord. And observe the similarity in melodic construction between bars 3 and 7: the solo is a carefully assembled, extended strain in which the smooth $\frac{12}{8}$ phrasing contributes to the relaxed feeling of the performance.

In *Basin Street Blues* (ex. 9.33) Hodges is at his melodic best. This composition by Spencer Williams, in truth not a blues sequence but a standard functional progression frequently employed in jazz and other popular music (and much earlier by Lizst in *Liebestraum*), provides the soloist with an interesting, smoothly modulating chordal pattern on which to build his improvisations. As in the preceding example, Hodges refers back in bars 9 and 10 to the constructions of the first two bars, with a subtle rephrasing in bar 9; and the cyclic pentatonic passage in bar 7 leads smoothly into bar 8, based in the dominant. The sixteenth-note flurry in bar 12, descending chromatically with highly syncopated accenting, is pure Hodges. His insinuation of the thirteenth into bars 8 and 14 provides added strength and attraction to his well-rounded improvisation. Both solos are delivered with an exquisite, silky tone, skillful glissandi, and impeccable intonation.

The dance band qualities of *Junior Hop* are consistent with Ellington's background. It may be recalled that Ellington began his career in music as the leader of a five-piece dance band in Washington in the early 1920s. Although for most of his career he gave performances and made recordings that aspired to high art, he still earned a living playing in ballrooms, casinos, and nightclubs. This is well illustrated by a recording made by Ellington in 1958.[9] This disc, recorded in a hotel ballroom, is characterized by smooth, singable strains and soothing sounds. It demonstrates clearly that Ellington never lost sight of the practical side of music: to survive commercially, one must keep a full date book.

Example 9.26

Example 9.27

Example 9.28

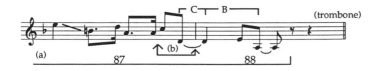

Example 9.29   13

Example 9.30   14

Example 9.31

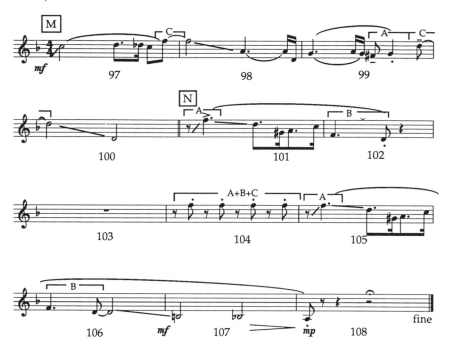

Example 9.32   *Weary Blues*

*= dissonant blue notes

✤= consonant blue notes

Example 9.33 *Basin Street Blues*

SUBTLE SLOUGH

On a long-playing record entitled *Things Ain't What They Used to Be*, one of many reissues of Ellington's recordings, side 1 is devoted to seven titles by Johnny Hodges and His Orchestra (a seven-piece band), including *Junior Hop* (see chapter 9). On side 2 are eight titles by another septet of Ellingtonians, this one led by the cornetist Rex Stewart. The final track on this side is *Subtle Slough*, recorded in Hollywood on 3 July 1941.[1] The soloist, Rex William Stewart (1907–67), was a master of an intriguing, often bizarre miscellany of instrumental tricks, tones, and effects well outside the legitimate limits of the cornet or trumpet. During the time Stewart worked with Ellington's orchestra (1934–45), Ellington exploited his versatility to the full. Stewart combined his own style with the simpler, more direct blues styles of Cootie Williams and Joe "Tricky Sam" Nanton to give Ellington an enormous choice of brass effects.

During the solo cornet passages in *Subtle Slough*, Stewart runs through his considerable repertoire of effects—a comprehensive catalogue of vocalized, blues-inspired devices which he learned from Williams,[2] Nanton,[3] and Bubber Miley.[4] Through the work of Stewart and Williams, and later of Ray Nance[5] and Clark Terry,[6] these techniques formed an integral part of Ellington's music until the end of his career. The following is a list of Stewart's principal devices, and of the symbols which I use to denote them in my transcription of *Subtle Slough*. In addition to describing the sounds which are produced, I give some information on how they are produced. These are techniques which I have learned in my own experience as a jazz trumpeter, and they will vary somewhat from one player to the next and from one instrument to the next. The basic mechanics, however, are constant.

A mute (either straight and made of fibrous material, or metal and pear-shaped) is inserted into the bell of the instrument and used in conjunc-

tion with a flexible rubber cup (the ordinary plumber's plunger tool is
ideal). The plunger-mute is manipulated by the free hand at varying distances from the bell: when it is held tightly against the bell the symbol +
is used; when it is a quarter-inch to a half-inch from the bell the symbol
½O (half-open) is used; and when it is an inch or an inch and a half from
the bell the symbol O (open) is used.

· The symbol +O is marked over single notes, successive notes, tied notes,
and sustained notes to denote the vocalized doo-wah effect. Where there
is a gradual opening, say over a long note, the score is annotated to
indicate the progress of this movement.

· The growl, a gruff effect produced by humming in the throat while
simultaneously producing the normal tone with the lip, is marked ♪ for
growls on short notes, and – –<u>GROWL</u>– → for growls on sustained notes (the
broken arrow indicates the duration of the effect).

· The half-valve effect, marked ½V, is produced by lip pressure alone
while the valve or valves which are usually depressed completely are
depressed only halfway. This short-circuits the length of tubing normally added by valve action to produce the legitimate chromatic range
available on the instrument. I frequently depress all three valves halfway at the same time, relying solely on lip and ear to achieve the desired
pitch. By using this method while blowing harder, I find that the desired
strangulated sound seems more emphatic. It is also possible with this
technique to play extended phrases in microtonal, completely variable
intervals.

· In a fall, notated as ⟍, the note is articulated either conventionally or
with half-valving, and then all three valves are half-depressed. The tone
disappears over a downward glissando, achieved by a slackening of lip
pressure and a diminution of the supply of air. The duration of the fall
is dictated by the value of the starting note (which may be as brief as an
eighth-note).

· The upward glissando is notated as ╱. This is executed like a fall, but
with a tightening of lip pressure throughout the ascent, culminating in
normal articulation of the top note.

· The downward glissando, notated ⟍, is a controlled descent made between two precise notes, executed like the fall, except that the lower note
is articulated and held for its full value.

The transcription of *Subtle Slough* in this chapter is notated as played. It
is accompanied by a bar-by-bar analysis of Rex Stewart's contributions to the
work, primarily as its featured soloist but also as a voice in the scored ensembles (see table 6). I have also described the manner in which he employed

Table 6

Section	Form	Score Reference	Bars	Structural Element	Number of Bars
A	Introduction	A	1–8	Unison ensemble riff	6
				Solo cornet break	2
		B	9–16	Same as A	8
B	A–A–B–A (popular-song form)	C	17–24	Ensemble riffing behind soloist; piano interpolates fragments of main strain in bars 23–24	8
		D	25–32	As in C, piano paraphrases main strain (as in section G)	8
		E	33–40	Soloist ad lib over piano chords and straight rhythm (middle eight)	8
		F	41–48	Same as D	8
Bᵃ	Same	G	49–56	Ensemble led by baritone saxophone states main theme of piece, for the the first time in its complete form; cornet interpolates solos	8
		H	57–64	Same as G, except that bar 64 differs from bar 56 harmonically and melodically	8
		I	65–72	Baritone and tenor saxophones in duet on	

Table 6 (continued)

Section	Form	Score Reference	Bars	Structural Element	Number of Bars
				theme of middle eight (its first appearance)	8
		J	73–80	Same as H	8
		K	81–88	Unison ensemble riff (as in A)	6
				Solo cornet break (a new construction entirely)	2
		L	89–96	Unison ensemble riff (as in A)	6
A	Coda			Ensemble on unison phrase to conclude the piece	2

[a] Ellington has delayed until this section the full exposition of his thirty-two-bar song strain (A–A–B–A).

various brass techniques in his solo passages. These are certainly not orthodox, and are contrary to most of the methods recommended to students of the trumpet, but they are perfect for reproducing the sounds of the blues.

General Observations

I decided to transcribe this composition because of what the recording offers: a definitive performance by a cornetist with an impressive repertoire of vocalized timbres stemming from traditional blues; an opportunity to expound on the technical as well as the aesthetic aspects of a blues brass player's repertoire; a chance to study Ellington's exploitation of the small group; and several clear instances of ideas deriving from Ellington's study of James P. Johnson's *Carolina Shout* being woven into the fabric of the work.[7]

Example 10.1

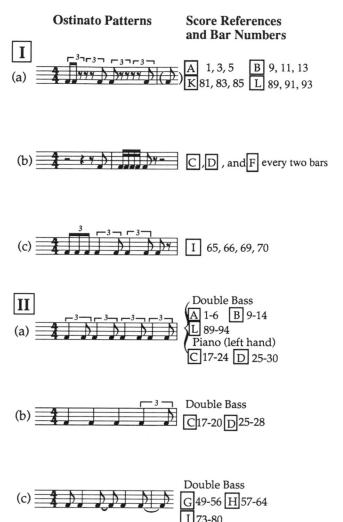

Overall, the ensemble phrasing and much of Ellington's own piano playing have a feel of $\frac{12}{8}$, and I have notated accordingly all passages where this is the case. But Stewart's impassioned snatching at certain phrases, his scurrying but evenly executed sixteenth-note breaks, and the rhythm of drums and brushes, rudimentary but unobtrusive, warrant using an underlying time signature of $\frac{4}{4}$. The progression on which Ellington built his composition is simple: the core of the work is in the thirty-two-bar pattern of popular song, A–A–B–A. Written in F major throughout, the piece has the following harmonic content (each section is eight bars long):

1. (A) Eight bars of I. A sustained tonic pedal is implied by the bass line and ensemble harmonies in all sections of the piece.
2. (A) As above.
3. (B) Two bars of I-dominant seventh, two of IV, two of II-dominant seventh, and two of V-dominant seventh.
4. (A) Eight bars of I, as above.

The tempo of the work is a relaxed thirty bars to the minute, allowing the soloist to play his sixteenth-note flurries without rushing.

As for the piece's rhythm, Ellington has used six principal motifs; three for the ensemble, three for the rhythm section (see ex. 10.1).

The ensemble's motifs may be found in the principal riff phrase in the introduction and coda, in the obsessive riff behind the trumpet solos and piano paraphrase of the main strain, and in the phrasing of the middle-eight melody (not stated until two-thirds of the way through the composition). The rhythm section's motifs are an eight-to-the-bar boogie pattern introduced by the double bass and taken up by the piano, a simplified boogie figure played by double bass only, and an eight-to-the-bar boogie shuffle rhythm set up by extended, anticipatory syncopation for the double bass against a straight, on-the-beat $\frac{4}{4}$ from the drums.

Over the first six bars of section A, Stewart plays a reiterated two-bar riff in octave unison with Ben Webster's tenor saxophone and Lawrence Brown's trombone (ex. 10.2). The principal motif here is constructed from a leap of a major seventh, from the minor sixth degree of the tonic scale of F major to the next perfect fifth degree above, and back again. Stewart imparts a gently growling quality to his sound, adding a bluesy flavor to his lead and some spice to the bland tones produced by the rest of the front line.

In his part writing for the baritone saxophone, Ellington inverted the upward leap of a major seventh which characterizes the riff. This variation is marked (a) to (a) on the music, on the first of the twelve occasions where it appears (in sections A, B, E, and L). This is particularly effective scoring, for it divides the C-naturals in the riff into three separate voices over two octaves, imparting a thicker and more resonant sound to the whole passage. Jimmy Blanton, on double bass, is given a relentless boogie ostinato rhythm of eight to the bar, bracketed (b), firmly underpinning the tonality of the passage on F, as is evidenced by his return to the tonic on the first and third beats of each of the first six bars of sections A and B. The alternating natural sixths and flattened sixths in Blanton's boogie bass contribute an interesting touch: the D-naturals reaffirm the F major tonality of the passage and the D-flats add

Example 10.2   *Subtle Slough*

Example 10.3   2

further substance to the two-octave unison noted above. This emphasis on the tonic extends into the stop-time bars set aside for Stewart's solo exclamations in bars 7 and 8 (p. 2 of the score) and bars 15 and 16 (p. 3). Additionally, there is a similarity in melodic construction between the ensemble figures and Blanton's ostinato bass rhythm in sections A and B and the unison riff for ensemble which first appears in section C (beginning on p. 3 of the transcription) and is repeated in sections D and F. (For a detailed comparison of how the three patterns are used see the discussion below of p. 3 of the score.)

Stewart's explosive extempore break over the stop-time bars 7 and 8 is full of blues inflections. Apart from the flattened thirds marked (a) in ex. 10.2, the break is fashioned out of the pentatonic scale in F, close to the blues scale. The passion and intensity of the blues are well represented in the dynamics of this two-bar fragment. From the tentative approach in bar 6, the break builds into a desperate, rasping cry in bar 8.

Under the soloist's improvised fill, Ellington's piano can be heard indistinctly (owing to poor recording), entering for the first time in bars 7 and 8 on quiet, offbeat, two-part chords formed from the tonic and the major third which are approached through parallel blue grace notes, marked (b). The blueness of Stewart's flattened third degrees, marked (a), is emphasized by Ellington's insistent commitment to the F major harmony. After his double-time legato flurry in bar 7, Stewart attacks the two mid-beat phrases in bar 8 with a growling ferocity heightened by his adept manipulation of the plunger. He plays variously in open, closed, and half-open positions, then plays all out at the phrase end in bar 8. His snatched, panicky phrase over the fifth and blued third degrees at the beginning of bar 8 provides an instant of high drama. Bars 9 to 12, which begin score section B, are a repeat of bars 1 to 4 in section A.

Bars 13 and 14 (ex. 10.3) substantially repeat bars 5 and 6 of section A. The only variance occurs in bar 14, where Ellington, although materially close to his earlier pattern of blued thirds (in bars 7 and 8, section A), now foreshadows his entry into bars 15 and 16 with a cross-bar chord of the major third at (a), but adds further two-part minor thirds at (b)—all are approached with parallel, blue-note appoggiaturas as before. Additionally, as a first step toward the assembly of the rhythm accompaniment in section C, he adds an eight-to-the-bar boogie figure in the left hand, shuttling in both bars between the dominant and submediant over the tonic in the bass.

After playing in the octave-unison ensemble in bars 13 and 14, Stewart plays a growling A-flat (the flattened third degree) against Ellington's insistent and deliberate A-naturals in the right hand and then holds it, before finally descending to the tonic with a fall lasting only a sixteenth-note. After two tacet bars in section C he repeats the process in bar 19: again there is a flattened third

Example 10.4

A = the new figure in section C (where the flatted 6th is notated
    as the augmented 5th)

B and C = the related figures from the beginning of the work

(a suppressed growl behind the closed plunger), a descent through a controlled glissando to the tonic, and a brief fall. (These glissandi are played by using half-valving.) Stewart's phrase leading into bar 21 (p. 3 of the score), which had mid-beat and cross-bar syncopation, is similarly ended, with a fall from the dominant (C-natural) which lasts a quarter note. Throughout sections C (bars 17 to 24) and D (bars 25 to 32), the tenor and baritone saxophones and the trombone play a new two-bar riff in octave unison. This is a particularly rhythmic construction: the phrase begins with a staccato C-sharp, followed by a legato sixteenth-note gruppetto and a final staccato articulation on the D-natural at phrase's end. The figure uses the sixth again, both flat and natural, so that it links to the first ensemble riff and boogie bass used in bar 1 and in subsequent bars throughout sections A and B (and repeated in sections K and L). The comparisons are clear in ex. 10.4.

At first sight this excited phrase, which extends over sections C, D, and F with no respite for the instrumentalists, seems to create problems for the slide trombone. In practice this is not the case: only a comfortable, minimal shift of slide position is necessary to execute the sixteenth-note turn easily and with true legato. Situated as it is in the path of the easily played glissando (much used by New Orleans and traditional ensembles), as illustrated in ex. 10.5 at (a), the turn may be negotiated by using the minimal slide movement indicated at (b).

Example 10.5

Slide trombone: an easily executed glissando

(a)

Slide commencing on the alternative 6th position on C, closing gradually
to the first position on F

The riff

(b)

slide positions   2d   1st 2d 1st 2d 1st

In the rhythm section, Blanton's predominantly pentatonic line joins
Ellington's left-hand ostinato to form a surging barrelhouse-boogie foundation for the interplay of solo cornet, ensemble, and piano treble figurations
over the next sixteen bars. This sixteen-bar passage illustrates how Ellington
as a composer, group leader, and participant achieved his customary, smooth
integration of extempore and written elements. Sections C and D, in which
the responsibilities for continuity are shifted from rhythm section to ensemble
with soloist and again to rhythm section, shows a high level of interaction
among soloist, ensemble, and Ellington himself, whose right-hand part is
probing and propulsive. This is clear from ex. 10.7, where except for the short
break in bar 21 (marked X), the three principal melodic elements used by this
little band achieve a continuous flow of phrases.

In the last four bars of section C (ex. 10.6), Stewart confines himself to a
brief wah-wah exclamation, marked (a), in bars 22 and 23, then remains silent
until two and a half beats into bar 24, where he introduces section D with
a restrained, tightly muted lead-in on the dominant over three eighth-notes.
The first overt use by Stewart of half-valving occurs in section D, bars 25 and
26, on the E-flat which is first played tightly muted and held for seven and a
half beats. During this sustained note the plunger is moved slowly away from
the bell, through half-open position to open position on a gradual crescendo,
culminating in the snatched sixteenth-note triplet in bar 27. The phrase ends
on a quick diminuendo, partly smothered by the plunger returning to the
half-open position. At the beginning of section D, Stewart's opening note
(sounding as D-natural on the cornet) is produced by completely depressing
the first valve, in the conventional manner. The second note in the phrase, a

Example 10.6   3

Example 10.7

An example of small group interaction, showing the interplay of improvised
solo, scored ensemble, and improvised piano interpolations

Example 10.8   4

consonant blue note marked (c), is played by allowing the valve to rise against the tension of its spring, pause halfway up to its normal resting position, and be released smartly at the triplet phrase in bar 27. (I have discovered that one can achieve the same effect by depressing all three valves halfway and holding them there for as long as necessary. This is feasible on most models of trumpet and cornet in this particular register.)

Another facet of Stewart's style appears at the center of the sixteenth-note triplet in bar 27, marked (d), where he implies rather than enunciates a D-natural, notated as X. It is rare to find a solo by Stewart that does not contain this trick somewhere. In bars 23 and 24 Ellington's right hand introduces the principal motif from the main strain of the work, which does not appear in its thirty-two-bar entirety of A–A–B–A (with a written middle eight) until sections G to J (bars 49 to 80) of the score. In ex. 10.23 this statement is compared with Ellington's fragmented piano quotation of his central strain, first played in section D. Throughout the first four bars of D, Ellington's paraphrasing of the principal theme is characterized by the employment of major and minor thirds in the two-part chords carrying the melody. The phrasing has a feel of $\frac{12}{8}$ throughout. In keeping with the prevailing boogie-woogie rhythm, Ellington returns to the dominant (C-natural), and the stylistic consistency is emphasized by his inclusion of the dissonant major seventh (E-natural) in the $\frac{6}{4}$ triads marked (e) in bars 25 and 27. In a further heightening of the bluesy atmosphere, parallel grace notes slide into the third and fifth degrees of the tonic scale in bars 23, 26, and 28, marked (b) on the score; the boogie partnership between Blanton's double bass and Ellington's left hand continues.

At (a) in bar 29 (ex. 10.8) Stewart plays a closely muted, even lip trill. This is more difficult to accomplish in the middle register, as here, than in the higher register, say above the cornet's G-natural, on the first space above the staff. Above that point the trill may be played fairly easily, either by shaking the instrument or by means of lip control alone. Stewart's phrase in bar 30, marked (b), contains four blue notes (A-flats) sounded against the natural third degree of the tonic scale in Blanton's bass line, which could either be following an underlying harmony of F major or be a C-dominant thirteenth. This inconclusiveness arises because after the clear and definite F-natural which begins the bar, Stewart ghosts the second and fourth notes of the sixteenth-note phrase on the second full beat of the bar. In bars 30 and 31 the plunger is deftly used to reproduce the near-human vowel sounds so close to the vocal blues.

Section E, the middle eight of the song form A–A–B–A, consists simply of the soloist accompanied by the rhythm section; the saxophones and trombone are silent. Stewart manipulates his plunger, alternating between the open and closed positions on the notes of the offbeat I^9 and IV^6 chords expressed by

Example 10.9   5

Example 10.10

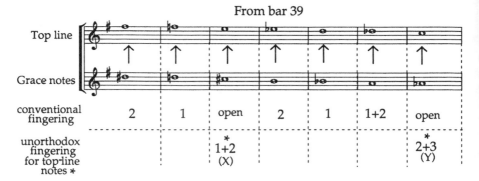

From bar 39

Top line						
Grace notes						
conventional fingering	2	1	open	2	1	1+2	open
unorthodox fingering for top-line notes *			*1+2 (X)				*2+3 (Y)

Ellington's piano (all three syncopation types are used). In the rhythm section there is a brief smear by the piano in bar 33, marked (c), and Blanton's accenting of the notes marked (d) in bars 35 and 36 sets up a one-to-one secondary pattern.

In bars 37 and 38 (ex 10.9) Blanton's bass supports Ellington's widely spaced G-dominant ninth and thirteenth chords. The sharply attacked dominant eleventh three and a half beats into bar 38, which foreshadows the V^7 harmony in bar 39, continues at (a) the augmented syncopation of bars 35 and 36 before commencing the scalar descent of bars 39 and 40. Ellington's addition to the dominant ninth chord in bar 40 of the major sixth provides a hint of abrasive dissonance.

Stewart's mid-bar syncopated phrase in bar 38, marked (b), is approached by an upward glissando from the D-natural in the preceding bar. This idea is continued in reverse by the downward smear back to D-natural at the phrase's end. Here it is smothered by the rapidly closed plunger, and cut off on a sharply attacked staccato. Bar 39 is of some interest to a brass player: Stewart has approached each note of his solo break, marked (c), with a brief but well defined grace note, each over a major or minor third. He has used the natural harmonics of the instrument in this register to achieve the effect, and at two points has surely sought additional help by using false fingering. In ex. 10.10 I have marked the fingering which I have found will almost guarantee the duplication of Stewart's performance in this break. The leap is of course accomplished by lip control, but false fingerings are of great help in playing the top notes, marked (x) and (y) in the example. Any slight falseness of intonation occasioned by these fingerings is hardly noticeable, owing to the brevity of the notes.

The first four bars of section F offer a compact exposition of the range of

Example 10.11

Jimmy Blanton

41   42   43   44

vocal impersonations employed: at (d) in bar 41, a half-valved A-natural (the second valve is depressed only halfway); at (e) in bars 42 and 43, a sustained throat growl, incorporating a rapid crescendo and diminuendo in step with the rise and fall of the seven-note construction (Stewart has opened his plunger wide, to give the growl full voice); and at (f) in bar 44, a fall from each of the first two notes of the quarter-note triplet (the third element is tied across the barline into bar 45).

The saxophones and trombone repeat the unison riffing, as in section C. Ellington's piano introduces a fragment of the principal strain of the piece during bars 41 to 44, with parallel appoggiaturas, marked (g). The functionally rhythmic bass accompaniment in $\frac{4}{4}$ in bars 41 to 44 is tuneful: the notes of the first three beats of each bar form a logically developing fragment of melody, bracketed in ex. 10.11 as (h), (i), (j), and (k) in bars 41 to 44.

Stewart sustains a robust, even, and well separated lip trill, marked (a) in ex. 10.12, throughout bars 45 to 47, with a decrescendo in bar 48 and a momentary space for breathing in the final eighth-note of this bar. The saxophones and trombone repeat their unison riff. Ellington is silent until bars 47 and 48, where he leads into section G with dissonant, offbeat chords of F major with an added major seventh, at (b), and a final C-dominant ninth/thirteenth, at (c).

In the ensemble's front line during section G the song strain of the work, in A–A–B–A form, is carried by Harry Carney's baritone saxophone. His lead, marked (d) on the score, is voiced on the lowest notes of the ensemble chords over the next thirty-two bars (comprising sections G to J). The phrasing of the front line is swung, using all three syncopation types. The quarter notes in bar 49 (and in the comparable bars to follow) have been marked in seemingly contradictory fashion with both a long accent and the short staccato. In performance these notes are attacked sharply and held for a fraction less than their full notated value: each note is detached, but not isolated from the note which follows. The "eyebrow" markings (e) over the syncopated phrases in bars 50 and 52, which appear also in bars 53 and 55, p. 7 of the score, indicate a bend: the lip lowers the pitch by a microtone at the point where the marking appears, then brings it back to its normal level. With the exception of the chord marked (f) in bar 52, Ellington's harmony is diatonic: a succession of parallel

Example 10.12   6

Example 10.13   7

Example 10.14

Jimmy Blanton

$^6_3$ triads over Carney's lead line. Stewart's muted cornet is written into the front line in bars 49 to 52 and in bar 53 (p. 7 of the score); it is variously a perfect fourth and an augmented fourth above the baritone saxophone melody. It is interesting that the tessitura of the identical A sections of this song-form piece is only a minor third, between A-natural and the C-natural above.

Throughout section G, as well as section H, Jimmy Blanton prefigures the straight, on-the-beat $^4_4$ from Sonny Greer's drums by half a beat (this must have required sustained concentration), setting up a boogie-woogie shuffle rhythm identical in form to the examples cited from James P. Johnson's *Carolina Shout*.[8] And if Blanton's bass part is rewritten as in ex. 10.14, the relationship of all three syncopation types is clearly defined (but in this section the syncopation is extended over sixteen bars—more jazz than rag).

Having dropped out of the ensemble in bar 53, Stewart contributes a solo break in bars 55 and 56 (ex. 10.13). The throat growl is employed throughout this descending construction, which incorporates blue notes at (a) and (b) and a ghosted (implied) F-sharp at (c). Stewart's plunger work on the first three notes of the break—a rapid movement on each note from closed position to open position—imparts a highly vocalized quality to his sound.

The ensemble trio in bar 55 (p. 7 of the score) is voiced on the second inversion tonic triad beneath Stewart's emphatic forte entry. The chromatic phrase at (d) in bar 56 leads in, on a delicate surge in volume, to section H. In bars 57 to 60 of section H the ensemble repeats the first four bars of section G. Blanton sustains his offbeat, anticipatory syncopation, but the line is varied from the original followed in section G (bars 49 to 52). Here again I perceive some melodic enhancement: there has been more rearrangement of the bass part, marked (e), (f), (g), and (h) on the music. It is interesting to compare the melodic pattern which emerges in bars 57 to 60 with the previously noted example from bars 41 to 44 in section F. The two constructions are closely related (ex. 10.16).

Stewart leaves the ensemble in bar 61 to breathe, then leads in on the dominant over a cross-bar phrase to a lip trill of decreasing power in bar 62, marked (a) in ex. 10.15. His solo wah-wah passage which commences at (b) in bar 63

Example 10.15   8

Example 10.16

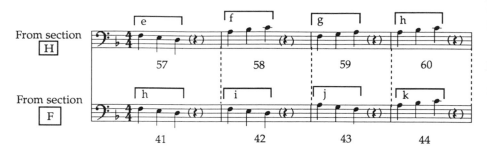

From section
H

From section
F

clashes briefly with the ensemble chord, in obvious anticipation of it: Stewart's E-natural against Lawrence Brown's F-natural. This dissonance is resolved during the mid-beat phrase at the beginning of bar 64, where the ensemble has been given in succession two parallel first-inversion triads in E major and F major.

In the rhythm section Ellington has remained silent; Blanton and Greer continue to provide a boogie beat. At (c) in Section I, and for all eight bars of this section (p. 9 of the score), Carney's baritone saxophone continues to play the melody in parallel major and minor thirds below Ben Webster's tenor saxophone. This is the first time the new chromatically inclined melody of the middle eight has appeared in the work. The trombone is silent throughout section I.

As Ellington remains silent, Blanton reverts to a straight, on-the-beat bass line. And Stewart's couplets, marked (d), which proceed alternately by leap and by step and have a growling, limping quality, are set against the sustained B-flat harmony implied by the saxophones and double bass in bar 68. They descend chromatically in each beat and represent a curious choice of material. This may be accounted for as follows: had the modulation from the B-flat major harmony in bar 68 to the G-dominant seventh in bar 69 (p. 9 of the score) been achieved through the progression B-flat major to B-flat seventh to A seventh to A-flat seventh to G seventh (a progression much overused in jazz and popular music in general), then Stewart's fill-in phrase would have been a model of harmonic propriety; perhaps Stewart heard these parallel dominants in his head (see ex. 10.18). Stewart ends the phrase on a D-natural, held on a diminuendo against the saxophones in bar 69 (p. 9 of the score).

The baritone and tenor saxophones complete the middle-eight theme; bars 69 and 70 are a transposition one tone higher of bars 65 and 66, over the implied dominant seventh on II (ex. 10.17). They resolve to a V^7 in bar 71, then through a cross-bar phrase to a V^9 in bar 72. There is an inventive arrange-

Example 10.17   9

Examples 10.18

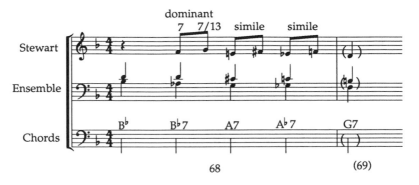

ment of the basic underpinning bass line in bars 71 and 72. The three-note descending phrases marked (bI) and (cI) point up the main motif of the two-bar sequence; at (bII) and (cII) one may see the similarity in construction between the two bars, which are complete constructions of four quarter notes each.

Stewart plays a subdued wah-wah phrase in bar 72, at (a). A brief and bluesy inflection is created by the grace note (G-sharp) which decorates the final note in the bar. Stewart's phrase follows through into the first bar of section J (bar 73), a ninth above the ensemble's tonic harmony.

Section H (bars 57 to 64) is repeated, except for three minor variations: the inclusion of Stewart's G-natural at (d) in bar 73; the phrasing of bar 78 (which looks forward to p. 11 of the score), where a mid-beat dotted quarter note replaces the two-note appoggiatura construction of bar 62, section H (p. 8); and the reversion at (e) by the double bass to sustained syncopation (as in section H), and its playing of an entirely new, predominantly scalar line until the end of the episode in bar 80.

Stewart resumes his solo role in bars 77 and 78 (ex. 10.19), repeating the lip trill which first appeared in bars 61 and 62 of section H. The material in bars 79 and 80 is new, and includes three blue notes, marked (a), against the underlying harmony of F major.

In section K, bars 81 to 86 repeat bars 1 to 6 of section A. Ellington is silent during bars 81 to 85, and the double bass does not immediately return to the eight-to-the-bar boogie figurations of section A (at the beginning of the work) but instead follows the blues-related pentatonic scale in bars 81 to 83, bracketed (b) on the music. The imitative melodic twists of bars 41–44 and 57–60 occur in similar fashion in bars 82 and 84, bracketed (c).

Stewart's solo break in bars 87 and 88 (ex. 10.20) is the most passionate explosion of blues rhetoric in the whole performance, and fittingly is the last solo passage on the recording. It is forcefully executed with a growling in-

Example 10.19   10

Example 10.20   II

Example 10.21   12

flection, and played forte to fortissimo, but the tightly closed plunger adds to the tension. In addition, Stewart half-valves the top A-flats, marked (a), producing a strangled, ethereal sound (in this register the first valve is depressed halfway to produce the cornet's B-flat). The flattened third degree is played repeatedly (as it is elsewhere) against the A-naturals in Ellington's two-part chords beneath, marked (b). Even there Ellington has made them blue with his G-sharp appoggiaturas. At (c) in bar 88 is an example of the "blue tritone" figure, resolving to the major third and fifth at (d). Section L repeats the first six bars of section A, and extends to the final page of the transcription.

The cornet and saxophones play a quirky unison break over the final two bars of the work (ex. 10.22). Their angular quality stems largely from the leaps of a major seventh which occur at (a) and again, transposed, at (b). The trombone has been omitted from the unison until the last note, apparently to avoid a slide shift (nearly impossible at this tempo) from seventh position to first; that is, from B-natural to B-flat, marked (c) and (d) on the baritone saxophone part. The final note of the piece, a gentle staccato unison on the tonic, is marked "push" on my score. In jazz practice, a note so marked is played with a nudge from the diaphragm—it is not tongued in the normal manner.

Example 10.22   13

The rhythm section is silent after the first beat of bar 95, until the piano and double bass play the final tonic, sounding an octave apart and underpinned by Sonny Greer's choked cymbal and bass drum beat.

Conclusions Drawn from the Analysis

Rex Stewart is never called on in *Subtle Slough* to indulge in pyrotechnics. Although the piece is designed to feature him as a soloist, there is no striving for theatrical effect; only once, in his final solo break, does he venture above the staff (bars 87 and 88, p. 11 of the score). He gives essentially a middle-register performance, in which his delicacy and occasionally bizarre delivery take precedence over displays of velocity and power. The quality of vocalized blueness is apparent in almost every bar he plays: the growls, smears, trills, and strangulated half-valve effects have a quality strongly suggestive of traditional black music. Only in one section, the middle eight (bars 33 to 40, section E, p. 5 of the score) does Stewart play solo for a full eight bars; the rest of the time he is allotted two- and four-bar solos, presented in straightforward antiphonal patterning with the ensemble.

Ben Webster and Harry Carney (saxophones), Lawrence Brown (trombone),

Example 10.23

(a)

Ellington
(piano right hand)

Ensemble cues

(b)

Ellington

Ensemble
cues

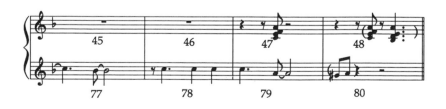

and Sonny Greer (drums) have been granted no freedom to improvise: they simply read what has been written (in Greer's case, it is doubtful that Ellington would even have bothered to sketch out his basic $\frac{4}{4}$ brush rhythm). The responsibilities for improvisation have therefore been left to Stewart and to a lesser degree to Ellington himself. Apart from his occasional rhythmic chords, Ellington's major contribution to the thematic development of the work occurs in sections D and F (pp. 4, 5, and 6 of the score). In these passages there is evidence of variation achieved during performance. In ex. 10.23 I have extracted the relevant bars of Ellington's right-hand part and compared them with the exposition of the main strain by the ensemble in sections H and J of the score.

The element of paraphrase in Ellington's contribution may be perceived by following his interpretations through (a) and (b) in the example. There is exact duplication in only three bars: 24 (leading into section D), and 26 and 28 (in section F). All the other bars show some variation, and section F displays the gradual phasing out of his involvement. A standard characteristic of Ellington's premeditations at D and F is the unanimity of phrasing with the later score ensemble passages at H and J. This is seen in the even-numbered bars leading up to and including bar 44 (in section F) and bar 76 (in section J).

Texturally, Ellington has made the most of his front-line quartet of two brass and two reed instruments, by means of the middle-register voicing of the octave- and two-octave unisons at the beginning and the end of the composition, and the parallel, diatonic triads in the exposition of the main song strain in sections G, H, and J (pp. 7, 8, and 10 of the score). The only exception is the eight-bar duet (in thirds) of the saxophones in section I (bars 65 to 72): this jaunty, raglike melody could perhaps have been better served if the trombone had been added and the passage given a more adventurous, three-part voicing. As it stands, however, it does possess a pleasant Mexican tinge.

Subtle Slough may be described as an impromptu. The term is not normally used in jazz, but it seems entirely appropriate for this miniature, which is a short, well-defined instrumental composition of a character that suggests improvisation.

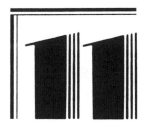

SOME CONCLUSIONS

AND COMPARISONS

Beauty of style, harmony and grace and good rhythm
depend on simplicity.
 —Plato

The foundations on which Ellington built his oeuvre are simple. His harmonic progressions are not complex, owing much to the conventions of archaic blues, and his rhythms are overtly influenced by the syncopation of ragtime, which in turn had its roots in African percussion and chant—the accompaniments to ritual and festive dancing and repetitive work movements. Ellington had a singular gift for melody, an ability to construct simple, singable, memorable tunes. Not only was this a key to his skill as a serious composer, but it also assured his commercial success and the acceptance of his work as pure entertainment.

But although Ellington's source materials were simple, his use of them was sophisticated. He combined the extended, decorated voicings and harmonies characteristic of classical music of the late nineteenth century and the early twentieth with the earlier sounds of folk-blues. This successful integration may be recognized in every one of the works analyzed in the preceding chapters.

Ellington's output was widely varied, as is clear from the five compositions analyzed in this book. But his works had certain common characteristics. Formally they used the sixteen-bar structures of ragtime, the thirty-two-bar structures of pop songs, and the eight- and twelve-bar structures of the blues; all these were favored as well by King Oliver and Jelly Roll Morton, and in the emergent swing styles of Bennie Moten and Count Basie. In Ellington's music the structure of the popular song predominated (A–A–B–A). Of his

Table 7

Blues and Ragtime in Five Works by Ellington

| | Number of Complete Bars (All in 4/4 Time) | Tempo (in Bars a Minute) | Blues — Number of Blue Notes on or around the Third, Fifth, and Seventh Degrees of the Scale | | | | | | Ragtime — Syncopation Types | | | | | |
| | | | Extemporized | | | Written | | | Extemporized | | | Written | | |
			Third	Fifth	Seventh	Third	Fifth	Seventh	A	B	C	A	B	C
Ko Ko	104	40	14	—	5	47	—	23	31	5	9	95	47	18
Mr. J. B. Blues	116	40	14	7	27	22	15	3	26	22	18	54	44	18
Concerto for Cootie	82	24	—	—	—	11	1	4	4	6	10	20	30	18
Junior Hop	108	36	—	—	—	24	11	1	—	—	—	30	23	22
Subtle Slough	96	30	37	6	7	—	1	1	21	17	18	34	23	9
Total	506	—	65	13	39	104	28	32	82	50	55	233	167	85

1,012 copyrighted works, 331 were in fact songs. But the distinctive sound of his ensemble brought life to these simple structures.

A Statistical Analysis

The statistical summary which follows deals both with Ellington's written work and with the improvised solos of Ellington and his sidemen. In some performances, notably in the duet for piano and double bass *Mr. J. B. Blues*, it is difficult to ascertain which passages were completely improvised, which were wholly or partly written out, and which fall somewhere in between (that is, they took a definite form after repeated rehearsal); even alternate takes do not always allow a clear distinction to be drawn. But this uncertainty is unlikely to affect the statistical analysis significantly, and the ambiguities themselves are of course integral to Ellington's style.

In table 7 the use of blues and ragtime devices is quantified for each of the five compositions analyzed earlier. I have also noted the tempo of each piece. These data reconfirm the omnipresence of the blues in the mature works of Ellington and in the performances of his musicians. And the stylized, offbeat phrasing of the ragtimers and barrelhouse bluesmen is equally well represented.

Where the blue notes are concerned, the ones around the third degree of the scale account for 60 percent of the total (56 percent of those extemporized, 63 percent of those written); the ones around the fifth degree, 14 percent (11 percent of those extemporized, 18 percent of those written); and the ones around the seventh degree, 26 percent (33 percent of those extemporized, 19 percent of those written). This is consistent with the prevailing style of the early 1940s: after the bebop revolution of the mid-1940s, blue notes created by the flattened fifth became more common, usually against a V-dominant seventh chord or included in one. As for the ragtime elements, type A accounts for 46 percent of all syncopations (44 percent of those extemporized, 48 percent of those written), type B for 30 percent (27 percent of those extemporized, 34 percent of those written), and type C for 24 percent (29 percent of those extemporized, 18 percent of those written). Type A (mid-beat syncopation), an offbeat displacement of untied form contained within the first two or last two beats of a bar in quadruple meter, was the most frequently used rhythmic motif in early ragtime and the foundation of mid-bar syncopation (B) and cross-bar syncopation (C). The predominance of mid-beat syncopation in early ragtime has been noted by Edward Berlin: "The pre-eminence of untied syncopation in early ragtime is evident from the following supporting statistics (selected from material published before 1901). Of the 200 early pieces sur-

Table 8

Ellington's Instrumental Mixes and Voicings

Title of Work	Score References		Details of Scoring
	Pages	Bars or Strains	
Ko Ko	15–17	49–60	High-register clarinet leads; saxophone quartet
	18–19	61–66	Full brass figures
	21–23	73–84	Full brass sustained chords
Concerto for Cootie	1	B–D	Saxophone quartet led by clarinet, with pizzicato double bass doubling baritone saxophone and sounding one octave lower
	2	E–G	As above, with valve trombone doubling baritone saxophone and two trumpets voiced within the saxophone quartet
	3	1–4	Trombone trio, with pizzicato double bass as extra voice
	5–6	11–14	Saxophone section led by clarinet, with pizzicato double bass as extra voice
	11	34–36	Saxophone section led by clarinet, this time with valve trombone doubling the clarinet lead one octave lower
Junior Hop	1	3–4, 7–8	Double bass phrases, with trio of plunger-muted trumpet, hat-muted trombone, and baritone saxophone sounding in

Table 8 (continued)

Ellington's Instrumental Mixes and Voicings

Title of Work	Score References		Details of Scoring
	Pages	Bars or Strains	
			parallel major sixths at octave unisons below. In other respects, the voicing of this piece follows the conventional block scoring of the dance band, within the octave, with frequent unisons and octave unisons.
Subtle Slough	1–3	1–16	Pizzicato double bass ostinato, in simple counterpoint with staccato ensemble in two-octave unison
	11–13	81–96	As above, but with a small variation to the bass figure
	7–9	49–64	Baritone saxophone lead, with melody line on the lowest notes of parallel first-inversion triads (fourth part added from time to time)
	9–10	65–72	Baritone saxophone melody, with tenor saxophone voiced in parallel major and minor thirds above it (trumpet and trombone tacet)

veyed: 59% are untied rhythms as the exclusive rag rhythm [type A], 17% are tied, or tied in conjunction with untied [types B and C]. The balance consists of pieces called rags that are totally unsyncopated (19%) and those pieces that emphasize dotted rhythms (5%)."[1]

The Ellington Mix and the Role of Ellington's Men

The instrumentation of Ellington's orchestra was firmly based in the tradition of the dance band, which began before the 1920s and was maintained by Paul Whiteman in the early 1920s, Guy Lombardo in the 1930s, and Glenn Miller from the mid-1930s to the mid-1940s. But whereas these bandleaders seldom departed in their scoring from tutti (trumpets on top, reeds in the middle, trombones below), Ellington stressed the individual nature of his trumpet, saxophone, and trombone sections. His tuttis were reserved chiefly for climactic passages and endings.

Ellington's brass sounds were varied by the use of mutes and nonstandard methods of tone production. His reeds generally produced rounded, pure tones, decorated only by the occasional portamento or glissando. His rhythm sections were functional:[2] steady, swinging, and unobtrusive.

In table 8 are shown some of the instrumental mixes and voicings used by Ellington in the works analyzed in chapters 6–10.

Apart from all-round musicianship, the principal qualification for membership in Ellington's band was an ability to play the blues. Ellington's keen grasp of each player's abilities enabled him to match the sound of the individual musician with that of the whole orchestra. Among those who spent a large part of their careers with Ellington are the trumpeters Bubber Miley, Cootie Williams, Rex Stewart, and Ray Nance; the trombonists Tricky Sam Nanton and Lawrence Brown; the saxophonists Johnny Hodges and Harry Carney, and the clarinettist Barney Bigard. Their individuality was such that any attempt to re-create Ellington's sound seems sure to fail. Duke Ellington's son Mercer began performing his father's repertoire in 1974 (with some new arrangements), but although his work is of a high quality it is no more than an affectionate imitation of the original.

What did Ellington contribute to twentieth-century music? First, he managed to liberate the music of Europe from the strictures of the twelve-note system. His special musicianship achieved a freedom which is noticeable on close examination of his representative performances. And this emancipation was achieved without recourse to musical anarchy: Ellington never subscribed to the dubious principle that creative brilliance could result from randomness

or coincidence. Ellington integrated free blues into a European musical formalism without diluting or caricaturing either genre; for me this constitutes
his greatest single contribution to twentieth-century music.

Derek Jewell has written poignantly of Russell Procope's reminiscences about
his relationship with Ellington:

> On 4 June 1976, Russell Procope and Wild Bill Davis (who played organ
> with Ellington from Autumn 1969 to early 1971) came to the '100' Club,
> London to play in a concert called 'Echoes of Ellington' along with the
> British jazzman Chris Barber. Procope sat in a tiny dressing-room playing
> his warm-up before taking the stand. He was edgy at first:
>> Well, I'm a sitting duck. Everybody asks me about Duke. I'm an
>> introvert. I don't like the spotlight.
> But after a while he relaxed:
>> Why did I stay 28 years? Well, hell, I joined him because I loved
>> his music. It was the greatest. Besides which, it was security. Sure,
>> security. What else are we here for? In a profession to do what you
>> like doing *and* getting paid for it—isn't that what everybody wants?
> To the question of why he wasn't playing in an Old Ellingtonians band,
> and particularly Mercer's band, he replied:
>> There aren't many Ellingtonians left. A lot of guys who played with
>> Ellington are *not* Ellingtonians. He achieved what he did *despite*
>> them rather than because of them. People say he didn't fire many
>> people. Yeah, and he didn't *hire* many either. It was special, very spe-
>> cial. So that's why I don't want to play in no "Ellington" band now.
>> There's nobody really left. Mercer isn't even playing the old book. If
>> only he would!
> It was getting time for the show. He hitched his sax up over his shirt front,
> picked up his clarinet and walked to the door. He turned:
>> Don't let nobody tell you any different. While it was happening,
>> it was the greatest thing that ever took hold of your soul. When it
>> ended, it ended.[3]

APPENDIX A

A CHRONOLOGY OF

DUKE ELLINGTON

I'm not old enough to be historical, and I'm too young to be biographical . . . Biographies are like tombstones; who wants one?
—Duke Ellington

1899   Born 29 April in Washington, D.C., to James Edward Ellington and Daisy Ellington, christened Edward Kennedy Ellington. His father is a butler at the White House and later a blueprint maker in a government department. The family is comfortably off and the Ellingtons are indulgent parents.

1904   Starts school. His ruling passion is baseball, but a potentially serious head injury convinces Daisy Ellington that her son should engage in gentler activities.

1907   Begins musical training—piano, harmony, and notation—apparently with little enthusiasm or satisfaction. Is given his nickname by a colleague. The next few years pass without much serious attention to music.

1914   Continues his education at Armstrong High School, Washington, where he displays a talent for draftsmanship. Also studies in the school's music department and with Harry Grant, music teacher at Dunbar High School, nearby. Invited to Grant's house for private lessons in musical theory, he later recalls the experience as follows: "It ended up a hidden course in harmony that lighted the direction to more highly-developed composition. It was a music foundation, and I jumped at the opportunity."[1]
Writes first composition, *Soda Fountain Rag.*

1915–16   Listens intently to the playing of ragtime and stride pianists in and around Washington: "Doc" Perry, Louis Brown, Lester Dishman, Shorty Mac. In later life often refers to this informal tuition as his "poolroom education." Plays his first professional job as an accompanist to a magician. "I did that, and was rather amazed at my ability to fall into the spirit of the very serious and sometimes mystical moods."[2] Influenced by the renowned stride, ragtime, and jazz pianist and composer James P. Johnson, he once performs Johnson's piece *The Carolina Shout* in the composer's presence after diligently studying the original piano-roll recording.

1917   Works as a sign painter by day, plays casual band engagements at night.

1918   Marries Edna Thompson on 2 July. Begins to organize bands in and around Washington.

1919–21   Duke Ellington's son Mercer born 11 March 1919. A band begins to evolve around a fairly stable nucleus of musicians.

1922   With Sonny Greer (drummer) and Otto Hardwick (reed player) moves to New York for a brief, unsuccessful engagement with the Wilbur Sweatman Orchestra. Soon returns to Washington for further informal study with Johnson and Willie "the Lion" Smith.

1923   On the advice of the pianist and composer Thomas "Fats" Waller, who is visiting Washington, decides to try New York again, taking with him his regular quintet (completed by Arthur Whetsol, trumpeter, and Elmer Snowden, banjoist). This band, the Washingtonians, plays at Barron's Club in Harlem and at the Hollywood Club (later the Kentucky Club) on Broadway. Makes his first recording, with the Kentucky Club Orchestra.

1924   Recruits an important instrumentalist, James "Bubber" Miley, exponent of the growl trumpet, and (for a brief period) Sidney Bechet, Creole soprano saxophonist and clarinetist in the New Orleans tradition.

1925   The rhythm section remains stable for the next nine years with the addition of Fred Guy, banjoist and guitarist.

1926   Engages Joe "Tricky Sam" Nanton, a trombonist adept at growl and jungle effects who becomes a partner of Bubber Miley. Encourages the talent of the two men for bizarre instrumental effects. Wellman Braud (double bass player) replaces Bass Edwards (tuba player). Irving Mills becomes Ellington's manager, also contributing lyrics to many of Ellington's songs during the fourteen years of their association.

1927   Harry Carney joins (baritone saxophonist, alto saxophonist, clarinetist, and bass clarinetist), as does Barney Bigard (clarinetist). Adelaide Hall contributes wordless vocal variation to *Creole Love Call*, as an additional "instrumental" voice, innovative in jazz at the time. Band plays at the Cotton Club, New York. This important engagement allows Ellington to compose and experiment under favorable conditions, and continues until 1932.

1928   Johnny Hodges (alto and soprano saxophonist) joins, Otto Hardwick leaves.

1929   Band appears in the short film *Black and Tan Fantasy* and the Ziegfeld revue *Show Girl*. Two individualists are recruited: Cootie Williams (trumpeter) and Juan Tizol (valve trombonist). Bubber Miley leaves owing to ill health. Recordings are made under a variety of pseudonyms.[3]

1930   *Mood Indigo* (original title *Dreamy Blues*), Ellington's first big hit, published and recorded. Band appears in Hollywood film *Check and Double Check*. The jungle style, by now firmly established, is developed and perpetuated by Williams and Nanton, in the tradition of Miley. These vocalized instrumental timbres influence Ellington throughout his career.

1931   Composes his first extended work, *Creole Rhapsody*, which takes up both sides of a 78 rpm disc. The singer Ivie Anderson joins the band.

1932   Through the efforts and recommendations of the Australian-born composer Percy Grainger, plays a jazz concert at Columbia University. Lawrence Brown (trombonist) joins, Otto Hardwick (reed player) returns.

1933   First European tour. Band plays a two-week engagement at the London Palladium.

1934   Band appears in two films, *Belle of the Nineties* and *Murder at the Vanities*. Tours the southern states. Rex Stewart (cornetist) joins.

1935   *Reminiscing in Tempo* composed in memory of Ellington's mother, who died this year. Work extends over two 78 rpm records.

1936   Contributes music to the Marx Brothers' film *A Day at the Races* (in which Ivie Anderson also appears). Wallace Jones (lead trumpeter) joins, Arthur Whetsol (trumpeter) leaves because of illness.

1937   Plays a season at the "New" Cotton Club, New York. His father dies. A year of much activity, both composing and recording. Plays at the Apollo Theatre, New York.

1938   Harold "Shorty" Baker (trumpeter) joins for the first of several terms of service. He is both a dependable lead player and a sensitive, sweet-toned soloist.

1939 Tours the Continent. Several of his sidemen record with Django Reinhardt (guitar) in Paris. Engages Billy Strayhorn (composer, arranger, lyricist, and second pianist, a close collaborator with Ellington) and Jimmy Blanton (double bass player).

1940 Ben Webster (tenor saxophonist) joins. Ray Nance (trumpeter and cornetist) replaces Cootie Williams (trumpeter), who leaves to join Benny Goodman's orchestra. Many memorable, durable compositions are written: *Junior Hop, Never No Lament, Harlem Air Shaft, Subtle Slough, Pitter Panther Patter, Mr. J. B. Blues,* and *Day Dream* (the last in collaboration with Billy Strayhorn).

1941 Writes score for the revue *Jump for Joy,* which includes some comment on racism. Band enjoys a three-month run in Hollywood, adopts Billy Strayhorn's *Take the "A" Train* as its signature tune in place of *East St. Louis Toodle-oo.*

1942 Orchestra appears in film *Cabin in the Sky* in which the singer Lena Horne is also featured; Mercer Ellington's twelve-bar blues *Things Ain't What They Used to Be* is included in the principal sequence of the film. Barney Bigard (clarinetist) leaves, Jimmy Blanton dies.

1943 Writes the suite *Black, Brown and Beige,* his first extended concert work, which is given its premiere in Carnegie Hall, New York, in January. At a second concert at Carnegie Hall in December marks the premiere of *New World A-Comin',* a vehicle for Ellington's piano. Annual concerts at Carnegie Hall continue until 1950, each the occasion for the premiere of an important new work. Jimmy Hamilton (clarinetist and tenor saxophonist) joins, taking Bigard's chair and solo responsibilities. Ben Webster (tenor saxophonist) leaves.

1944 Orchestra plays in New York for extended engagements at the Capitol Theatre and Hurricane Club. The lead trumpeter and high-note specialist William "Cat" Anderson joins the band, and Al Sears (tenor saxophonist) completes the reed section. Juan Tizol (valve trombonist) leaves.

1945 *The Perfume Suite* is given its premiere at Carnegie Hall.

1946 Premiere at Carnegie Hall of *The Deep South Suite,* based on theme of black aspirations and ambitions. Russell Procope (alto saxophonist and clarinetist) replaces Otto Hardwick. Joe "Tricky Sam" Nanton dies.

1947 *The Liberian Suite* performed at Carnegie Hall, also a work dealing with social inequality. Tyree Glenn (trombonist, vibraphonist) joins, to take the place of Tricky Sam Nanton.

1948   Writes the suite *The Tattooed Bride* for concert at Carnegie Hall. Tours England, accompanied only by Ray Nance (trumpeter, cornetist, and violinist) and Kay Davis (soprano). Plays at the London Palladium and visits other European cities with a quintet completed by British musicians. Ben Webster (tenor saxophonist) rejoins in autumn.

1949   The orchestra suffers some decline in popularity, like other big bands after the war. Very little creative effort shown this year. Ben Webster (tenor saxophonist) leaves after six months.

1950   Orchestra tours the Continent. Paul Gonsalves (tenor saxophonist), brilliant soloist and technician, joins.

1951   *Harlem Suite* first performed at the Metropolitan Opera House, New York. There is some reorganization of the band's membership.

1952   Little new material produced this year by either Ellington or Strayhorn.

1953–54 Recordings include much material not by Ellington, with an atypical commercial bias and a revamping of old works, but there are signs of a renewed interest in composition. The orchestra still suffers from the continuing popularity of bebop, which is ideally suited to performance by smaller, cheaper groups.

1955   Orchestra accompanies a summer show, in a subordinate role which did not even require Ellington to be present at the performances. He writes a play, *Man with Four Sides*, and presents a new, ambitious work, *Night Creature*, at Carnegie Hall, joining forces for this performance with the radio orchestra Symphony of the Air. This work, calling for full strings, woodwinds, brass, and percussion in addition to Ellington's regular players, is not recorded until 1963: the first and second movements with the Stockholm Symphony, the third with the Paris Symphony. Johnny Hodges (alto saxophonist) returns.

1956   A resurgence of popularity, as Paul Gonsalves (tenor saxophonist) gives a frenetic, impassioned performance of *Diminuendo and Crescendo in Blue* at the Newport Jazz Festival which causes a sensation. Ellington's picture appears on the cover of *Time*. He composes with renewed enthusiasm and creativity, aided by Billy Strayhorn.

1957   Ellington, the orchestra, and the soloists are back on form and in demand. Collaborates with Strayhorn on *Such Sweet Thunder* (after Shakespeare) and *Royal Ancestry* (a portrait of Ella Fitzgerald), both well received.

1958   European tour, with important date at Leeds Festival in the presence
              of Queen Elizabeth II, the Duke of Edinburgh, and other members
              of the royal family. Great success again at Newport Jazz Festival with
              new work, *Toot Suite.*

1959   Writes first complete film score, for *Anatomy of a Murder*, performed
              by the orchestra. *The Queen's Suite*, written in honor of Queen Eliza-
              beth, is recorded at his own expense, the only record pressed is sent to
              Buckingham Palace, and there is no commercial release until 1976.

1960   Appearance at the Monterey Jazz Festival marked by the premiere
              of *Suite Thursday* (inspired by John Steinbeck's novel *Sweet Thurs-
              day*). Two months in Paris, where Ellington writes and records music
              for the film *Paris Blues*. Two efforts with Strayhorn reshape works
              by Tchaikovsky (*Nutcracker Suite*) and Grieg (*Peer Gynt* suite) with
              wit and ingenuity, and surprisingly little objection from the world of
              "serious" music.

1961   A year of diversification: a recording session combining the orches-
              tras of Ellington and Count Basie; two records with Ellington at the
              piano in the Louis Armstrong All Stars, a six-piece band; and two
              recordings with the tenor saxophonists Coleman Hawkins and John
              Coltrane, the first made by Ellington with a sextet of his sidemen and
              the second with a rhythm section only.

1962   Records a trio album, *Money Jungle*, with the drummer Max Roach
              and the double bass player Charlie Mingus, prominent and innova-
              tive bebop performers. Cootie Williams returns.

1963   Tours Europe, the Middle East, and the Far East. Completes *My
              People*, an extended choral and orchestral work celebrating the cente-
              nary of the Emancipation Proclamation (1863).

1964   Tours Europe and Japan.

1965   Tours Europe. Appears in the Virgin Islands (a new suite is written
              especially for this visit).
              First sacred concert, *In The Beginning, God*, has its first performance
              in Grace Cathedral, San Francisco.
              Pulitzer Prize Committee rejects a recommendation to award a spe-
              cial citation to Ellington, who is greatly disappointed. Billy Strayhorn
              admitted to hospital, suffering from cancer. Ellington's only son,
              Mercer, joins him as his road manager and as a member of the brass
              section (trumpet).

1966   Awarded President's Gold Medal of Honor by President Lyndon
              Johnson. Tours Europe, performs *First Sacred Concert* in Coventry
              Cathedral, England, and tours Senegal and Japan. Edna Ellington,
              estranged wife, dies.

1967   Billy Strayhorn dies.
            European tour includes concerts with Ella Fitzgerald.
            Awarded honorary doctorate in music at Yale University.
            Records album of Strayhorn's compositions in his memory (*And His Mother Called Him Bill*).

1968   *Second Sacred Concert* receives first performance at Cathedral of St. John the Divine, New York, with the Swedish soprano Alice Babs singing.
            Tours South America and Mexico.
            Harold Ashby (tenor saxophonist and clarinetist) replaces Jimmy Hamilton.

1969   President Richard Nixon invites Ellington to celebrate his seventieth birthday at the White House, awards him the Medal of Freedom.
            Orchestra tours Eastern and Western Europe and the West Indies.

1970   Tours Europe, Australasia, and the Far East.
            Writes music for the American Ballet Theatre (*The River*), performed in New York. Johnny Hodges dies. Lawrence Brown leaves.

1971   Three overseas tours: Russia (five weeks), Europe (five weeks), Latin America (three weeks).
            Appearances at Newport Jazz Festival and Lincoln Center, New York.
            William "Cat" Anderson (trumpeter) leaves.

1972   Extended tour of the Far East.
            Hardly any new music written this year.

1973   Third sacred concert, *The Majesty of God*, predominantly for solo voices, choir, and Ellington's piano, receives its first performance in Westminster Abbey, London. Alice Babs is the principal solo singer.
            Royal Command Performance at the London Palladium.
            Tours of the Continent, Zambia, and Ethiopia.

1974   Enters hospital in January, suffering from cancer.
            Dies on 24 May.

APPENDIX B

ELLINGTON'S PRINCIPAL

SIDEMEN

The cats who came into this band are probably unique in the aural realm. When someone falls out of the band—temporarily or permanently—it naturally becomes a matter of "Whom shall we get?" or "Whom can we get?" It is not just a matter of replacing the cat who left, because we are concerned with a highly personalized kind of music. It is written to suit the character of an instrumentalist, the man who has the responsibility of playing it, and it is almost impossible to match his character identically. Also, if the new man is sufficiently interesting tonally, why insist upon his copying or matching his predecessor's style?

. . . When a man is needed, I personally scarcely know which way to look for a replacement. I haven't the slightest idea whether the grass next door is greener or leaner. So someone suggests so-and-so, and we send for so-and-so, and get him. We play together for a day or two, and then I enquire whether or not the new cat likes what we are doing, having already watched his reaction to the band. If he likes it, he is invited to stay.

　—Duke Ellington

The quotation above is taken from Ellington's autobiography *Music Is My Mistress*, which contains Ellington's evaluations of many of his sidemen. All the quoted matter in the following paragraphs is taken from this source. The dates are those of membership in Ellington's band.

Alvis, Hayes
(double bass player), January 1935 to February 1938.
A player of great power and drive. During his stay he worked in a double bass duo with Billy Taylor.

Anderson, Ivie

(singer), February 1931 to August 1942.

An emotional singer, equally at home in slow and fast tempos. Was Ellington's favorite of all his singers. "She had great dignity . . . [and] became one of our mainstays and our highlights . . . every girl singer we've had since has had to try to prevail over the Ivie Anderson image" (p. 124).

Anderson, William "Cat"

(trumpeter), September 1944 to February 1947, December 1950 to July 1951, December 1951 to November 1959, April 1961 to March 1963, July 1963 to June 1969, August 1969 to January 1971.

Played lead trumpet with a sensational range, far beyond the limits imposed by normal embouchure. Dependable and punctual. His wide range was exploited to the full by Ellington and Billy Strayhorn. He was also capable of lyrical middle-register solos in the style of Louis Armstrong, and coloratura acrobatics with a Latin American flavor. Was often criticized for displaying poor musical taste, but Ellington was evidently pleased with his prodigious technique. "He had a good musical education and had really mastered the trumpet . . . Never a no-show artist, for a while he became an essential ingredient—*le super grand splang de l'acrobatique*" (p. 216).

Ashby, Harold

(tenor saxophonist and clarinetist), three weeks in December 1963, July 1968 to April 1974.

Played on recording *My People* in 1963. Joined band five years later and stayed to the end. A melodic improviser in the style of Ben Webster, also adept at edgy, swinging solos. An admirable foil to Paul Gonsalves. "He has been a great contributor in ensemble sound, on both tenor and clarinet. Originally, he came out of the Kansas City community which has produced so many outstanding swingers, and he has never lost that kind of impetus and feeling" (p. 404).

Babs, Alice

(singer), occasionally between 1963 and 1973.

Swedish-born coloratura soprano with spectacular range, tone, and intonation. Never sang regularly with the band, but appeared as a guest whenever Ellington needed her virtuoso singing. Extensively featured in the second and third sacred concerts, which contain material expressly written for her. "She sings opera, lieder, what we call jazz and blues, she sings like an instrument . . . she sight-reads and sings it as if she had rehearsed it a month . . . a composer's dream" (p. 287).

Baker, Harold "Shorty"

(trumpeter), February 1938 to April 1938, autumn 1942 to April 1944, May 1946 to December 1946, March 1947 to December 1951, May 1957 to September 1959, December 1961 to March 1962.

A brilliant lead trumpeter with a firm, masculine tone. As a soloist excelled both at hot, up-tempo playing and at simple, dreamy blues. "His way of playing a melody was absolutely personal, and he had no bad notes at all" (p. 221).

Bechet, Sidney

(soprano saxophonist and clarinetist), summer 1924.
Masterly blues player born in New Orleans in 1897. Played forcefully, with a throbbing, pronounced vibrato. Often toured worldwide. Was recognized as a major creative force by the conductor Ernest Ansermet as early as 1919. "Sidney Bechet was one of the truly great originals. I shall never forget the first time I heard him [in 1921] . . . I had never heard anything like it . . . a completely new sound and conception to me . . . He took Johnny Hodges under his arm and taught him everything, and Johnny's approach to saxophone was very much in that direction . . . so it was easy for him to absorb from Bechet, whom he loved and really idolized" (pp. 47–49).

Bigard, Barney

(clarinetist and tenor saxophonist), December 1927 to July 1942.
A native of New Orleans, he played with the early jazz pioneers Joe "King" Oliver and Luis Russell before he joined Ellington. Had a fluid, facile technique and a pure tone. Often featured as a soloist and as an improviser with the ensemble. Collaborated with Ellington on many works, notably *Mood Indigo*. "He is a very original and imaginative clarinet player, and he gave our band another of its distinctive sound identities. He was invaluable for putting the filigree work into an arrangement and sometimes it would remind you of all that delicate wrought iron you see in his home town" (p. 115).

Blanton, Jimmy

(double bass player), December 1939 to October 1941.
The first true virtuoso double bass player in jazz. He had a brilliant, rapid pizzicato technique and the discipline to use it tastefully and melodically. Died at the age of twenty-one, shortly after leaving Ellington's band. "Jimmy Blanton revolutionized bass-playing, and it has not been the same since. He played melodies that belonged to the bass, and always had a foundation quality . . . We were doing wonderfully with him. He had given us something new; a new beat and new sounds . . . altogether it was a great period" (p. 164).

Braud, Wellman

(double bass player), 1926 and late 1935.
Had a solid, persuasive beat. Played simple bass lines in the New Orleans style and was an expert with the bow. "He believed in crowding the microphone, and when you got ready to blow a chorus, Mr. Braud would already have established so compelling a beat that you simply could not miss . . . [he] also made many valuable suggestions . . . particularly about style and tempo . . . a major contributor to our budding style" (p. 115).

Brown, Lawrence

(trombonist), spring 1932 to June 1943, August 1943 to February 1951, May 1960 to January 1970.
Smooth, melodic player with the purest of tones. A devout, abstemious man whose playing displayed a gentle discipline. "As a soloist, his taste is impeccable, but his greatest role is that of an accompanist . . . the accompanist par excellence" (p. 122).

Carney, Harry
(baritone saxophonist, clarinetist, and bass clarinetist), June 1927 to April 1974.
Principally a baritone saxophonist with a massive tone and a direct, melodic style free of clichés. An important contributor to the depth and tonal richness of the reed section. For decades recognized as the premier soloist on the baritone saxophone. He introduced Johnny Hodges to the band and was Ellington's constant traveling companion and confidant.

Ellington, Mercer
(trumpeter, arranger, composer, and manager), January 1965 to April 1974.
A section player, never featured as a soloist. Composed and arranged many items for the band (*Moon Mist* and *Things Ain't What They Used to Be* are two notable examples). "My son, Mercer Ellington, is dedicated to maintaining the lustre of his father's image . . . he seeks out the best, and only the best musicians . . . He accepts the responsibility on any occasion he thinks might . . . lead to unhappiness for the Old Man, and sees that he gets the respect that is ever due to him" (p. 41).

Gaskin, Victor
(double bass player), March 1969 to mid-1970.
A technically accomplished player with a penchant for melodic ornamentation. Never obscured the basic pulse.

Glenn, Tyree
(trombonist and vibraphonist), May 1947 to April 1950.
A versatile soloist, expert in the growling, plunger-muted techniques of Tricky Sam Nanton, whom he effectively replaced.

Gonsalves, Paul
(tenor saxophonist), September 1950 to January 1970, December 1972 to May 1974.
One of Ellington's most important soloists, capable of playing delicate, lyrical blues, ballads, and frenetic up-tempo compositions. Had a dazzling technique and a fine tone. His virtuoso playing of *Diminuendo and Crescendo in Blue* at the Newport Jazz Festival in 1956 was largely responsible for a revival of interest in Ellington's work. A disciple of Ben Webster, whom he succeeded. Often featured in later, large-scale works. "He had good musical education, has great solo taste and plays with profound authority" (p. 221).

Greer, Sonny
(drummer), 1923 to October 1944, March 1945 to February 1951.
"A natural supporting artist, . . . he kept time . . . and he dug the value of teamwork all the way back. Everything in his life, I think, has always been done in a happy way, even though not according to Hoyle . . . He was the world's best percussion reactor. When he heard a ping he responded with the most apropos pong. Any tune he was backing up had the benefit of rhythmic ornamentation that was sometimes unbelievable" (pp. 51, 53).

Guy, Freddy
(banjoist and guitarist), spring 1925 to May 1949.

Never featured as a soloist, but his sound was an important segment of Ellington's early rhythm section. "He was a rather serious type of fellow, and was always giving us advice, but his guitar was a metronome and the beat was always where it was supposed to be" (p. 109).

Hall, Adelaide
(singer), 1928.
In 1927 recorded the wordless obbligato to Ellington's *Creole Love Call*.

Hamilton, Jimmy
(clarinetist and tenor saxophonist), June 1943 to July 1968.
Eventually replaced Barney Bigard in the band. An exceptionally well schooled musician and a clarinetist of academic technique and tone, much used by Ellington in complex situations. "He usually manages anything musical that he sets his hand to, and there, I think, is the key to any attempt at describing him. He practices endlessly and scarcely ever gets away from the school rules . . . He was very important to us throughout the 25 years he was in the band" (pp. 220–21).

Hardwick, Otto
(alto saxophonist), 1923 to spring 1928, April 1932 to June 1943, autumn 1943 to June 1946.
A founding member of the band. He made his principal contribution as the leader of the reeds. Specialized in the "sweet" exposition of themes until Johnny Hodges joined. "He read very well and played even better" (p. 50).

Hodges, Johnny
(alto saxophonist), May 1928 to February 1951, August 1955 to December 1957, March 1958 to May 1970.
Undoubtedly Ellington's most important soloist and interpreter of his music. A peerless saxophonist with a silky tone, an exceptional command of glissandi and portamenti, and a large supply of ravishing melodic phrases. His serene, simple, majestic playing was instantly recognizable and has been widely imitated. "His sultry solos were not done in an attempt to blow more notes than anybody else. He just wanted to play them in true character, reaching into his soul for them, and automatically reaching everybody else's soul . . . [He had] a tone so beautiful it sometimes brought tears to the eyes" (pp. 118–19).

Jenkins, Freddy
(trumpeter), October 1928 to December 1934.
A showman influenced by Louis Armstrong and a brilliant technician. "He brought us a new kind of sparkle; his every move was a picture. Even a cliche in his solos had an extra unique flair, a personality ploy. He was total 'theatre'" (p. 121).

Jones, Rufus "Speedy"
(drummer), December 1966 to March 1967, March 1968 to July 1973.
Had a powerful, confident sound. "His role . . . in African, jungle and Oriental pieces has led to demands from the audience for him to be featured solo . . . his drum solos have been show-stoppers" (p. 401).

Jones, Wallace

(trumpeter), autumn 1936 to February 1944, January 1947 to March 1947.
Lead trumpeter, not featured as a soloist.

Marshall, Wendell

(double bass player), September 1948 to January 1953, March 1953 to September 1954.
A player in the manner of his first cousin Jimmy Blanton, full-toned and rhythmic,
with an acrobatic and accurate pizzicato facility.

Miley, James "Bubber"

(trumpeter), autumn 1924 to early 1929.
A durable influence on Ellington's musical thinking throughout his career. His use of
the plunger mute and growl effects brought the sound of the trumpet very close to that
of the human voice and had a profound influence in jazz. Collaborated with Ellington
on early "jungle" compositions. "Every note he played was soul filled with the pulse
of compulsion. *It don't mean a thing if it ain't got that swing* was his credo. His growl
solos with the plunger mute were another of our early sound identities, . . . and he laid
the foundation of a tradition that has been maintained ever since by men like Cootie
Williams and Ray Nance" (p. 106; italics in original).

Nance, Ray

(trumpeter, cornetist, violinist, and singer), November 1940 to September 1945, April
1946 to November 1961, January 1962 to September 1963, January 1965 to June 1965,
a few days in September 1973.
Cornetist with a sweet tone and melodic style. Used growl-and-plunger techniques. An
adept violinist with an approach ranging from the highly rhapsodic to the brutal and
gritty. Had a mischievous vocal style. "Ray Nance never played a 'bad' note in his life,
so this makes him unique among artists who practice freedom of expression in music.
Singer, violinist, cornetist . . . he is constantly a 'gas' (a revelation!). He is a pure artist
at heart and no trumpet-player ever takes an ad. lib. chorus on Strayhorn's *Take The
"A" Train* without falling back on some of the original 'licks' introduced by Ray Nance
on the first recording of it" (p. 162).

Nanton, Joe "Tricky Sam"

(trombonist), summer 1926 to July 1946.
Best-known for his adroitness with the plunger and wah-wah mutes. Using these and
playing in the top register almost exclusively, he produced tonal effects uncannily close
to the timbre of the human speaking voice, as did his mentor Bubber Miley. His blues
playing was moving and passionate, his contribution to the jungle sound considerable.
He influenced almost all his successors in the band. "Bubber Miley was the right mate
for 'Tricky.' 'Now you've got it,' he'd say, and we gave 'Tricky' the opportunity to play
more . . . a chance to develop his 'tricks.' That's what we called them, and he was
'Tricky' because he wasn't stupid. When he played his thing, that was the end of it"
(p. 108).

Procope, Russell

(alto saxophonist and clarinetist), June 1946 to April 1974.

A capable, all-round musician, his principal contribution was his lead and section work with the reeds. Had a smooth, melodic style. In the 1930s he was prominent as a swing alto saxophone soloist in John Kirby's neat, polished sextet. His clarinet playing was inspired by the New Orleans style, with a distinctive, pleasant, woody tone in the chalumeau register. A fine bluesman. "Russell Procope . . . a man of dignity . . . of clean and gentlemanly appearance . . . one always to be relied upon" (p. 222).

Raglin, Alvin, Jr.

(double bass player), November 1941 to October 1945, December 1947, a brief period in 1955.
He replaced Jimmy Blanton, who was ailing. A vigorous player with powerful swing and a full tone, although less agile and inventive than his predecessor.

Sears, Al

(tenor saxophonist), May 1944 to May 1949.
A hard-driving musician who played glissandi and legato phrases that recalled the work of Johnny Hodges, though at a lower pitch. In more hurried tempi he played in a spiky, violent, staccato manner.

Stewart, Rex

(cornetist), December 1934 to June 1943, September 1943 to December 1945.
Had a hot, impassioned approach to up-tempo material, but was also adept at gentle, melodic playing in the manner of Bix Beiderbecke. Employed a whole range of in-strumental effects: growls, glissandi, and notably a strangled, stifled effect obtained by blowing the note firmly while holding down halfway the valve or valves. A versatile player frequently and effectively exploited by Ellington.

Stone, Fred

(trumpeter, composer, and arranger), May 1970 to September 1970.
Canadian session musician and composer, a modernist who joined Ellington's orches-tra for its tour of fifteen European countries. An experienced player who wrote some revealing memoirs of his experiences with the band.

Strayhorn, Billy

(composer, arranger, lyricist, and pianist), March 1939 to May 1967.
Ellington's consistent collaborator throughout their association. Younger than Elling-ton and learned much from him. He inclined occasionally toward experimental mod-ernism in his own work. The combination of Ellington's "poolroom education" and Strayhorn's classical training produced a highly individual blend of the self-taught and the academic. Strayhorn's piano playing, although obviously influenced by Ellington's approach to the keyboard, was lighter and airier but still swinging. "His patience was incomparable, and unlimited. He had no aspirations to enter into any kind of compe-tition, yet the legacy he leaves, his oeuvre, will never be less than the ultimate on the highest plateau of culture (whether by comparison or not)" (p. 161).

Taylor, Billy

(double bass player), January 1935 to October 1939.

Teamed with Hayes Alvis during the greater part of his stay with Ellington. He produced a light, full-toned pizzicato without using the slap techniques of the older players, thus moving the double bass style closer to the modern conception. Jimmy Blanton replaced the duo of Alvis and Taylor.

Terry, Clark
(trumpeter and flugelhorn player), November 1951 to October 1959.
A player equipped with a prodigious legato technique on both instruments. He excelled at rapid, double-tempo improvisations, perfectly articulated, and in economical, bluesy playing, in which he often imitated Rex Stewart's half-valve effects and growls. His solos were often puckish and humorous, punctuated by unusual intervals and employing the whole of his three-octave range. "He is a busy man, but he always finds time to help the college bands around the country, and I am sure many a youngster has been inspired by him, both as a man and a musician" (p. 229).

Tizol, Juan
(valve trombonist), September 1929 to April 1944, March 1951 to December 1953, March 1960 to May 1960, May 1961 to July 1961.
Born in Puerto Rico, he worked well in Latin American idioms. In essence not a jazz-man, but a fine section player. He was strongest in the unembroidered statement of themes, particularly those with a Latin flavor. Composer with Ellington of the Latin pieces *Caravan*, *Bakif*, and *Congo Brava*, and also of *Perdido*, which is thoroughly a jazz composition. Worked closely with Ellington on the editing of scores. "He was a tremendous asset to our band" (p. 56).

Turney, Norris
(alto saxophonist, clarinetist, and flutist), 1969 to 1972.
A lyrical soloist, he was strongly influenced by Johnny Hodges. Frequently a flute soloist (a function availed of only belatedly by Ellington's band).

Webster, Ben
(tenor saxophonist), February 1940 to August 1943, November 1948 to June 1949.
Had a profound influence on the jazz saxophone. Played with a huge tone, by turns forceful and almost guttural, and breathy and smooth. His solos ranged from ones of great power and directness to lyrical, sinuous ornamentations of Ellington's themes and sequences. "His enthusiasm and drive had an especially important influence on the saxophone section . . . [which] didn't end when he left either, because when Paul Gonsalves came into the band he knew all of Ben's solos note-for-note . . . We now have Harold Ashby as well, and 'Ash' is both a Webster protege and a disciple" (p. 163).

Whetsol, Arthur
(trumpeter), 1923 to summer 1924, March 1928 to autumn 1936.
Lead trumpeter with a fine tone. Played melodies sensitively, but his solos lacked swing. "He had a tonal personality that has never really been duplicated. Sweet, but not syrupy . . . and he was one of the really good readers . . . He left behind an echo of aural charisma that I can still hear" (p. 54).

Williams, Charles "Cootie"
(trumpeter), March 1929 to November 1940, September 1962 to May 1973.
Brilliant player, with a style forged from those of Bubber Miley and Louis Armstrong. On the open trumpet he produced a magnificent, round, full, thick tone, and on the muted trumpet played growls in the jungle tradition of Miley. Always played lines of great delicacy and beauty. His solos had massive authority. One of Ellington's most important and influential players. "He soon became one of our most outstanding soloists. He began to use the plunger mute, one of our major tonal devices, and he used it very well" (p. 121).

Woodyard, Sam
(drummer), July 1955 to March 1959, July 1959 to September 1959, April 1960 to June 1965, February 1966 to November 1966, September 1967 to early 1968, spring 1973 to July 1973.
Played with a strong, driving beat and an excellent technique. His versatility was exploited by Ellington, who took advantage of his numerous percussion specialties, one of which was hand drumming. He played in Ellington's orchestra at the Newport Jazz Festival of 1956, behind Paul Gonsalves's solo tour de force in *Diminuendo and Crescendo in Blue*. "When he is playing, he just about has an affair with his drums" (p. 227).

APPENDIX C

A SELECTIVE DISCOGRAPHY

There are several comprehensive discographies of Duke Ellington. *Duke Ellington's Story on Records,* by Luciano Massagli, Liberio Pusateri, and Giovanni M. Volonté (Milan: Musica Jazz, 1981), has been issued as a series of booklets, each devoted to a short period. The greater part of each booklet is a chronological listing of commercial recordings, radio and television performances, public concerts, and some soundtracks. The following information on each session is provided: place and date of performance, names of musicians, matrix and take numbers, titles, original issues and reissues on LP, structure of piece performed (including succession of choruses), and names of soloists (in order of their solos). The discography also contains an index of composers, and a listing of musicians (giving the duration of their service with the orchestra). *The "Wax Works" of Duke Ellington,* by Benny Aasland (Järfälla, Sweden: Duke Ellington Music Society, 1978–79), was first published in two volumes. The first covers the period from 6 March 1940 to 30 July 1942 (when Ellington recorded for RCA-Victor), and the second covers the period of the wartime recording ban, from 31 July 1942 to 11 November 1944. The period from 1939 to 1941 therefore benefits from double coverage. Aasland's discography contains precisely the same information as that of Massagli, Pusateri, and Volonté, as well as many facsimiles of record sleeves and reprints from the frequent bulletins issued by the Duke Ellington Music Society. There are also some interesting memorabilia, such as reproductions of recording schedules and many fine photographs. The Duke Ellington Music Society frequently issues additions and corrections. *Duke Ellington,* by Barry Ulanov (London: Musicians' Press, 1947), includes a discography covering the period from late 1925 to October 1945. The lists of titles and musicians are comprehensive, but occasionally the chronology is vague: sessions that took place in the same year are often grouped together, without specific dates. In addition to these three discographies, the catalogue of the Library of Congress contains valuable information.

About four-fifths of the music recorded by Ellington between 1939 and 1941 was written by Ellington himself and his associates, as may be seen from the following listing:

Ellington as sole composer	86
Ellington in collaboration with Billy Strayhorn	6

Ellington in collaboration with members of his orchestra   28
Ellington in collaboration with others   5
Ellington's musicians as sole composers:

Barney Bigard	4	
Harry Carney	1	
Mercer Ellington	6	
Johnny Hodges	13	
Rex Stewart	3	
Billy Strayhorn	11	
Juan Tizol	2	
Cootie Williams	4	44

Barney Bigard in collaboration with Billy Strayhorn   2
Arrangement of traditional tune ("Frankie and Johnny")   1
Total number of works by Ellington and his associates   172
Total number of works by other writers   42

Total of all works recorded   214

Many items were of course recorded more than once, in differing versions, and a large amount of Ellington's recorded work has been reissued repeatedly in anthologies and collections.

The discography which follows includes only those recordings cited in this book. The ordering of the items accords with the order of their mention in the text, and is therefore not strictly chronological.

Key to Instruments

as	alto saxophone		p	piano
b	double bass		ss	soprano saxophone
bjo	banjo		t	trumpet
bs	baritone saxophone		tb	trombone
cl	clarinet		tc	trumpet-cornet
ct	cornet		ts	tenor saxophone
dr	drums		tu	tuba
fl	flugelhorn		v	violin
g	guitar		voc	vocals

Key to Record Labels

At	Atlantic		HMV	His Master's Voice
BA	Blue Ace		OK	Okeh
Bb	Bluebird		PaE	English Parlophone
Bi	Biograph		Ph	Philips
Br	Brunswick		Pt	Paramount
BrE	English Brunswick		RCA	Radio Corporation of America
BYG	BYG (Paris)			and RCA (Victor)

CBS	Columbia Broadcasting System	Sav	Savoy
Cd	Camden	SCCJ	Smithsonian Collection of
Co	Columbia		Classic Jazz
CoE	English Columbia	Se	Sentry
De	Decca	TL	Time Life
Ea	Electrola	VDP	VDP
Ep	Epic	Vi	Victor
FDC	For Discriminate Collectors	Vo	Vocalion
Fw	Folkways	VSA	VSA
Gr	Gramophone	VSM	Voix de Son Maître
Gro	Groove	"X"	"X"

Chapter 1.
An Introduction to Ellingtonia

Creole Rhapsody, parts 1 and 2

Duke Ellington and His Orchestra
First version: New York City / Early
1931
Second version: New York City /
11 June 1931

Arthur Whetsol, Freddy Jenkins,
Cootie Williams (t), Joe Nanton, Juan
Tizol (tb), Johnny Hodges (as), Barney
Bigard (cl), Harry Carney (as, bs),
Duke Ellington (p), Fred Guy (bjo),
Wellman Braud (b), Sonny Greer (dr)
(The same musicians play on both
versions.)

First Version: parts 1 and 2 (both sides
of a ten-inch, 78 rpm disc) Br 6093,
80047; BrE 1145
Second version: parts 1 and 2 (both
sides of a twelve-inch, 78 rpm disc)

HMV C.4870; Vi 36049

Reminiscin' in Tempo

Duke Ellington and His Orchestra
New York / 12 September 1935

Arthur Whetsol, Cootie Williams (t),
Rex Stewart (ct), Lawrence Brown,
Juan Tizol, Joe Nanton (tb), Otto
Hardwick, Johnny Hodges (as), Harry

Carney (bs), Barney Bigard (cl), Duke
Ellington (p), Fred Guy (g), Hayes
Alvis and/or Billy Taylor (b), Sonny
Greer (dr)
Parts 1 and 2 (both sides of a ten-inch,
78 rpm disc)
Br 7546; Co 36114; BrE 02103
Parts 3 and 4 (both sides of a ten-inch,
78 rpm disc)
Br 7547; Co 36115; BrE 02104

Chapter 2. The "Ellington Effect"

Creole Love Call

Duke Ellington and His Orchestra
New York / 27 October 1927

Bubber Miley, Louis Metcalf (t), Joe
Nanton (tb), Otto Hardwick, Rudy
Jackson (as, cl), Harry Carney (as, bs),
Duke Ellington (p), Fred Guy (bjo),
Wellman Braud (b), Sonny Greer (dr),
Adelaide Hall (voc)

HMV B.6252, B.4895; Vi 24861, 21137

East St. Louis Toodle-oo

Duke Ellington and His Cotton Club
Orchestra
New York / 19 December 1927

Bubber Miley, Louis Metcalf (t), Joe
"Tricky Sam" Nanton (tb), Otto

Hardwick (as, cl), Harry Carney (as, bs), Rudy Jackson (as, cl), Duke Ellington (p), Fred Guy (bjo), Wellman Braud (b), Sonny Greer (dr)

HMV B.4958, B.8649; Vi 21703, 20-1531

Black and Tan Fantasy

Duke Ellington and His Orchestra
New York / 26 October 1927

Same musicians as East St. Louis Toodle-oo

HMV B.6356, B.4869; Vi 21137, 24861

Misty Mornin'

Duke Ellington and His Cotton Club Orchestra
New York / ca. 15 November 1928

Arthur Whetsol, Bubber Miley, Freddy Jenkins (t), Joe "Tricky Sam" Nanton (tb), Johnny Hodges (as), Barney Bigard (ts, cl), Harry Carney (bs), Duke Ellington (p), Fred Guy (bjo), Wellman Braud (b), Sonny Greer (dr)

Co 35955; OK 8662; PaE R.2258

Mood Indigo

Duke Ellington and His Orchestra
Three versions of this work were recorded in New York during 1930 (see below), each time with the same musicians.

Arthur Whetsol, Freddy Jenkins, Cootie Williams (t), Joe "Tricky Sam" Nanton, Juan Tizol (tb), Johnny Hodges (as), Barney Bigard (ts, cl), Harry Carney (bs), Duke Ellington (p), Fred Guy (bjo), Wellman Braud (b), Sonny Greer (dr)

1. Br 4952. 6732; BrE 1068 (date obscure)
2. OK 8440; PaE R.866 (date obscure)
3. HMV B.6354; Vi 22587, 24486, 20-1532 (10 December 1930)

Chapter 3.
The Influence of the Blues

Gully Low Blues

Louis Armstrong Hot Seven
Chicago / 14 May 1927

Armstrong (ct), John Thomas (tb), Johnny Dodds (cl), Lil Armstrong (p), Johnny St. Cyr (bjo), Pete Briggs (tu), Baby Dodds (dr)

OK 8474

Parker's Mood

Charlie Parker All Stars
New York / 18 September 1948

Parker (as), John Lewis (p), Curley Russell (b), Max Roach (dr)
Sav MG 12000

Take It Easy

Duke Ellington and His Cotton Club Orchestra
New York / Early 1928

Bubber Miley, Louis Metcalf (t), Joe Nanton (tb), Otto Hardwick (as), Harry Carney (bs), Barney Bigard (cl), Duke Ellington (p), Fred Guy (bjo), Wellman Braud (b), Sonny Greer (dr)

OK 41013; Br 7670; PaE R144, R2304; CBS LP 62611/66302 (first record of a three-record set)

Sweet Chariot

Duke Ellington and His Orchestra
New York / Late 1930

Arthur Whetsol, Freddy Jenkins,
Cootie Williams (t), Joe Nanton, Juan
Tizol (tb), Johnny Hodges (as), Barney
Bigard (ts, cl), Harry Carney (as, bs),
Duke Ellington (p), Fred Guy (bjo),
Wellman Braud (b), Sonny Greer (dr)

OK 8840; PaE R1615; CBS LP
62611/66302 (first record of a
three-record set)

Anthology of the Country Blues

"Roots of the Blues," At 1348
"Jazz II, The Blues," Fw FB55

Things Ain't What They Used to Be

Johnny Hodges and His Orchestra
Hollywood, California / 3 July 1941

Ray Nance (tc), Lawrence Brown (tb),
Johnny Hodges (as), Harry Carney (bs),
Duke Ellington (p), Jimmy
Blanton (b), Sonny Greer (dr)

Bb 11447; Gro 5007; HMV B9283,
7EG8030, 7EG8045, DLP 1025,
EA 3245, Jo 313; RCA 75617, 430629,
LPV 533, RD7829, WPT/EPBT/LPT 3000,
FXM1-7274 (first edition); Vi EPBT 300,
947-0068, 42-0159

Chapter 4.
The Influence of Ragtime

Maple Leaf Rag: Ragtime In Rural America

(an anthology of rural ragtime, issued
in 1976)

In the black tradition:
Dallas String Band (Dallas Rag)

Blind Blake (Southern Rag)
Sugar Underwood (Dewdrop Alley)
Blind Ben Fuller (Piccolo Rag)
Cow Cow Davenport (Atlanta Rag)
Blind Willie McTell (Kill It Kid)
Bunk Johnson Band (The Entertainer)
Rev. Gary Davis (Maple Leaf Rag)
In the white tradition:
Jimmy Tarleton (Mexican Rag)
Gil Tanner & His Skillet Lickers
(Hawkins Rag)
Harvey Johnson (Guitar Rag)
The Spooney Five (Chinese Rag)
China Poplin (Summer Rag/Steel
Guitar Rag)
Merle Travis (Cannon Ball Rag/ Bugle
Call Rag)
Flatt & Scruggs & the Foggy
Mountain Boys (Randy Lynn Rag)

New World Records 235

Black, Brown and Beige

(only four excerpts recorded)

Duke Ellington and His Famous
Orchestra
New York / 11 and 12 December 1944

Ray Nance, Taft Jordan, Shelton
Hemphill, William "Cat"
Anderson (t), Lawrence Brown,
Claude Jones, Joe Nanton (tb), Johnny
Hodges (as, ss), Otto Hardwick (as), Al
Sears (ts), Jimmy Hamilton (ts, cl),
Harry Carney (bs, cl), Duke
Ellington (p), Fred Guy (g), Alvin
Raglin, Jr. (b), Sonny Greer (dr), Joya
Sherrill (voc, on "The Blues")

11 December 1944:
"Work Song": HMV C.3504;
Vi 28-0400 A
"Come Sunday": HMV C.3504;
Vi 28-0401 A

12 December 1944:
"The Blues": HMV C.3505;
Vi 28-0401 B

"Three Dances": HMV C.3505;
Vi 0400 B

All four titles reissued on RCA LAS 3071

Eubie Blake: Rags to Classics

(piano solos)

Charleston Rag (recorded 1921)
Charleston Rag (recorded 1971)

All the following titles were recorded during 1971 and 1972:

Capricious Harlem (Blake)
Rustles of Spring (Sinding, arr. Blake)
You're Lucky to Me (Blake and Razaf)
You Do Something to Me (Cole Porter)
Rain Drops (Blake)
Pork and Beans (Luckyeth Roberts)
Valse Marrion (Blake)
Classical Rag (Blake)
Scarf Dance (Chaminade, arr. Blake)
Butterfly (Blake)
Junk Man Rag (Roberts)

Eubie Blake Music 2

Jelly Roll Morton and His Red Hot Peppers

(asterisks denote compositions by Morton)

Chicago / 15 September 1926

The Chant/Black Bottom Stomp*/
Smoke House Blues.
George Mitchell (ct), Omer
Simeon (cl), Edward "Kid" Ory (tb),
Jelly Roll Morton (p), Johnny St.
Cyr (bjo), John Lindsay (b), Andrew
Hilaire (dr)

Chicago / 21 September 1926
Steamboat Stomp/Sidewalk Blues*/
Dead Man Blues*
Same musicians as 15 September
1926, plus Lee Collins (t), Darnell
Howard (cl), Barney Bigard (cl)

Chicago / 16 December 1926
Cannon Ball Blues*/Granpa's Spells*/
Original Jelly Roll Blues*/Doctor Jazz
Same musicians as 15 September 1926
Chicago / 4 June 1927
Jungle Blues*/The Pearls*/Beale
Street Blues
George Mitchell (t), George
Bryant (tb), Johnny Dodds (cl), Stomp
Evans (as), Jelly Roll Morton (p),
Johnny St. Cyr (bjo), Quinn
Wilson (tu), Baby Dodds (dr)

New York / 11 June 1928
Kansas City Stomp*/Shoe Shiners
Drag*/Georgia Swing*
Ward Pinkett (t), Geechy Fields (tb),
Omer Simeon (cl), Jelly Roll
Morton (p), Lee Blair (bjo), Bill
Benford (tuba), Tommy Benford (dr)

RAC International INTS 5092 (NL 43434)

The Carolina Shout

(piano solo recordings and piano rolls made by the composer, James P. Johnson)

Solo recordings: OK 4495 (October 1921) (on the LP *The Father of Stride Piano*, Co CL 1780), SCCJ II/4
Rolls: Artempo 12975 (February 1918, on the LP *Parlour Piano Solos, 1917– 21*, Bi BLP 1003Q), QRS 100999 (1918, also on the LP Bi BLP 1003Q)

The A section of this composition is a descending progression derived from a floating folk strain which was modified and adapted by rag composers and jazz musicians alike, most particularly in the A strains of Wild Cherries (Ted Snyder, 1908), Perfect Rag (Jelly Roll Morton, 1924), Buddy's Habits (Arnett Nelson, 1923), and Little Rock Getaway (Joe Sullivan, 1935).

Jig Walk (Jig Walk Charleston)

Piano Roll by Duke Ellington
New York / 1923 or 1924

BYG Records 529071 (Duke Ellington
Archive of Jazz, vol. 21); FDC 1003;
Pt 14027

This item was discovered on the LP
listed above, issued by BYG. According
to the liner notes, the piece was
reproduced from a piano-roll playback,
and constitutes Ellington's "recording
debut in the 1920s." It is the first track
on side 1 of the record, followed by
"It's Gonna Be a Cold Winter" by the
singer Alberta Prime (Alberta Hunter),
who is accompanied by Ellington at
the piano (this track bears the date
November 1924). I was greatly helped
in my research into this piece by the
collector and archivist Ron Clough of
Abergele, Wales, and I quote from his
reply to my enquiries (in a letter dated
2 August 1982):

> I have an acetate copy of it which
> came from a French LP, FDC 1003.
> According to Luigi Sanfilippo's 1966
> discography, comparison of the
> Paramount catalogue numbers
> would seem to confirm the actual
> time of processing the roll and
> issuing it, as being 1924, or even in
> 1923, and it was also issued on
> Paramount 14027 ("78" disc),
> Master No. 607, date mentioned,
> April 1926.
>   However, in the Massagli
> Discography, it says "unknown
> date." There, the Paramount issue
> and master numbers are as above. It
> also states "accompanied by Sonny
> Greer, drums," and that the original
> "78" is a dubbing from a piano roll.
>   However, here are my
> observations: Could drums be put
> on to a piano roll? I've just played
> my copy and certainly found a funny

> noise in places, similar to drums on
> a fairground organ. So that must be
> it [Clough's supposition is correct;
> see chapter 4]. I'm sure the
> Paramount catalogue is suspect. I
> have checked my discographies, and
> the highest Paramount catalogue
> number I can find is 13141 (Jabbo
> Williams's "Jab's Blues"). The
> closest Paramount master number I
> can find is 677 (Jimmy O'Bryant's
> "Red Hot Mamma," recorded
> Chicago, November 1924, and the
> Para. Cat. No. for this is 12246).
> Many discographers copy other
> discographers' errors. This is
> probably the case here.

Chapter 5.
The Influence of Tin Pan Alley

Hot Feet

Duke Ellington and His Orchestra
New York / 7 March 1929

Arthur Whetsol, Cootie Williams,
Freddy Jenkins (t), Joe "Tricky Sam"
Nanton (tb), Otto Hardwick, Barney
Bigard, Harry Carney (reeds), Duke
Ellington (p), Fred Guy (bjo), Sonny
Greer (dr)

Bb 6335; HMV B.4865, B.6343;
Vi 38065

Serenade to Sweden

Duke Ellington and His Famous
Orchestra
New York / 6 June 1939

Cootie Williams, Wallace Jones, (t),
Rex Stewart (ct), Lawrence Brown,
Juan Tizol, Joe "Tricky Sam"
Nanton (tb), Johnny Hodges, Otto
Hardwick (as), Barney Bigard (ts, cl),
Harry Carney (bs), Duke Ellington (p),
Fred Guy (g), Sonny Greer (dr)

Co 35214, C 3L-39, CLO2365; CBS BPG-62613

Chapter 6. Ko Ko

Ko Ko

Duke Ellington and His Famous Orchestra
Chicago / 6 March 1940

Wallace Jones, Cootie Williams (t), Rex Stewart (ct), Lawrence Brown, Joe Nanton, Juan Tizol (tb), Johnny Hodges, Otto Hardwick (as), Ben Webster (ts), Harry Carney (bs), Duke Ellington (p), Fred Guy (g), Jimmy Blanton (b), Sonny Greer (dr)

BA 208; Ea2766; Gr DA 4977; HMV B.9078, DLP 1034, ALS 2764, TG 186; RCA 75541, RD 27133, 730565, FMP1-7002, DPM-2-0351 (Special Products), LPM 1715; Se 4001; SCCJ P6-11891 (Columbia Special Products); TL STL-Jo2-P 3-14729; Vi 26577, LPT 3017, EPBT 3017, 947-0047; VSA GY 417; VSM FOLP-8002, K-8732, 7 EMF27

Boogie Woogie

The Count Basie Quintet
Chicago / 9 October 1936

Carl Jones (t), Lester Young (ts), Count Basie (p), Walter Page (b), Jo Jones (dr), Jimmy Rushing (voc)

CoE SEG 7576; Ep LN 3107; PaE R 2874; Vo 3459

Jumping at the Woodside

Count Basie and His Orchestra
New York City / 22 August 1938

Buck Clayton, Harry Edison, Ed Lewis (t), Dan Minor, Eddie Durham, Benny Morton (tb), Earl Warren (as),

Herschel Evans, Lester Young (ts), Jack Washington (bs), Count Basie (p), Freddie Greene (g), Walter Page (b), Jo Jones (dr)

BrE o.2684; De 2212

Main Stem

Duke Ellington and His Famous Orchestra
Hollywood, California / 26 June 1942

Wallace Jones (t), Ray Nance (tc), Rex Stewart (ct), Lawrence Brown, Joe Nanton, Juan Tizol (tb), Johnny Hodges, Otto Hardwick (as), Barney Bigard (cl), Ben Webster (ts), Harry Carney (bs), Duke Ellington or Billy Strayhorn (p), Fred Guy (g), Alvin Raglin, Jr. (b), Sonny Greer (dr)

HMV B.9386, N.14002, EA 3735, JK 2369, SG 318; RCA Rd 27134, LPM 1364, FXMI 7301; Vi KLVP 184; VSM FFLP 1035, 7 EMF-28

Midnight Call Blues

Lonnie Johnson and Eddie Lang (guitars)
(Eddie Lang recorded under the pseudonym Blind Willie Dunn on this session.)
New York / 9 October 1929

OK 8818

Weather Bird

Louis Armstrong (t), Earl Hines (p)
Chicago / 5 December 1928

OK 41454

Chapter 7. Mr. J. B. Blues

Mr. J. B. Blues (take 1)

Duke Ellington (p), Jimmy Blanton (b)
Chicago / 1 October 1940

HMV B.9211, 7EG 8189, EA 3279, JK
2314; RCA 75489, RD 27258, FXMI-7072
(take 2); Vi 27406, EPA 619, LPM
6009-1; RCA Jazz Tribune PM.45352

Chapter 8.
Concerto for Cootie

Concerto for Cootie

Duke Ellington and His Famous
Orchestra
Chicago / 15 March 1940

Wallace Jones, Cootie Williams (t),
Rex Stewart (ct), Lawrence Brown, Joe
Nanton, Juan Tizol (tb), Johnny
Hodges, Otto Hardwick (as), Barney
Bigard (cl), Ben Webster (ts), Harry
Carney (bs), Jimmy Blanton (b), Sonny
Greer (dr)
(piano and guitar tacet throughout)

Cd 60207; HMV B.9104, EA 2896, JK
2117, TG 189, X 8002, DLP 1034; RCA
75541, DPM 2-0351, RD 27133, LPM
10063, LPT 3017, EPBT 3017-1,
730565, VPM 6042-2, FMPI-7042; VDP
GW 2026; SCCJ P6-11891 (Columbia
Special Products); TL STL-J02-P3-
14729; Vi 26598, 947-0046, LPM 1715,
68-0380, 82-0220

Chapter 9. Junior Hop

Junior Hop

Johnny Hodges and His Orchestra
Chicago / 2 November 1940

Cootie Williams (t), Lawrence
Brown (tb), Johnny Hodges (as), Harry
Carney (bs), Duke Ellington (p),
Jimmy Blanton (b), Sonny Greer (dr)

Bb 11021; HMV B.9184, 7EG 8030, EA
3015, JK 2574; RCA 75665, 430629, RD
7829, LPT 3000, EPBT 3000, B.21038-
2, 430732, LPV 533, FXMI 7094; Vi
947-0069, 20-2541, 42-0161

Duke Ellington, His Piano and His Orchestra

Miami Beach, Florida / Recorded 20
March to 1 April 1958 during an
engagement at the Bal Masque, supper
club at the Americana Hotel

Co CL. 1282, CS.8098; Ph 840-060 BY
(SBBL 543)

Alice Blue Gown/Who's Afraid of the
Big Bad Wolf?/Got a Date with an
Angel/Poor Butterfly/Spooky Takes a
Holiday/The Peanut Vendor/Satin
Doll/The Lady in Red/Indian Love
Call/The Donkey Serenade/Gipsy
Love Song/Laugh, Clown, Laugh
(Satin Doll is the only composition by
Ellington.)
Harold "Shorty" Baker, Clark Terry
(t and fl), Ray Nance (t and v), Cat
Anderson, Andres Ford (t), Quentin
Jackson, Britt Woodman (tb), John
Sanders (valve tb), Jimmy
Hamilton (cl), Johnny Hodges, Russell
Procope (as), Paul Gonsalves (ts),
Harry Carney (bs), Duke Ellington (p),
Jimmy Woode (b), Sam Woodyard (dr)

Weary Blues/Basin Street Blues

Issued as Back to Back: Duke Ellington
and Johnny Hodges Play the Blues
New York / 20 February 1959

Ellington (p), Hodges (as), Harry
Edison (t), Leslie Spann (g), Al

Hall (b, on "Weary Blues"), Sam Jones (b, on "Basin Street Blues"), Jo Jones (dr)

EMI (Verve Series) CLP 1316

Chapter 10. *Subtle Slough*

Subtle Slough (Just Squeeze Me)

Rex Stewart and His Orchestra
Hollywood, California / 3 July 1941

Rex Stewart (ct), Lawrence Brown (tb), Ben Webster (ts), Harry Carney (bs), Duke Ellington (p), Jimmy Blanton (b), Sonny Greer (dr)

Bb B.11258; Ea WDLP 1025; HMV B.9260, DLP 1925, JK 2489; RCA 130254, 75713, LPV 533, 430629, RD 7829, 430732, FXMI-7201; "X" LX 3001, EVAB 3001

Chapter 11.
Some Conclusions and Comparisons

Swampy River

Duke Ellington and His Famous Orchestra
New York / 17 May 1932

Arthur Whetsol, Freddy Jenkins, Cootie Williams (t), Juan Tizol, Joe "Tricky Sam" Nanton (tb), Johnny Hodges (as), Harry Carney (bs), Barney Bigard (ts, cl), Duke Ellington (p), Fred Guy (g), Wellman Braud (b), Sonny Greer (dr)

Br 6355; BrE 01727

Duke Ellington had earlier recorded this item as a piano solo (New York, 1 October 1928, OK 8636 and PaE R.582).

APPENDIX D

ELLINGTON'S COPYRIGHTED

WORKS

The data in this appendix are drawn from the following sources: Ellington's autobiography *Music Is My Mistress*, pp. 493–522; Mercer Ellington and Stanley Dance, *Duke Ellington in Person*, pp. 222–23 (this includes items which had been inadvertently omitted from the autobiography); and the catalogue of Ellingtonia compiled in 1981 by United Artists Music, New York and London (managers of the music on behalf of Ellington's estate), from the files of Tempo Music, Inc., New York (Ellington's own publishing house), Robbins Music Corp., New York, and Leo Feist, Inc., New York. The 1,012 works attributable to Ellington may be categorized as follows:

Ellington as sole composer	769		
Ellington in collaboration with		Oscar Pettiford (double bass	
musicians in his employ:		player, cellist)	1
Hayes Alvis (double bass player)	1	John Sanders (trombonist)	2
Cat Anderson (trumpeter)	2	Al Sears (tenor saxophonist)	1
Aaron Bell (double bass player)	1	Willie Smith (alto saxophonist)	1
Barney Bigard (clarinetist)	10	Rex Stewart (cornetist)	8
Lawrence Brown (trombonist)	2	Billy Strayhorn (composer,	
Harry Carney (baritone saxophonist)	1	arranger, and pianist)	102
Mercer Ellington (trumpeter)	1	Clark Terry (trumpeter and	
Matthew Gee (trombonist)	2	flugelhorn player)	4
Tyree Glenn (trombonist)	1	Juan Tizol (valve trombonist)	8
Paul Gonsalves (tenor saxophonist)	1	Arthur Whetsol (trumpeter)	1
Jimmy Hamilton (clarinetist)	2	Cootie Williams (trumpeter)	9
Otto Hardwick (alto saxophonist)	1		
Rick Henderson (alto saxophonist)	1		191
Johnny Hodges (alto saxophonist)	23	Ellington in collaboration	
Bubber Miley (trumpeter)	5	with others	52
		Total number of works	1,012

The following list gives the number of compositions copyrighted each year from 1923 to 1973 (the year of copyright is not necessarily the date of composition):

Year	Number of Works	Year	Number of Works
1923	1	1949	7
1924	2	1950	8
1925	13	1951	7
1926	1	1952	8
1927	12	1953	7
1928	8	1954	15
1929	22	1955	12
1930	14	1956	33
1931	3	1957	24
1932	6	1958	27
1933	3	1959	41
1934	7	1960	16
1935	21	1961	13
1936	7	1962	51
1937	15	1963	45
1938	31	1964	44
1939	50	1965	28
1940	29	1966	16
1941	24	1967	51
1942	27	1968	27
1943	20	1969	9
1944	17	1970	33
1945	30	1971	42
1946	21	1972	5
1947	41	1973	10
1948	18	Total	1,012

APPENDIX E

EVIDENCE OF THE BLUES

IN CLASSIC PIANO RAGTIME

Trilby Rag (Carey Morgan, 1915), Trio, bars 17 to 32

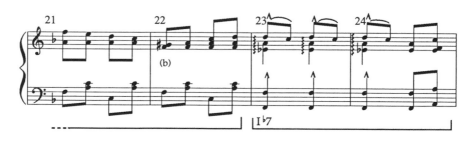

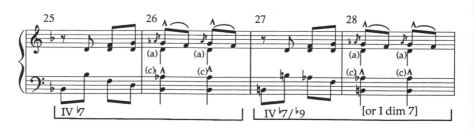

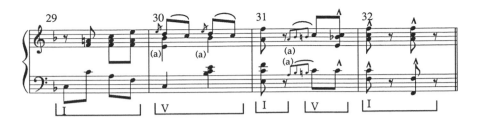

Chordally, this trio follows the classic eight-bar blues sequence, repeated to form a sequence of sixteen bars. The basic changes are as follows: eight bars of tonic, four bars of subdominant, one bar of tonic, one bar of dominant, one bar of tonic and dominant, one bar of tonic.

On the score, (a) denotes grace notes used to simulate glissandi and portamenti; (b) denotes blued mediants against implied tonic major triads; and at (c) is the strongest melodic blues inflection in the extract—a descent from the A-flats to the F-naturals through the dominant thirteenths on IV in bars 26 and 28. There is an example of one-to-one (augmented) syncopation in bar 20 of the treble strain, and the heavily accented dominant thirteenths in bars 23 and 24 help to sustain the bluesy flavor of the example.

NOTES

Chapter 1. An Introduction to Ellingtonia

1. Ellington, *Music Is My Mistress*, p. 447.
2. Duke Ellington, *Music Is My Mistress*, pp. 493–522.
3. Ellington and Dance, *Duke Ellington in Person*, pp. 222–23.
4. See appendix D for a detailed breakdown of the catalogue.
5. McLuhan and Fiore, *The Medium and the Message*, p. 93.
6. Waterman, "African Influence on the Music of the Americas," p. 214.
7. Tirro, *Jazz*, p. 47.
8. See chapter 4.
9. Downtown New Orleans comprised the richer districts of the city, where better-schooled musicians played. Uptown, in the poorer sections, was where largely self-taught groups were employed. Robichaux, a Creole of color, would have been more readily accepted into a society dominated by whites and Creoles than a black bandleader would have. Robichaux's orchestra occasionally engaged "hot" musicians, but overall it played little black music and much popular dance music of the period: quadrilles, cakewalks, square dances. It performed both at open-air concerts and at polite society balls, notably in Antoine's Restaurant (which remains in business).
10. Mellers, *Music in a New Found Land*, p. 316.
11. Hobson, *American Jazz Music*, pp. 78–79.
12. Ellington, "The Duke Steps Out," *Rhythm*, March 1931: 20–22. *Rhythm*, a British jazz magazine, ceased publication during the Second World War.
13. "Since the breakdown of the primitive work-democratic form of social organization, the biological core of man has been without social representation. The 'natural' and 'sublime' in man, which links him to his cosmos has found expression only in great works of art, especially in music and painting." Jack Diether, "Gustav Mahler and Orgonomy," *Journal of Orgonomy* (November 1974): 216–17. Diether again, quoting from Wilhelm Reich: "Every musical individual knows the state of emotion created by great music; yet it is impossible to put this emotion into words. Music is wordless." Reich, *Character Analysis*, 2d ed. (New York: Orgone Institute Press, 1945), p. 361. (This statement ignores that well-modulated speech contains cadences, which are very musical indeed.) Reich continues: "Nevertheless [the music] is an expression of movement and creates in the listener the expression of being 'moved' . . . The natural-scientific interpretation is that musical expression

comes from the very depths of the being." Diether then offers his own corollary: "Music is, or can be, then, a form of direct, immediate contact with the living, i.e., with the biological core," and again cites Reich: "[The listener's] biologic organization prompts him to construct a musical instrument, an organ, the sound of which is capable of evoking [the vegetative somatic] currents in the body." Diether concludes: "This quotation demonstrates Reich's awareness of the direct visceral effect of music on people, which can indeed be plainly seen in the historical line extending from tribal dance to rock-and-roll. Here, he states directly and categorically . . . that musical sounds are capable of evoking the vegetative currents of the body, an observation which can be corroborated by any person who responds to music. I suggest that no other form of art, except the allied medium of the dance (and, essentially, there can be no dance without music), has such a direct somatic effect on the living organism—what might be crudely called the 'gut' reaction."

14. Mellers, *Music in a New Found Land*, p. 315.

Chapter 2. The "Ellington Effect"

1. Transcribed from a private recording of the broadcast which has survived.
2. *Melody Maker*, 15 July 1939.
3. See appendix B.
4. Ellington, *Music Is My Mistress*, pp. 120–25.
5. Feather, *The Book of Jazz*, p. 198.
6. Finkelstein, *Jazz*, p. 191.
7. Finkelstein, *Jazz*, p. 202.
8. Mellers, *Music in a New Found Land*, p. 318.
9. Berendt, *The New Jazz Book*, p. 50. Berendt, a respected jazz aficionado and historian, is the head of the jazz division of a major German television and radio network.
10. Dolph, *Michigan Adviser*, 8 November 1972.
11. Ellington and Dance, *Duke Ellington in Person*, pp. 158–59.
12. Transcribed from the soundtrack of Russell Davies's documentary film *Duke Ellington and His Famous Orchestra*, broadcast by BBC television on 12 January 1983.
13. Also from Davies's film.
14. Shapiro and Hentoff, *Hear Me Talkin' to Ya*. "Gutbucket" is musicians' slang for down-to-earth, bluesy music.
15. Schuller, *Early Jazz*, p. 326.
16. Included in an album of songs and piano arrangements of instrumental pieces, *The Great Music of Duke Ellington*, pp. 92–93.
17. Ellington, *Music Is My Mistress*, p. 493.
18. Strayhorn's observations on this subject are quoted at length later in this chapter.
19. Schuller, *Early Jazz*, pp. 327–28.
20. Newton, *The Jazz Scene*, p. 110.
21. Shapiro and Hentoff, *Hear Me Talkin' to Ya*, p. 215.
22. In the performance referred to earlier in this chapter.
23. Lees, "Ellington Remembered," pp. 28–34.

24. Interview, *Hi Fi and Music Review*, July 1958.
25. Roger Moore, *Kansas City Star*, 13 May 1973.
26. Jewell, *Duke*, p. 80.
27. Stone, "My Life with the Duke."
28. Stone, "My Life with the Duke."
29. This short extract was transcribed from a recording dating from 1940. Compare the following in part II: p. 1 of the score of *Ko Ko*, p. 20 of the score of *Concerto for Cootie*, and p. 7 of the score of *Subtle Slough*.
30. Schuller, *Early Jazz*, pp. 318–57.
31. Schuller, *Early Jazz*, p. 342.
32. Schuller, *Early Jazz*, pp. 342–43.
33. For an analysis of *Jig Walk* (1923) see chapter 4; for an analysis of *Ko Ko* (1940) see chapter 6; for an analysis of *Mr. J. B. Blues* (1940) see chapter 7.
34. Lambert, *Music Ho!*, pp. 194–95.
35. The example is taken from p. 1 of the piano arrangement published in 1927 by Chappell & Co., London.
36. Lambert, *Music Ho!*, p. 187.
37. Lambert, *Music Ho!*, p. 188.

Chapter 3. The Influence of the Blues

Epigraph. Jones, *Blues People*, p. 17.
1. Hitchcock, *Music in the United States*, p. 123.
2. Oliver, *Blues Fell This Morning*, p. 5.
3. Oliver, *Blues Fell This Morning*, p. 6.
4. Epstein, *Sinful Tunes and Spirituals*, p. 236.
5. Epstein, *Sinful Tunes and Spirituals*, p. 291.
6. Epstein, *Sinful Tunes and Spirituals*, p. 347.
7. Krehbiel, *Afro-American Folksongs*, p. 73.
8. Krehbiel, *Afro-American Folksongs*, p. 73.
9. Borneman, "The Roots of Jazz," p. 13.
10. Oliver, *Blues Fell This Morning*, p. 11.
11. "Few childhoods can have been as idyllic as Edward Kennedy Ellington made *his* sound. He worshipped his mother and father (as well as his sister, Ruth) . . . From the moment of his birth, on 29 April 1899, he was, in his own words, spoiled rotten by a multitude of relatives, mostly female. He was no child of the ghetto . . . As a youngster, Ellington ate well and lived a pampered, civilised existence" (italics in original). Jewell, *Duke*, p. 27.
12. Ellington, *Music Is My Mistress*, pp. 23–24.
13. Born in 1903, Hopkins was a well-known, blues-oriented leader and pianist who led his own group in Washington in the early 1920s. He moved to New York in 1924 with Wilbur Sweatman and traveled to Europe in 1925 as the music director for Josephine Baker (the band included Sidney Bechet). In later years Hopkins organized his own improvising bands, which included such musicians as Edmond Hall (clarinet) and Vic Dickenson (trombone).
14. Ellington, *Music Is My Mistress*, p. 33.
15. Ellington, *Music Is My Mistress*, pp. 33–34.

16. Nordell, "Duke, a Man Who Used to Light Up the Place."

17. Mellers, *Music in a New Found Land*, p. 317.

18. See "The Scalar Structure of Jazz," in Sergeant, *Jazz, Hot and Hybrid*, pp. 147–72.

19. Borneman, "The Roots of Jazz," p. 13.

20. Mellers, *Music in a New Found Land*, p. 324.

21. Nordell, "Duke, a Man Who Used to Light Up the Place."

22. Berendt, *The New Jazz Book*, pp. 94–95.

23. Mellers, *Music in a New Found Land*, p. 317.

24. Mellers, *Music in a New Found Land*, p. 371.

25. Good examples are the recordings *The Roots of the Blues* (Atlantic 1348, 1959) and *Jazz II: The Blues* (Folkways FB55, 1959). See also the discography in appendix C.

26. Recorded in Hollywood by Johnny Hodges and His Orchestra, 3 July 1941. See appendix C.

Chapter 4. The Influence of Ragtime

1. Mellers, *Music in a New Found Land*, pp. 272, 276–77.

2. See appendix E.

3. Lawrence Cohn, notes to the recorded anthology *Maple Leaf Rag: Ragtime in Rural America*, (New World Records 235, 1976). See also the discography in appendix C.

4. Joplin (1868–1917), the son of former slaves, published sixty-eight ragtime compositions between 1899 and 1915. (An additional piece, *The Silver Swan Rag*, discovered on a piano roll [National Music Roll Co./QRS 31553] and attributed to Joplin, appeared in 1971.) Scott (1886–1938) was a black composer of thirty rags and seven other published works. Lamb (1887–1960), of Irish descent, wrote forty-one rags between 1908 and 1919, only twelve of which were published. See *The Collected Works of Scott Joplin*, ed. Vera Brodsky Lawrence, vol. 1, p. vii; Blesh and Janis; *They All Played Ragtime*, pp. 285–87.

5. Schaefer and Reidel, *The Art of Ragtime*, p. xvii.

6. Blesh and Janis, *They All Played Ragtime*, p. 248.

7. Rudi Blesh, "Scott Joplin, Black American Classicist," preface to *The Collected Works of Scott Joplin*, ed. Vera Brodsky Lawrence, vol. 1, p. xxxix.

8. See appendix C.

9. Horricks, "The Orchestral Suites," p. 124.

10. Joplin, *School of Ragtime*.

11. Mellers, *Music in a New Found Land*, pp. 318–19.

12. Mellers, *Music in a New Found Land*, p. 291.

13. I am indebted for the descriptions of mid-beat, mid-bar, and cross-bar syncopation to *Achievements of Ragtime: An Introductory Study*, by the British composer Peter Dickinson, Proceedings of the Royal Musical Association, vol. 105 (1978–79), pp. 63–76; and for the categorization of tied and untied syncopation to Berlin, *Ragtime*, p. 83.

14. Sargeant, *Jazz, Hot and Hybrid*, pp. 58–59.

15. Knowlton, "The Anatomy of Jazz," *Harper's Magazine*, April 1926, p. 581.

16. Both versions of *The Charleston Rag* are included on the LP recording *Eubie Blake:*

Rags to Classics (Eubie Blake Music; see appendix C). The sheet music for this and eight other rags written by Blake and transcribed by Terry Waldo is included in the album *Sincerely, Eubie Blake*; the other compositions are *Eubie's Classical Rag, Rhapsody in Ragtime, Poor Jimmy Green, Eubie Dubie, Brittwood Rag, Poor Katie Redd, Kitchen Tom,* and *The Baltimore Todolo.*

17. See chapter 8.
18. Berlin, *Ragtime*, pp. 14–15.
19. Ellington, *Music Is My Mistress*, pp. 94–95.
20. Ellington, *Music Is My Mistress*, pp. 94–95.
21. Ellington, *Music Is My Mistress*, pp. 94–95.
22. Ellington, *Music Is My Mistress*, pp. 94–95.
23. Kirkeby, *Ain't Misbehavin'*, pp. 32–33.
24. Jewell, *Duke*, p. 141.
25. See appendix D for works recorded at Morton's sessions, dates of recording, and musicians who took part.
26. Tirro, *Jazz*, p. 433.
27. Tirro, *Jazz*, p. 434.
28. Jasen and Tichenor, *Rags and Ragtime*, p. 240.
29. Jasen and Tichenor, *Rags and Ragtime*, p. 240.
30. Ellington, *Music Is My Mistress*, p. 93. See appendix C for information on rolls issued by QRS and other firms.
31. The Leeds Music Company, London, has been helpful in making available a photographic facsimile of a file copy of the rag, long out of print. This is the original sheet music issued by the Clarence Williams Music Publishing Co., New York, in 1925.
32. QRS Piano Roll no. 100999 (1918). See appendix C for details of this and other recordings of *The Carolina Shout* made by James P. Johnson.
33. The ring shout is named after and derived from an African dance in which singers circle a leader counterclockwise while performing a ritual or religious chant. A solo phrase is delivered by the leader and echoed immediately by the choir, all in rhythmic fashion. This call-and-response routine was transplanted to the field hollers and work chants, antecedents of the vocal blues which functioned as a partial anodyne against the cruelly repetitive tasks required of black slaves in the South. In church the same device appeared in the spontaneous gospel exchanges between minister and congregation. The jazz riff is a short, melodic, forcefully rhythmic phrase, repeated frequently.
34. Ellington, *Music Is My Mistress*, p. 20.
35. Ellington, *Music Is My Mistress*, p. 510.
36. See ex. 3.4.
37. See ex. 3.4.
38. See chapter 8.
39. Ulanov, *Duke Ellington*, p. 16.
40. I have been unable to unearth any proof that the notes were punched into the master roll by Ellington himself (see appendix D).
41. Jewell, *Duke*, p. 35.
42. Ellington, *Music Is My Mistress*, pp. 493–522.
43. The Charleston was a variety of foxtrot, a kind of ragtime in march style, slow or quick, which became popular among blacks in the South from around 1913. It

enjoyed several years of spectacular success in American and European ballrooms from about 1924 and then faded. The principal rhythm was based on the obsessive repetition of type B syncopation (tied, mid-bar), which may be regarded more as a popular-music device of the day than as having stemmed from classic ragtime. James P. Johnson composed the definitive Charleston song, *Charleston, South Carolina*, in 1923. The type B phrasing appears in twenty-eight of the thirty-two measures of melody in this A–B–A–C song.

44. The transcription was made from the LP *Duke Ellington, Archives of Jazz Vol.* 21 (BYG Records 529071). See appendix D for details of the research into the dating of this item.

45. Published by Mills Music, Inc., New York, in 1921.

46. The three song form episodes are identical in every melodic, rhythmic, and pianistic detail, which strongly suggests that the notes of the first chorus were punched into the original master roll by the performer and then mechanically reproduced twice, reading from the score.

47. I am indebted to Mr. D. Thistlethwaite, of Rugeley, Staffordshire, England, a restorer of player pianos and collector of piano rolls, for the following information: "[May I] explain to you the drum-roll effect achieved on player pianos? Those instruments with extras, such as drum, triangle etc., were generally nickelodeons [coin-operated] . . . These repetition pneumatics were often used on players, operating in the same manner as the 88 pneumatics which strike the notes."

Chapter 5. The Influence of Tin Pan Alley

Epigraph. Williams, *Where's The Melody?*, p. 4.

1. See appendix D.

2. Scholes, *Oxford Companion to Music*, p. 881.

3. The chorus of the old, sentimental "plantation" song *Carry Me Back to Old Virginny* (published in 1878), by James Bland (1854–1911), has a strict A–A–B–A construction. (A facsimile of the original sheet music is reproduced on pp. 22–25 of Tirro, *Jazz*.)

4. "Often there is more than one theme in a blues, for the additive nature of blues composing allows for movement from one subject to another. The binary character of the individual blues line is reflected in the content, and it is also evident in the relationship of the repeated line and the third, rhyming line. The blues stanza, frequently summarized as an A–A–B form, is thus binary in nature; the first line repeated emphasizes its distinction from the third line, which often has an opposing content and which is frequently the vehicle for the point of the verse. As I have noted, the individual line is broken with a fleeting pause which divides its contour and also very often divides its content. This may apply to the first line and its repeat, but not to the rhyming parts of the stanza." Oliver, "Blues and the Binary Principle," p. 170.

5. *The Great Music of Duke Ellington* (New York: Belwin-Mills, 1973); *The Genius of Duke Ellington* (New York: Big 3 Music, 1980); *Duke Ellington at the Piano* (Los Angeles: United Artists Music, 1980).

6. Lambert, *Music Ho!*, p. 95.

7. Lambert, *Music Ho!*, p. 95.

8. Lambert, *Music Ho!*, p. 95.
9. Lambert, *Music Ho!*, p. 95.
10. Goldberg, *Tin Pan Alley*, p. x.
11. See p. 00.
12. Transcribed from Russell Davies's documentary film *Duke Ellington and His Famous Orchestra*, broadcast by BBC television on 12 January 1983. Mills was Ellington's business manager from 1926 to 1940, a publisher, and occasionally a lyricist who worked with Ellington and others.
13. Also from Davies's film.
14. Also from Davies's film.
15. See also appendix C.
16. Ellington, *Music Is My Mistress*, p. 294.
17. Ulanov, *Duke Ellington*, pp. 216–17.
18. See appendix C.

Introduction to Part II: The Music of the Mature Period, 1939 to 1941

1. See appendix D.
2. I gratefully acknowledge the assistance afforded by the scores of *Ko Ko* and *Concerto for Cootie* transcribed by Dave Berger and Alan Campbell, published in 1980–81 by the Big 3 Music Corp.

Chapter 6. Ko Ko

1. *Black, Brown and Beige,* Ellington's first extended concert work, was given its premiere in Carnegie Hall, New York, on 23 January 1943. It was described by Ellington on that occasion as "a tone-parallel to the history of the American Negro," which had also been the intended subject of *Boola.*
2. RCA's recording schedule for 6 March 1940 gives the name as *Kalina* in typescript, altered to *Ko Ko* in longhand; a photocopy of the document appears in Aasland's *"Wax Works" of Duke Ellington* (see Bibliography).
3. See appendix C.
4. See appendix C.
5. Clar, "Ellington Style," p. 7.
6. See ex. 3.4.
7. Williams, *The Jazz Tradition*, pp. 100–101.
8. Schuller, *Musings*, p. 285.

Chapter 7. Mr. J. B. Blues

1. *Mr. J. B. Blues* was reissued on an extended-play (45 rpm) disc by RCA as part of its "Collector's Issue Series" (EPA G19, 1945). The other three titles on the record, all from 1 October 1940, are *Pitter Panther Patter, Sophisticated Lady,* and *Body and Soul* (composed by John W. Green). Two takes of each title were retained; all eight were issued in 1983 by RCA as part of the Jazz Tribune Series (PM 45352). See appendix C.

2. See appendix C.
3. See appendix C.
4. See appendix B for more information on Blanton.
5. For an analysis of *Jig Walk* see chapter 4.
6. See chapter 10, in particular the discussions of sections A and B of *Subtle Slough* (pp. 1 to 3 of the transcription score).
7. See chapter 10. The score of *Subtle Slough* is written and played almost exclusively as if it were in $\frac{12}{8}$.
8. See chapter 4 on forms predating jazz and ragtime.
9. See ex. 3.1.
10. See ex. 3.1.
11. The alternate take, not issued until 1983, confirms this supposition: whereas the overall plan is substantially the same episodically and harmonically, and the blues influence equally apparent, the performance itself suffers by comparison with the issued version—it is a little scrappy and fragmented.

Chapter 8. *Concerto for Cootie*

1. Leon Bismarck "Bix" Beiderbecke (1903–31) was born in Davenport, Iowa, came to New York with his own recording group in 1923, and played in Charlie Straight's and Frankie Trumbauer's bands in 1925 and 1926. He belonged to the Paul Whiteman Orchestra from 1928 to 1930 and briefly to Glen Gray's Casa Loma Orchestra in 1931. He died in Davenport.
2. From p. 2 of the album *Bix Beiderbecke's Modern Piano Suite* (consisting of four pieces: *In a Mist, Candlelights, Flashes,* and *In the Dark*), published by Robbins Music Corp., New York, 1928.
3. Example 8.4 is from p. 2 of the sheet music published by Chappell & Co., London, in 1937.
4. See p. 2 of the sheet music of *Soda Fountain Rag* in chapter 4.
5. See the transcription of *Subtle Slough* (measures 17–20 and 25–28) in chapter 10.
6. It is possible to play pedal notes in the extremely low bass register, well below the legitimate range of the instrument, by using a slack embouchure which produces a buzzing sound. The effect is a little vulgar, however.
7. See ex. 8.8, which shows similar voicing for the reeds in measure D of the introduction (p. 1 of the score).
8. See ex. 8.6.
9. Hodeir, *Jazz*, pp. 77–98.
10. See chapter 6.
11. Hodeir, *Jazz*, pp. 97–98.
12. The song is included in *The Great Music of Duke Ellington*, pp. 86–88.

Chapter 9. *Junior Hop*

1. See appendix B.
2. See appendix B for information on Bechet.
3. From 1928 to 1951 and from 1955 to 1970.

4. Ellington, *Music Is My Mistress*, pp. 118–19.
5. See the transcription and analysis in chapter 3 of Hodges's solo on *Things Ain't What They Used to Be*.
6. This is confirmed on virtually every page of the transcription score.
7. See exx. 9.1–9.6.
8. The album, *Back to Back: Duke Ellington and Johnny Hodges Play the Blues*, was recorded in conjunction with Harry Edison (trumpet), Les Spann (guitar), Sam Jones and Al Hall (double bass; Jones plays on some tracks, Hall on others), and Jo Jones (drums).
9. *Duke Ellington, His Piano and His Orchestra at the Bal Masque*. See appendix C for a list of the tracks on the album, which seem to have been chosen primarily for their popular appeal.

Chapter 10. *Subtle Slough*

1. Ellington did not copyright this work until 1945, and in the following year lyrics by Lee Gaines were added and the composition was retitled *Just Squeeze Me, but Please Don't Tease Me*. This version became a hit for the cornetist and singer Ray Nance (see appendix B).
2. See chapter 3.
3. See chapter 3.
4. See chapter 8.
5. See appendix B.
6. See appendix B.
7. See chapter 4.
8. See chapter 4.

Chapter 11. Some Conclusions and Comparisons

1. Berlin, *Ragtime*, p. 88.
2. See chapter 1.
3. Jewell, *Duke*, pp. 182–83. Italics in original.

Appendix A. A Chronology of Duke Ellington

Epigraph. Jewell, *Duke*, p. 24.
1. Ellington, *Music Is My Mistress*, p. 28.
2. Ellington, *Music Is My Mistress*, p. 30.
3. Eleven pseudonyms were used by twelve record labels. Ellington and Dance, *Duke Ellington in Person*, p. 33.

Appendix B. Ellington's Principal Sidemen

Epigraph. Ellington, *Music Is My Mistress*, p. 214.

BIBLIOGRAPHY

Aasland, Benny. *The "Wax Works" of Duke Ellington*. Järfälla, Sweden: Duke Ellington Music Society, 1978–79. Discography of the period 6 March 1940 to 11 November 1944.

Beiderbecke, Bix. *Modern Piano Solos*. New York: Robbins Music Corp., 1928. Four pieces: *In a Mist, Candlelights, Flashes,* and *In the Dark*.

Berendt, Joachim-Ernst. *The New Jazz Book*. London: Jazz Book Club, 1965.

———. *Jazz: A Photo History*. New York: Schirmer, 1979.

Berlin, Edward A. *Ragtime: A Musical and Cultural History*. Berkeley and Los Angeles: University of California Press, 1980.

Blake, Eubie. *Sincerely, Eubie Blake*. New York: Edward B. Marks/Belwin-Mills, 1975. Nine original compositions for piano solo, transcribed by Terry Waldo.

Blesh, Rudi, and Harriet Janis. *They All Played Ragtime*. London: Jazz Book Club, 1960.

Borneman, Ernest. "The Roots of Jazz." In *Jazz*, ed. Nat Hentoff and Albert J. McCarthy. New York: Rinehart, 1959.

Clar, Mimi. "Ellington Style." *Jazz Review*, April 1959.

Collier, James Lincoln. *Duke Ellington*. New York: Viking Penguin, 1987.

Confrey, Zez. *Kitten on the Keys*. New York: Mills Music, 1921.

Dance, Stanley. "I Let a Song Go Out of My Heart." In *Decca Book of Jazz*, ed. Peter Gammond. London: Jazz Book Club, 1960.

Dickinson, Peter. "The Achievement of Ragtime." *Proceedings of the Royal Musical Association*, vol. 105. London, 1978–79.

Dolph, L. R. "Ellington on Composition." *Michigan Advertiser*, 8 November 1972.

Ellington, Duke. "The Duke Steps Out." *Rhythm*, March 1931.

———. "On 'Swing.'" *Melody Maker*, 15 July 1939.

———. *The Great Music of Duke Ellington*. New York: Belwin-Mills.

———. "On the Question of Retirement." *Kansas City Star*, 13 May 1973.

———. *Music Is My Mistress*. London: W. H. Allen, 1974.

———. *The Genius of Duke Ellington*. New York: Big 3 Music Corp., 1980.

———. *Duke Ellington at the Piano*. Los Angeles: United Artists Music, 1980.

———. *Ko Ko* and *Concerto for Cootie*. Los Angeles, Nashville, and New York: Big 3 Music Corp./United Artists Music, 1980–81. Transcriptions in full score by Dave Berger and Alan Campbell.

Ellington, Mercer, and Stanley Dance. *Duke Ellington in Person: An Intimate Memoir*. London: Hutchinsons, 1978.

Epstein, Dena J. *Sinful Tunes and Spirituals: Black Folk Music to the Civil War.*
    Chicago: University of Illinois Press, 1977.
Feather, Leonard. *The Encyclopedia of Jazz.* London: Arthur Barker, 1956.
————. *The Book of Jazz.* London: Jazz Book Club, 1964.
Finkelstein, Sidney. *Jazz: A People's Music.* London: Jazz Book Club, 1964.
George, Don. *The Real Duke Ellington.* London: Robson, 1982.
Gershwin, George. *Rhapsody in Blue.* Los Angeles: Warner/Chappell, 1927.
————. *Nice Work if You Can Get It.* Los Angeles: Warner/Chappell, 1937.
Goldberg, Isaac. *Tin Pan Alley: A Chronicle of American Popular Music.* New York:
    Frederick Ungar, 1961. First published 1930.
Harris, Rex. *Jazz: Its Origins and Growth.* 4th. ed. Harmondsworth: Penguin, 1956.
Hentoff, Nat, and Albert J. McCarthy, eds. *Jazz.* New York: Rinehart, 1959.
Hitchcock, H. Wiley. *Music in the United States: A Historical Introduction.*
    Englewood Cliffs, N.J.: Prentice-Hall, 1962.
Hobson, Wilder. *American Jazz Music.* London: Jazz Book Club, 1956.
Hodeir, André. *Jazz: Its Evolution and Essence.* London: Secker and Warburg, 1956.
Horricks, Raymond. "The Orchestral Suites." In *Duke Ellington,* ed. Peter
    Gammond. London: Jazz Book Club, 1959.
James, Burnett. *Essays on Jazz.* London: Jazz Book Club, 1962.
Jasen, David A., and Trebor Jay Tichenor. *Rags and Ragtime: A Musical History.*
    New York: Seabury, 1978.
Jewell, Derek. *Duke: A Portrait of Duke Ellington.* London: Elm Tree Books, 1977.
Johnson, James P. *The Carolina Shout.* New York: Clarence Williams Music, 1925.
Jones, LeRoi. *Blues People: Negro Music in White America.* London: Jazz Book
    Club, 1966.
Joplin, Scott. *The School of Ragtime: Six Exercises for Piano.* New York: Scott Joplin,
    1908.
————. *The Collected Works of Scott Joplin,* ed. Vera Brodsky Lawrence. New York:
    New York Public Library, 1971.
Kirkeby, W. T. ("Ed"). *Ain't Misbehavin': A Biography of Thomas "Fats" Waller.*
    London: Jazz Book Club, 1967.
Knowlton, Don. "The Anatomy of Jazz." *Harper's Magazine,* April 1926.
Krehbiel, H. E. *Afro-American Folksongs.* New York: Schirmer Books, 1914.
Lambert, Constant. *Music Ho! A Study of Music in Decline.* London: Faber and
    Faber, 1966. First published 1934.
Lambert, G. E. ("Eddie"). *Duke Ellington.* London: Cassell, 1959.
Lees, Gene. "Ellington Remembered: A Minority Report." *High Fidelity,* November
    1974.
Massagli, Luciano, Liborio Pusateri, and Giovanno M. Volonté. *Duke Ellington's
    Story on Records.* Milan: Musica Jazz, 1981. Discography.
McLuhan, Marshall, and Quentin Fiore. *The Medium and the Message.* New York:
    Bantam, 1967.
Mellers, Wilfrid. *Music in a New Found Land.* New York: Stonehill, 1964.
Newton, Francis. *The Jazz Scene.* London: Jazz Book Club, 1964.
Nordell, Roderick. "Duke, a Man Who Used to Light Up the Place." *Christian
    Science Monitor,* 30 May 1974. Obituary.
Oliver, Paul. *Blues Fell This Morning.* London: Jazz Book Club, 1963.
————. "Blues and the Binary Principle." Paper delivered at the First International

Conference of Popular Music Research, Amsterdam, June 1981. Conference report, ed. David Horn and Philip Tagg, Göteborg and Exeter, 1982

Sandved, K. B., ed. *The World of Music*. London: Waverley, 1965.

Sargeant, Winthrop. *Jazz, Hot and Hybrid*. London: Jazz Book Club, 1959.

Schaefer, William J., and Johannes Reidel. *The Art of Ragtime*. Baton Rouge: Louisiana State University Press, 1973.

Scholes, Percy A., ed. *The Oxford Companion to Music*. 6th ed. New York, Toronto, and London: Oxford University Press, 1946.

Schuller, Gunther. *Early Jazz: Its Roots and Early Development*. New York: Oxford University Press, 1968.

———. *Musings: The Musical Worlds of Gunther Schuller*. New York: Oxford University Press, 1986.

Shapiro, Nat, and Nat Hentoff, eds. *Hear Me Talkin' to Ya*. London: Peter Davies, 1955.

Stone, Fred. "My Life with the Duke." *Canadian Composer*, October 1970.

Tirro, Frank. *Jazz: A History*. London: J. M. Dent and Sons, 1979.

Ulanov, Barry. *Duke Ellington*. London: Musicians' Press, 1947.

Waterman, Richard A. "African Influence on the Music of the Americas." In *Acculturation in the Americas*, ed. Sol Tax. Chicago: University of Chicago Press, 1952.

Williams, Martin. *Where's the Melody? A Listener's Introduction to Jazz*. New York: Funk and Wagnalls, 1967.

———. *The Jazz Tradition*. New York: Oxford University Press, 1983.

INDEX